I fell in love with you and I cried

I fell in love with you and I cried

Rachel Hill

For Anthony John Hill
My anchor and my guide

'We look down on people who choose themselves first, people who make the most of the lives they've been given.'
                    - Natalie Swift, The Darkest Tunnel, WordPress

'The coop is guarded from the inside.'

- Aravind Adiga, *The White Tiger*

Contents

Nothing to lose but our dignity: Harleston, UK

It was a weekend morning, I was standing in the hallway between the bedroom and the bathroom, my husband Anthony was in bed. He said, 'What kind of people would we have to be to sell the house and just leave everything and everyone and go off on an adventure?'

'Strong', I said, 'We'd have to be so strong'. Electricity ran up the length of my spine.

'Wow,' Anthony said, 'I just felt a tingle go right through my body.'

I was forty-seven years old. In terms of career and property, I had gone as far as I could and as far as I wanted to. Head of Occupational Therapy at a specialist secure hospital and living in a nice house in a pleasant little town on the Norfolk-Suffolk border. But now what? Was I just going to keep on working and living there until I retired, grew old and died? And that was if I was lucky.

The house was near my job, near my mum. For the first time in years, Anthony had a job he loved, caring for people with learning disabilities as part of a lovely team, several of whom became friends.

We were happy and we both began to dream. Just over a year after we had moved in and supposedly settled for life we began to roll around the idea of dismantling it all, selling the house, buying a camper van and travelling the world or going to live in a healing centre in Mexico run by an old friend of Anthony's.

Anthony had been to India twenty years earlier, before he had kids, and had always meant to go back. Funnily enough I got a new manager who actually asked me, apropos of nothing, if I were planning to carry on working until I retired, 'Or was I going to go off to India or something?'

I began to ask myself, what would I do if I didn't have to do anything? What would I do if anything was possible? What would I do if I could do whatever I wanted?

When we first had the conversation and I experienced the glittering thrill of possibility, it was the first time in recent memory that I had allowed myself to think about what I actually might want. Since becoming pregnant at the age of eighteen my life had revolved around my son in one way or another. Even though he was now twenty-seven years old, I hadn't seriously thought about leaving Norfolk until very recently, when an advertisement had jumped out at me for a job in Guernsey. We went to Guernsey for my interview, I was offered the job but neither of us wanted to live there.

Looking back, this was practical action that shifted us. It got us both wondering if we could live away from our kids. That trip to Guernsey marked the start of a shift in mental attitude that ultimately was to propel us all the way to India.

Anthony's two children lived with their mum in London and were now teenagers and rarely came to stay with us anymore. Anthony's daughter had her own room at last but she never even put a picture up. Like most parents, we misjudged how fast the kids grew up. Even so, going off and leaving the kids for a year was unthinkable at first.

We had bought the house in Harleston from a widow who had lived in it with her husband from when it was first built in 1952, with many of the original features and it hadn't been decorated since the 1980s. I was besotted with the original glass lampshades, small chandeliers and kitsch garden ornaments.

We realised that if we didn't do anything we'd get old and die there.

I thought about old people whose homes haven't been decorated for years and who have had the same things around them for decades. As they do less outside the home and spend more time inside, maybe the wallpaper, the furniture, the ornaments all loom larger because those things are given more attention and are tied with the memories they hold. People say that possessions and objects are important because they *hold our memories.* When people customise their homes they say they *put something of themselves into it.*

It was at this time that we began to discuss what we needed, something big enough and no bigger, a one bedroom flat, a caravan, a boat. To have a solid shelter, with heat that comes on with the flick of a switch, clean drinking water, hot running water, comfortable seating and sleeping areas, plenty of bedding and warm clothes, a washing machine. These things are denied to many. Even one thing off this list would represent enormous progress, even luxury, to some. Many of us who have these things do not fully appreciate them.

Not only that, the progress and comfort they represent and provide becomes grossly extended, with people changing their furniture before it has even worn out and painting the inside of their homes a different colour according to what is deemed fashionable that season. 'Needs updating,' such a spurious phrase that has helped give rise to the largely unnecessary industries of producing new 'kitchens' and 'bathrooms' and the mind boggling array of paint colours on offer.

Of course, we need to have shelter but there's probably an optimum level of comfort. If things are too hard, that takes so much time and energy that there's no space for creativity. If things get too comfortable, one can be lulled into a false sense of security. Somehow by being too comfortable we become less aware: in our centrally heated comfort zones it's easy to fall back to sleep.

Everything is arranged so that our biggest and best experiences are early in our lives and this, plus the emphasis on youth in film, television shows and advertising means that people spend most of their lives looking back to 'the good old days,' and taking their power and energy away from the present. You can see this in young people's gap year travels before they 'settle down' to work, marry, have children and in big event weddings, 'the best day of your life' with just the photographs on the mantelpiece to sustain you for the rest of your 'less good' life.

We had met eight years previously. Meeting Anthony and falling in love had triggered a full on tripped out spiritual awakening for me. Because his children were still young and my son still needed quite a bit of support, we explored ideas of spirituality and personal growth from the comfort of our living room. We were lucky, that we both had the same ideas.

At the start it wasn't even about selling the house and leaving the kids (that was too scary at first) it was just about getting to a position where we could. The decluttering came first, before the travelling was a solid plan and caused the mental shifts required in order for the travel to become a solid plan.

I was petrified of the idea of doing something so unthinkable, of giving up the security of property. Yet at the same time I was really excited about the idea of letting go of possessions and leaving with just a backpack each and no keys. I wrote at the time: 'For me it's not really about travelling per se, it's about testing my long felt urge to trust-fall into the Universe, to let my fingertips peel from the cliff face and slip into the unknown. Mainly, it is about freedom; about realising where I am, what I have and therefore what I am able to do with a bit of guts and imagination. The thought of just going off for a while with no plan other than to go travelling and keep writing is thrilling.'

In the UK there's such a drive towards home ownership as a goal that selling a property goes against the grain; family and home owning friends were dead against the idea. We had to sell up to liquidate capital to have sufficient money for the trip. Not only that, we wanted to simplify, practise minimalism. Renting out the house and returning wasn't what I had in mind even if we could have afforded to do that. I didn't want to have, as an acquaintance at work had had, a life changing experience in Southeast Asia for a year only to return to the same life.

Because you are choosing to have less, and no matter what all the memes say you are going completely against the herd, who are all focused on getting more, so it feels weird and hard. You are going against the conditioning of the society you have been brought up in. That was why during the several months of thinking, planning and putting the house on the market I was mentally quite aggressive. I said to myself, 'I need to smash this down with a sledgehammer; I need to tear it up by the roots.'

I ruthlessly decluttered sentimental items. The bigger the action, the stronger I felt. It took a lot more energy than I had anticipated. I found that I did a splurge on something then had to stop for a bit. It was like going up steps or stages. We got tired. At other times decluttering would seem to release a spurt of energy that propelled us forward. It was a balance between theory and practical steps, between wrapping our minds around it and then taking the necessary action, interspersed with rest. And of course all the time we were going to work and doing the normal stuff of life.

The more I got rid of the lighter I felt, the more energy I had and the more I began to feel like a traveller. As the objects from my old life were left behind, I felt that I could become someone new, the kind of person who can do this.

***

'This' turned out to be selling the house, leaving our jobs, buying a narrowboat for our return to the UK and going off on a year of slow travel in India and Southeast Asia. Anthony's son Jude came with us to India for the first month. We arranged for Maeve, Anthony's daughter to come out to Thailand during her summer holiday. My son Siris stayed in the UK to finish his Fine Art Degree and build his career as an artist.

Welcome to India greeted us in big shiny letters at Arrivals. Arriving at 5am UK time and 9.30am India time, to Delhi heat and a visual overload we were all pretty quiet in the taxi, just absorbing it all. My first impressions were all good. A short trip to Morocco a few months previously had got me used to the style of driving and traffic. The pollution didn't seem as bad as I had feared. Billboards outside the police station described measures being taken to improve safety for women. A lot of the taxis and auto rickshaws- autos- had stickers on the back saying 'This taxi respects women.' Best of all, we saw monkeys out of the window, just there at the side of the road, wandering free!

We had looked up some footage of Main Bazaar on YouTube in advance, after realising that it was impossible for Anthony to adequately describe it to me. Arriving in Main Bazaar, it was like the YouTube video and like Marrakech; with stalls selling hippie/Indian goods, full of colour, noise and busyness with autos, bicycles and people.

The hotel staff didn't speak much English and we were unfamiliar with the money. We ended up with three bottles of orange Fanta, which was fine really but I was tired, probably a bit overwhelmed, and anxious about us, especially Jude, drinking enough in the heat. Going outside to get water just seemed an impossible task and I ended up lying in bed fretting about us all getting dehydrated yet too petrified to go out. I got annoyed with Anthony and laid on the bed and fell asleep. After a nap, when it was cooler we went out to get dinner and water. As soon as we stepped outside there was a man selling water from a cart right in front of our hotel. That was probably as good a lesson as any.

It was getting dark and Main Bazaar felt warm and dusty. There were lots of shops, street sellers, people, cows just wandering or sitting, cars, mopeds, autos and the continual noise of horns. Main Bazaar was lit with neon signs, including one which said *All Is Well*.

After dinner I walked on past our hotel alone, I wanted to go out by myself and buy some fruit and chai tea and practice my few words of Hindi. I was unsure about prices, money and etiquette but I managed to buy some small oranges and some chai. I felt completely safe and comfortable, aside from my ever-present mild anxiety about getting lost. The man at the chai stall gave me my tea in a plastic bag done up with a knot, like how goldfish used to be sold at fairs, with three little striped coloured paper cups to take back. The tea burned my fingers as I poured it out but it didn't matter. Jude said it was the best thing he had ever tasted.

Our room was on the second floor with a balcony that looked out onto Main Bazaar. Often in the morning we would be woken by traffic or the bells and chanting of religious processions. Stepping out into the bright white heat of the balcony the stone floor was too hot to walk on barefoot and the sunlight was too bright without sunglasses. We used to smoke out on the balcony and just stand and watch; the clothes, the cows, the autos, the mopeds, the honking of horns, a colour and sensory overload.

There were heavy faded navy drapes at the balcony door and windows. With the doors and windows closed, the drapes drawn and the fan on we could stay reasonably cool. If we got too hot, we could always take a cold shower. We stayed indoors in the afternoons, resting, sleeping and avoiding the heat. One afternoon I did some yoga in the hallway of our room. It was only a few stretches on a rug rather than a proper mat but it felt good. It was good to stretch after the tension of travelling. And of course I couldn't help thinking while I was doing it, '*I'm doing yoga. In India,*' which made me well up a little.

The water seller, the restaurant and the staff at the hotel all quickly became so familiar that the stress of our arrival and the first few hours blurred and receded into the past. The creation of a little comfort zone for ourselves, a bit of familiarity with our surroundings, a nice place to eat. Even though we were aware that we would soon undo it and have to do it over again, be out of our comfort zones, up against our edges, then the creation of a new comfort zone and so on and so on. But that was what coming to India was all about.

One evening we got a rickshaw to Connaught Place, the smart shopping area. Going by auto in Delhi is a good metaphor for the need to just let go while being in India. The ride seemed at times like a seriously grown up version of the dodgems and felt risky at times. But whatever it looks like to Western eyes the traffic seems to work. Lanes merge all the time, horns are used continually but to say, 'I'm coming,' rather than in anger. We saw near misses and slight bumps but we didn't seen anyone getting angry, and every moment there were the types of driving interactions that would lead to serious road rage in the UK.

At night the sign for the Hare Krishna hotel beside our balcony was lit up. Standing looking at the white neon sign from our balcony reminded me of when I used to do different spiritual practices. I thought, *'All that was to get me to here.'* I'm not saying I'll never do any spiritual practices again but right now it is about the practical application of all that theoretical and spiritual exploration.

Jude and I stood outside on the balcony, smoking a cigarette and looking at the view, feeling good, 'Yeah, it's okay here isn't it', Jude said.

'I actually feel okay here, confident, like I've been here for ages.' I said.

'We've got a long way to go yet,' Anthony said. He was right, of course.

On our third day in Delhi I didn't feel right all day and in the afternoon I felt my mood dip. I lay on the bed fretting about my to do list (which was just a few creative things and a few shopping/admin tasks), and couldn't understand what was the matter with me. I didn't recognise the feeling of overwhelm as a symptom of illness.

I spent the night sitting on the toilet with the shower bucket in front of me, interspersed with trying to sleep. At some point in the night I woke up really hot, even the stone floor near my bed felt warm so I went and laid on the rug on the stone floor in the hallway where I had so happily done yoga only the day before. I watched an insect walk along the strip of lit up doorway between the hallway and the bathroom, it felt like having a pet, a little bit of company.

Anthony got sick a few hours after me and it was touch and go as to whether we'd make it onto our train to Goa. In the morning I was over the worst, Anthony was lying on the bed looking awful, Jude came in.

'We are going aren't we?' he said. The three of us were ready to get out of Delhi by that time. We all really liked Delhi but by day three I had started really noticing the pollution, especially in the evenings. It seemed to get hotter while we were there and the water in the bathroom ran out regularly.

We had booked two tier AC sleeper. This is a soft option, I think hardened backpackers use three tier non AC- fans with windows and less space. Being ill it was a blessing that we'd booked this. The train was one of the best in India, the Rajdhani Express, with clean, firm blue beds, a paper packet of thick white cotton sheets, a towel, a pillow and a woollen blanket. We were glad to leave our hot sick room in Delhi and just rest, with no demands. Our carriage was almost empty, the toilets were plentiful and nearby, the staff were attentive, bringing us food we could barely touch and checking on us through the night. Although we couldn't eat the big meals, they brought us cartons of lemon and lime juice, clear tomato soup, bread sticks, tea and plain biscuits, perfect for people who had been sick. Being ill we slept through a lot of the journey but we went past cities, skyscrapers and very poor dwellings, rivers and mountains and miles and miles of green and trees.

Twenty five hours later we arrived in Madgaon, Goa and stepped out of our AC carriage into bright sunlight and midday heat. The place we were staying in Colva was like a hostel, with a shared toilet and shower room. We ate at a beach front restaurant, 'Hey Jude' was playing. After we had eaten we had a little paddle. The sea was like bath water, I had never felt sea that warm before.

I had been very apprehensive of going to India, or anywhere in Southeast Asia, at that time of year. Most people go to India between November and February, when it is not so hot. But if we're going to be out for a year, we are going to be in the hottest time at some point. And we had to go when we could, when the house sold, and so we arrived in Delhi at the end of March.

We moved to Agonda the next day. It was too early to check in so we walked along the beach. It was very hot but I was beginning to feel a bit better and didn't want to miss out or feel left out; being ill made me really pathetic. We turned and walked back and went to one of the many beach front restaurants to have breakfast. Sitting outside yet shaded from the sun, with the breeze blowing in off the sea it was entirely bearable. I breathed a huge sigh of relief; I wouldn't be shut indoors for months after all.

Agonda is touristy but in a palm trees, beautiful sandy beach, luxury-holiday kind of way. The buildings are tasteful, temporary structures made of natural materials and set back behind the line of palm trees. The beach is long and framed at each end by lush green tree covered mountains.

I had imagined beach huts like we get in English seaside towns but these were more like wooden chalets with proper washrooms and fittings and the incredible thing is that they aren't allowed to stay there permanently so they all get dismantled at the end of April. I wondered how they go about that, do they label all the bits, or do they just know? I used to struggle to remember how to put my tent up once a year.

Our beach hut had a veranda that was shaded and cool enough to sit out on even in the middle of the day, which was good as inside was very hot. The owner said, 'Don't worry that it's hot inside in the day, at night it will be okay.' And it was. It was the first time I had slept under a mosquito net, a proper fixed one like the coverings of a four poster bed.

We would have happily stayed on in our first hut but it was booked. Anthony went off to look for somewhere else and found us an even better place. The new hut was up high, up some steps, with more space in the room and a big veranda shaded with palm trees, cool, secluded and right on the beach. I was so relieved to be able to unpack properly. I am a real homebody but I can make myself at home easily too, putting my things out and doing some pampering- okay basic grooming- for the first time since leaving the UK.

On my first day in Agonda I did a bit of yoga out on the veranda and then without even thinking about it just dropped into meditation, sitting half against the door frame, resting after a set of one of those super strong hip opener poses, pulling the ends of the rug so as to buffer my ankle bones from the wooden floor. I adjusted my position away from the door frame but otherwise I sat still for quite a while despite the fact that I hadn't meditated for ages. I did nothing other than just check in with myself, deep inside. And what I noticed was fear. Fearful breathing, anyway, which I took to mean that fear was the thing going on for me.

I had read a blog post only a day or two before about how if you calm your breathing so it isn't fearful then you won't feel fear. Try as I might my breathing remained shallow, tight and almost painful and seemed to get worse the more I focussed on trying to calm it. I remembered what the post had said about if you have a pounding heartbeat- just observe it, and observing it will naturally calm it. I didn't have a pounding heartbeat but I used this approach for my breathing and eventually I broke through to a place where I felt at peace and with no fear.

As often used to happen to me in meditation, images came to mind; me opening a door, only to drop down an empty lift shaft and arrive sitting on a seat, in a room and then again, dropping down and arriving somewhere different.

We've done a lot of moving about- our house in Harleston, the Travelodge in Norwich, the boat in Northamptonshire, London, Delhi, the sleeper train, Colva, Agonda- and I'm a real homebody as I've said. I've not done much travelling before and coupled with the pre leaving stress it's not surprising there's fear in me. And of course I've been sick, but then tummies are emotional too.

On day eight of my traveller's diarrhoea Anthony took two auto rides to find a pharmacy and came back with antibiotics for me. I started feeling better from the first tablet. Antibiotics are good and strong here in India, I think. Anthony has looked after me all the way through and apart from the first night in Delhi when I went out to buy fruit and once when I went to the very nearby shops to buy water I hadn't done anything on my own up until taking the antibiotics. I also haven't always been that nice. I began to realise how much I hurt Anthony's feelings when I get annoyed with him when all he is doing is trying to look after me.

My problem is that I don't often know until later what it is I am unhappy about and even then I struggle to express it. I am inconsistent and emotional. I tend to come across as annoyed when in fact I am feeling overwhelmed or vulnerable, I just don't like to admit it. A couple of times recently, if I'd stopped and thought about it I could have said, 'That's a great idea but I can't manage that just yet.' Or, 'Actually, can you come with me, I'd rather not be on my own.'

We are both much worse and much better than we realise, is a Buddhist quote I read about becoming more aware of ourselves.

India has a lot to teach me, which is good, because I have a lot to learn.

As I got better I felt my capabilities returning. I went from being unable to even think about moving and the journey to Hampi (just the thought of the travelling and the heat made me feel sick), to talking about Vietnam, Japan, the whole trip. Anthony and I went out to dinner and had a good talk and reconnected. It was nice to talk and feel understood and with us reconnected and feeling better again all seemed brighter.

Leaving the demands, mental stimulation, pressures and deadlines of my job was like coming off a motorway and finding myself suddenly in a 30mph zone. It was bound to be an adjustment. It also forced me to face up to myself, my thoughts and feelings no longer subsumed beneath the work role. Even in the beach hut in Agonda I wrote lists and worried about getting things done, just like I always have. I always feel an urge to have things done as soon as possible even if I don't have the wherewithal or motivation to actually do them. In the heat, you are lucky if you get one thing done a day.

With plenty of time for writing the biggest obstacle to it all, as usual was my own mind. I put myself under pressure which of course made writing anything at all feel like a chore. This demonstrates what a brain can do; it can cause anxiety about nothing, even when one is ensconced in paradise with nothing at all to worry about. I realised I can just relax and enjoy myself. Write when and if I feel like it. Write nothing at all some days.

But mostly I will write, of course. As Elizabeth Gilbert, author of *Eat Pray Love,* my long time personal bible says, having a creative mind is like having a border collie for a pet. If you don't give it something to do, it will find itself something, and you may not like what it finds. This is probably why I have OCD, anxiety. I check taps, electrics, ashtrays, purse, cards. I get very, very anxious to the point of near panic sometimes. I have intrusive thoughts. There's no easy answer though, because even when I do keep my mind occupied with writing, I am still capable of getting anxious about that.

At the same time I am processing what it all means. I have sold my house, left my job, abandoned everything and everyone and just gone off. I had a lot of dreams in the first month about packing, moving, being back, going back, saying goodbye, not saying goodbye, my mum, the house, about to leave, my last day at work, thinking I was in one place but was in the other, the UK bleeding into India.

It's not about going travelling, not really. Or rather, the travelling is a tool. It gets me away, breaks me away from my old life and when I return I will be living in a new area quite far away, far enough that no family will ever come and visit probably. It's not as if my family was bad. It's not as if my life was bad. In fact it was good by any standard, and way, way better than I would have envisioned as a suicidal teenager or a freakish, teased child. But it wasn't really me, or it wasn't me anymore and the only way I could be me was to get right away from it and do something so big and so different that I would become unrecognisable to everyone, even to myself.

As a child I wanted to be a writer. I used to stay in at break times to finish my stories instead of going out to play. Even as a child I saw myself as different. The local kids were all very conventional, from a new housing estate whereas we lived in a big old farmhouse which my mum was renovating. My sister and I were teased at school. Yet even as the kids teased me about my jumble sale clothes, even as I hated some of my clothes, I felt superior in a way. At times I felt almost dissociated; looking out of the window in class, thinking of myself as a tiny speck in the enormity of space and feeling that nothing mattered. I liked the idea of doing something unique, like an artist or a writer does. Like someone who does something amazing does.

As a teenager on my bedroom wall beside the window I had cardboard butterflies, their wings weighted with tiny magnets, handwritten lyrics by the band The Cult blu-tacked amongst them, *'Her painted wings proclaim my suicide.'* I dressed and did my hair and makeup in a really wild, alternative way. I had a lot of sex and I drank to excess out of a desire to break on through to the other side, although it didn't work. In my twenties I 'went normal,' for a while when my son started nursery but I wasn't at ease, I didn't fit in. I made so many compromises to fit in that I just ended up feeling even more alienated.

***

My energy returned and with it my drive to get everything done immediately. 'Okay I'm back,' I said.

'Don't do your boom and bust,' Anthony said.

'I won't,' I said, 'Look, I'm fine, I'm having a break, I'm not doing anything, I'm sitting still... but I am super excited!'

'I can tell,' he said.

Our routine in Agonda was to get up around 7am, have a paddle and a walk on the beach then go and have breakfast at the beach front restaurant. By mid morning the sand burned the soles of our feet. Sometimes Jude would join us for breakfast, mostly we'd see him a little later. The beach front restaurant was smarter and more expensive than going into the village but it was very convenient and they did fruit salad for breakfast; a big white oval dish of all kinds of fruit with white curls of coconut on top, a work of art as well as being delicious. In the evening the cows all came and slept on the beach. In the mornings we watched from the restaurant as a woman with a broom swept the beach and removed the cow pats and any rubbish so that the beach was always perfect.

Incredible people, I assumed they must be teachers, did yoga on the beach in the mornings; it was awesome what they could do with their bodies. For my part, a short walk in the waves or a few stretches in the afternoon were all I could manage.

After breakfast we retreated to the veranda or indoors until the evening, with the exception of going out for lunch or snacks. Crisps and Maaza- a sugary mango drink- were the new staples; we naturally craved the salt and sugars for rehydration, and fresh coconuts and little sweet bananas. We ate snacks on the veranda and fed cashew nuts to the crows, half heartedly trying to tame them. Once we left a bag of the small bananas outside and the crows ate them, slitting them lengthways and hollowing out the insides.

Alleyways led to 'the village,' a few streets with shops for tourists, cafes, guesthouses and laundry facilities. At a cheap cafe with a dusty floor, an outside loo and mosquito coils under the table we drank sweet lime sodas and I had my first ever eaten-in-India masala dosa.

We got friendly with the waiter who was from Kerala and we swapped Instagram contacts. His dad owned the restaurant and wanted him to settle down but he wanted to travel, make films, design clothes and be an artist. 'He wants me to be settled, I am not settled,' he said.

Sometimes I felt like one of those proper writers you read about who have a regular routine or like Ian Fleming who used to live in paradise in Hawaii and swim each morning before sitting down to write. We ate meals with Jude, vegetable fried rice served with little silver pots of chilli and soy sauce; onion bhajis and Bombay potatoes and hung out together playing cards in the restaurant or on the veranda, me and Jude smoking and drinking. Goa was a holiday and a chance for us all to spend some real time together. Agonda was as easy as easy can be. Quiet except for the sound of coconuts crashing on the ground, the endless caw caw of the crows and the sound of the sea which grew louder the closer it came to the monsoon. I was conscious of making the most of the luxurious, quiet easiness and the sea breeze in readiness for going on an eight-hour sleeper coach to Hampi where I had heard it was 40°C. 'Be brave, Rachel,' I said to myself.

***

To my past self, and to anyone packing to go on a long trip to India I would say now: You don't need anything except passport, visa, money and tech, a few basic toiletries and a change of clothes. You really can buy everything there: clothes, products, even medication. I had been told that, I knew I was doing it as a security blanket but I still couldn't resist packing every product I use or thought I might need.

Which was funny, because I had been so good at getting rid of stuff from my old life. In the middle of the decluttering one day we were getting ready to go somewhere, I was wondering what to wear. Anthony said how about such and such skirt, I told him it had gone. He looked in my wardrobe and realised how much I had got rid of. 'Is that all the clothes you have left?' he said. I got rid of my gold wedding shoes then later my wedding dress, my grandmother's costume jewellery and her handmade 1960s dresses, my own jewellery and vintage dresses. I was left with only a minimalist wardrobe of work clothes, warm clothes and India clothes, the rings, silver bangles and ear studs I wear every day and one pair of gold sparkly earrings for weekends.

The more I let go of, the more I could let go of. I looked back and laughed at how hard I found it to do the bedding. Pah, bedding! I would never have believed attachments to sheets and pillowcases could be so strong; maybe it's the memories of all those nights, babies, and sick children. Those things have been everywhere with you, seen everything.

I simplified my finances. To do this I had to log into the work benefits site. As well as the pension contributions there were loads of other things: childcare vouchers, cycle to work schemes, purchasing of electronic goods in instalments. It reminded me that for every single thing you can think of, there is layer upon layer of complexity and choice and detail designed into it.

Anthony said he would do the stationery drawer. I was pleased. There are probably a couple of things I am attached to, a calculator I've had for as long as I can remember and a scented eraser in a box. I could let go of it all but it's easier if someone else does it. He said, 'There's all this stuff in there that we keep because we live in a house and we've got cupboards and drawers, things like hole punches and staplers, but I can't remember the last time I used a hole punch or a stapler at home'. He's right, me neither.

Anthony stayed up until the early hours for weeks, digitalising all the music so we could get rid of our CDs. Tech and computer problems beset him; my son gave him lots of advice on the phone, he had to buy a new (second hand) computer, it turned out to be broken and he had to buy another one, as well as the emotional difficulty of letting go of a music collection, the thing he was most attached to.

I spent a weekend sorting out all my old photographs. 'Good luck with that', my friend said when I told her what I was planning to do. She was right, it was hard. All the old tattered colour-bled albums, the kooky photo frames I used to collect, the wallets of photographs that had never been sorted. Sitting on the floor of the spare room for the best part of two days, my back aching, surrounded by piles and piles of photographs; thirty years of memories and people. Seeing the past fly by, the bits I could just put in the bin; my farewell lunch of my first job, me with a bouquet. A night out with friends I don't see any more. The fruits of my labours: two brand new albums of family photographs and three wastepaper bins of photographs thrown out without a backward glance. I dropped the old photo albums and frames off at the charity shop, arriving moments before it closed.

I already knew that decluttering and minimalism were much more than just an interior design ascetic. I felt a buzz every time I dropped a bag off at the charity shop. After finishing the photo albums I felt a surge of energy course through me, the like of which I hadn't experienced. I arrived home, went for an hour's fast walk across the fields, moved a large pile of bricks from the side of the house, washed the kitchen floor and then stayed up, wired, not hungry, until 1 am. It made me so light, gave me such a burst of energy and gave me all the proof I needed that this theory really is true, that decluttering, letting go really does do something.

Nature abhors a vacuum, so as soon as you get rid of the clutter and unnecessary possessions, awareness floods in instead, along with purpose, change, movement, aliveness and a new sense of identity. I found myself enjoying friendships more, finding friendships more satisfying. Noticing things, a black and white cat using a zebra crossing- the woman in the car behind me saw it too; I caught her eye in the rear-view mirror, both of us laughing.

The process of decluttering had far reaching effects. It made me immune, or almost immune to the lure of shopping and mindless consumerism. If I'm getting rid of things, why would I buy anything? I found the city so tiring. I made excuses or told my friends upfront, 'Let's just meet for coffee instead of going round the shops', or, 'I'm avoiding malls, too much stimulation'.

This new found attitude, if that's what it was, insulated me somehow. Waking up one Saturday morning Anthony and I decided on a whim to drive into the city to go out for vegan breakfast. I went out in the previous day's clothes and yoga pants and we walked through the city in our own little pocket of stillness.

Anthony and I noticed how our awareness changed as the process went on. The more we got rid of the more we became aware that we had more room than we needed; the house was too big, the garden was too big. It became obvious that even if you have ten rooms they will get full. Even though we aren't very materialistic we had found stuff for each room and we didn't need half of it. I used to walk from room to room and think, Oh, here's another one; the red living room downstairs, the dove grey dining room the same colour as the cats, our bedroom, the big white spare room where I did my yoga, and Anthony's daughter's room, a dear little back bedroom, the only one with a view out onto the beautiful long garden with the walnut tree and squirrels playing and eating on the shed roof. We began to rattle around. We started getting on better; I felt like I didn't need so much space. I found that I could sit in a room with Anthony and write. I started writing blogs in the living room on my tablet rather than at my desk on my laptop in preparation for travelling.

I read Elizabeth's Gilbert's book *Big Magic*, about creativity. In it she mentions *'-those dreams where you discover a previously unknown room in your house-',* and I thought, really, that's a thing? I have those dreams regularly. I usually dream about the same flat, not one I have ever had in real life, but in my dreams I return to the same one over and over. It's one of those old terraced houses divided into flats; messy, lots of other flats around. Each time I dream it, I rediscover a whole other set of rooms that are a bit neglected and that I have simply forgotten about. In the dream I wonder what to do with them, which room to sleep in, what to use the rooms for, I suddenly have all this extra space I don't know what to do with.

Sometimes I dream about caged animals that I have forgotten to look after, that I have somehow inexplicably forgotten I had and that are mercifully still alive despite no food or water. I thought all these dreams were about shame, or being messy and disorganised. So when I continued reading and Elizabeth Gilbert went on to say that those dreams are all about *'- that expansive feeling that your life has more possibility to it than you thought it did.'* that was very pleasing to me. I realised I had it wrong: those dreams weren't about me being irresponsible or my buried shames, they were about the hitherto unknown expansiveness and potential of my own life. I have nothing to be ashamed of. At worst, the unfed animals were a gentle chide or reminder about my sometimes neglected creative work.

When I was seventeen I left home and went to live in a gypsy caravan in someone's garden. I was desperate to leave home and some acquaintances of my mum let me live in it for £10 a week. It was beautiful, wooden with narrow bunk beds that came down from the ceiling on metal chains. I ate tinned marrowfat peas, tinned tomatoes and crispbread and sort of made do. I loved it but I was drinking, going out and sleeping around and I got kicked out for having too many visitors.

I had intended to go and live in a commune when I left home; I'm not sure why I didn't, it was probably because I was too shy to ask! I'd been to a party there and heard The Smiths for the first time. Some women who lived there had been friendly to me. Also there was a good looking guy in a black jumper who came up behind me and danced with me.

During my few months at the caravan I had been self medicating my general ennui or long term existential depression unsuccessfully with Kalms from the health food shop. One of the guys I was seeing persuaded me to go to the doctor. I probably hoped for pills but the doctor wanted me to try counselling. A woman turned up at the caravan. I think I was surprised to see her- maybe she had turned up unannounced or maybe I hadn't got the letter. The first thing she asked me was did I know x, from the commune. It was the guy I had a crush on, who had danced with me. She told me he had died, I can't remember now whether it was a road traffic accident or suicide. After that my vague sense of ennui and existentialist woe became all the more difficult to describe, and obviously impossible to compare with her having just lost her son. There followed a long awkward silence. 'Well if you're not going to talk,' she said, 'There's no point in me being here,' and she left. It was the only time I've ever been to see a doctor about my mental health and it would be another twenty-seven years until I sought any kind of help again.

***

Although initially I had dreamt of getting rid of everything and just leaving with a backpack, in the middle of all the decluttering and house selling we bought a narrowboat to come back to. It wasn't a gypsy caravan but it had a red wooden arch separating the rooms and the hatches were decorated with, wait for it, gypsy caravans!

Before we decided to do this, I read articles about voluntary simplicity, downsizing and living a simple life. I was no stranger to decluttering, making do, anti consumerism and wanting to live with less stuff. I believed in it all. But actually putting theory into practice was much harder than we expected. I realised that 'escaping the matrix' isn't just about making one decision or taking one big step, it's a process. There is a period of transition that takes time and in our experience involved our resolve being continually tested. Even when we actually did it, it was still hard, right up until the end. It was like we were being challenged, Are you ready? Are you sure?

On moving day we moved in a blizzard and thick snow, the UK experiencing the worst weather conditions for forty years. Several roads were closed and we tried three different routes into Norwich before we found one which was open.

We were determined to get there. That's what you have to do. If you decide to change your path, your script, you get obstacles and you get tempted back. That's why you have to keep taking steps. Sell house- can't go back- literally, we had posted the keys through the estate agent's door so couldn't have gone back for the last night anyway.

We stayed five nights in Norwich Travelodge completing all the admin and last minute tasks associated with selling the house, buying the boat and going off travelling for a year, then we moved onto the boat for two weeks.

Immediately there were hiccups. We couldn't fill up the water tank. Then the first time we turned on the water we discovered a leaking pipe under the sink. We had only been on the boat for a day or two. We were probably both thinking, should we have done that, given up the house. But the good thing about taking steps or having taken steps is that your previous actions propel you onwards even when you have a wobbly moment. You sell your house, you buy a boat. That means that now you live on a boat, this is your new life and you have to get used to that. You have to hold your resolve and you have to keep going.

Our main concern was whether the two of us could live in such a small space but that two weeks living on the boat felt good for both of us. I really enjoyed cooking in the kitchen, making simple cheap food out of what we had in the cupboards, making do, and writing. One evening Anthony said to me, 'What's good is you can sit in one place and look around and see everything all the time.' It's like voluntary simplicity for the mind, as compared to a three bedroom house, having to hold it all in one's mind. For a little while Anthony even thought the boat might be 'the thing.' I felt almost wistful about having to tear myself away to go to India.

Happy Hippies: Hampi, India

During the night we crossed from Goa into Karnataka which is a dry state. Twice police came on to check for alcohol, woozily I showed them my bag and my water bottles and afterwards I couldn't remember if it was a dream or not.

We arrived at Hampi around seven-thirty am. Outside the coach was a big crowd of men- auto drivers all wanting to take us to our destination; we had to push our way through to get off the coach.

We met a man- Anaconda, a name we couldn't forget who took us in his auto to Hampi village and a cafe- the Chillout. We had banana and peanut butter on toast while looking out of the open sides of the cafe onto a surreal landscape of banana palms and huge boulders.

Our guesthouse was on the other side of the river. At the river the temple elephant was being given a ceremonial bath, this happens every morning apparently. There were huge boulders in and around the river. People were washing clothes in the water. In the background were the temples. I hadn't realised but it's not just the temples in Hampi that are amazing, it's everything.

The ferry operates only in the daytime and goes back and forth only when it has twenty passengers waiting for it. We waited patiently and then stepped carefully onto the planks and into the boat with our backpacks. The small ferry took us across the river, past the elephant having its bath. It was so surreal and amazing that we just watched, we didn't even take photographs.

From the bank on the other side of the river it was a short, hot walk up a bit of a hill with stone steps with flat bits at the sides for mopeds to use; I could hardly watch as they went up the steep slope.

It was still early and we had to wait while they got our rooms ready. We sat downstairs in the communal area, a shaded area with low tables and floor cushions, sweating, drinking water and chatting. We met Elle, an outdoors instructor who had lived and worked in the Middle East and Africa and was reassuringly unfazed by the heat and by travelling in general. Elle was smart, confident, super fit, friendly and so well travelled and experienced especially for someone so young; quite inspirational, if we could get over how unfit we felt next to her! She invited Jude out to go swimming, which they did later on, and she invited us all to go bouldering which we very politely declined.

Our rooms were nice, off a cool shaded veranda with swing beds just outside the rooms. There was even a cat with three cute kittens. Jude and I sat out there keeping cool, him lying on the swing bed and me sitting on my yoga mat on the cool stone floor, chatting and writing and sorting and posting photos, while Anthony slept inside.

Just beyond the veranda was a hot concrete patio surrounded by mango trees. Jude and I saw a monkey on the patio; the housekeeping woman was shooing it away. When she saw me and Jude with our cameras she stopped and gestured to us and the monkey, handing over the task to us. We took some photos and then had to shoo the monkey away. I clapped my hands. It bared its teeth at me before disappearing off into the trees.

Unintentionally we had booked to stay on 'the other side' of the river, meaning the other side to the main temples. We were pleased to find out that this was apparently the 'cool' side, where the hippies hang out but we quickly realised none of them wanted to even say hello let alone hang out with us. Presumably because Anthony and I were too old and none of us were dressed right. I was surprised about how much it bothered me to walk past some tall, blond yoga bodied hippy-ish traveller, say hello and be completely ignored, but we all felt it and the three of us discussed it at length.

Near our guesthouse was a little food place with just a couple of tables outside and floor cushions and low tables indoors. People would lie in there in the afternoons. The first day I was a bit too shy to go in there with the cool hippies. The next day I went with Elle and we ate lunch together. I had a masala dosa. Elle, the super confident outdoor instructor-traveller chatted to me, sharing her story, which included many difficult personal challenges, and reminded me yet again that there's always more to people than meets the eye.

The little cafe was super cheap, which was why it later bothered Anthony to see two young Western men quibbling over the bill, not wanting to pay for two chapattis when they had only ordered one, even though they had actually eaten both; we are talking ten pence here! Some people make a thing of spending as little as possible in India as if it's part of the experience but that just seemed mean. We ate there several times after that; vegetable noodles with sweet chilli sauces on the side and big vegetable spring rolls, beginning a spring roll love affair.

We got up early to beat the heat and cross over the river to go and look at the temples, the ruins and the huge boulders and the many, many monkeys that live in the temple grounds. It isn't that you might see a monkey if you are lucky, or that if you look carefully you may see one or two in the distance. There are monkeys everywhere, climbing up the carved walls of the temple, sitting calmly at the foot of statues; grooming each other or eating bananas. Right there, feet, inches away and completely unfazed by the many tourists walking past or taking photographs. Tens of monkeys, hundreds probably, adult monkeys and family groups, baby monkeys suckling or riding on their mothers' backs. Ever since he was little, Jude has loved monkeys. At one point he went out. Anthony told me afterwards that Jude had said to him, 'I had to go outside for a while; it was just so overwhelming seeing so many monkeys.'

By eleven it was almost too hot to walk on the stone floors barefoot. On the way back, waiting in the heat for the ferry, I bought coconuts, my first shy purchase from a street stall. I also bought several newspaper cones of what I thought were grapes but which turned out to be some kind of sour green fruit that we couldn't eat.

On our side of the river was a place where people go bouldering, in the evening we went for a walk there and were waylaid by a group of three children selling chai. We bought some, not realising they were all working separately; one ended up taking all the money and we had to give more to another one, the three of them descending into a big argument with lots of shouting.

We came to the bouldering place and walked amongst the huge boulders on the rock slopes, they looked as though they might fall but have probably been there forever, balanced on each other like strange rock snowmen. Surrounding it all, walls of sandy coloured boulders and rocks, almost polystyrene looking, like the set of Planet of the Apes or Star Trek. The place seemed to look almost unreal, as if the world began there. Looking around it was easy to imagine that there was a big explosion and everything fell to Earth as it was created.

Even us, I whispered to myself. In moments like that, when everything seems unreal, where the unusualness or the beauty of my surroundings is so intense that it takes on an unreal quality, I can believe that I am living in a created universe. Some people call it a simulation, a hologram or even a computer game. Bill Hicks called it a dream. We sat on the huge flat rocks. They were still so warm from the day's sun that I had to put my bag under the contact points of my feet to stop them from burning. We watched the sun set behind the clouds. I felt that I was absorbing the sun's energy in a safe way, as well as absorbing power and energy from those huge rocks.

In the beach hut in Agonda I had meditated for a second time, again dropping into it easily after a little yoga. I couldn't help remembering that when I had meditated a few days earlier, the overriding sensation had been FEAR. This time, it wasn't there and although I may have initially suggested it to myself (it's hard in meditation to know if an idea has come from my thinking brain or from deep inside me) it felt true and stayed with me for the whole practice. The new word was STRONG.

Sitting on the rocks, although it was more reflection, mindfulness and energy absorption rather than actual meditation, there was still definitely no fear.

Of course, just being in India did not mean I was automatically a different person from who I was in the UK. I still got anxious and had some OCD. However lots of stuff was okay or much better than I had expected. I coped fine with the heat in Hampi which had been my biggest fear. The weather reports said it was '39°C but felt like 42°C,' whatever that means. Hot, anyway, hot enough that when I heard it was 32°C in Goa I thought that sounded fine. I even came to kind of enjoy the feeling of sweat pouring off me, as if I were being detoxified which I suppose I was. I also learned to accept and enjoy the sense of languidness which was essential to embrace, and which often included a nap in the afternoons.

I wrote at the time: I haven't shaved my arm pits since a week or two before we came out. I haven't done anything with my hair other than wear it in a bun all the time. Even in the hottest weather my clothes work and feel really comfortable. I have hardly any clothes, but they are all functional and all go together. During the day I wear very baggy black linen trousers, 'white' (well, they were when I bought them) shirts, a lilac hat and a cream scarf. The scarf I put across my shoulders and the back of my neck or on the hottest days over the top of the hat, creating a kind of bonnet effect shading the sides of my face, like a Victorian colonial lady. All fine, as long as I don't look in a mirror! In the evenings when it cools down a little I do my best to look nice, I shower, brush my hair and put it up into a fresh bun, put on a clean black vest top and my black knee-length skirt, ditch the hat and drape my cream scarf over my shoulders. By my standards I look good, or as good as I can in this heat.

My tummy is fine (although I have developed a new standard of fine since being in India). I have stopped caring about products. I've stopped needing to moisturise as much and decided that when I run out of Oil of Olay (which I have used every day for the past twenty years) I will just buy something else, whatever is available. Likewise even with my beloved Body Shop hemp hand cream I only experience mild anxiety regarding what to do when it runs out.

***

It was too hot to walk everywhere so one day we got an auto for the day, driven by Anaconda's cousin to see the more spread out temples and ruins. We saw the Lion God Narasimha with his jewelled eyes and broken hands. We stopped for coconuts at a street stall when we got too hot. At the huge statue of Ganesh, carved from a single piece of stone, we arrived at the exact moment that the woman who works there cleaning and minding the statue arrived. She opened the gates and we went inside and walked around and hugged the huge warm belly of Ganesh.

Meeting Indian people was nice. There were lots of Indian tourists who were very friendly and even took our photographs and took selfies with us. A Catholic nun stopped us to talk in the main temple, she was concerned about us being too hot; she advised me to wear a piece of onion in my hair to stop me getting heat stroke. We had met people in Goa but that was largely a pop up population, there only for the season before packing up and going home to places including Kerala and Nepal. In Hampi almost everyone we met had been born there and lived there all their lives. Our driver had lived amongst the ruins as a child before the people were moved out from there and his family moved into the town.

When we had to wait for the ferry we bought tea from a small chai stall and the man spread out a blanket in the shade for us to sit on. He introduced us to his family and told us his story. He had to get married at nineteen as his mother was sick and couldn't cook. Before his two sons were born he had a daughter who was born at seven months and died; his wife had to go to a hospital in the city for an operation which cost an enormous amount of money.

***

On the temple side is a well known sunset point, getting there involves walking and then clambering up a path of boulders to the top. It got increasingly scary, with bigger gaps between the boulders, and I got scared and had to stop. Jude was way ahead of us and continued to the top. Anthony stayed with me. Even just halfway up was a great view; seeing Hampi spread out we got a sense of how big it is. I was worried about Jude especially as he hadn't taken any water. But he came down blessed and buzzing; he had met the holy man at the top, been given a blessing and some other tourists had given him some water. He said there were crazy moments of jumping across gaps in the boulders but he had just gone with it; the other people climbing and jumping in flip flops.

It was his second blessing; he had also been given one at the main temple. Jude loved Hampi, we all did. He had spent some time alone near the temples, just sitting amongst the ruins and having a moment. Already he had noticed the effect of being in a country where religion is very important to people. India and Hampi in particular is so steeped in spirituality it wasn't surprising that it had an effect on us.

We got the ferry over the river each day, it is just a short distance and the man does this back and forth all day. We were reminded of Siddhartha. In a similar vein, we met the man who takes the money at the main temple, he told us that he has worked there caring for the temple for forty years.

We moved to the temple side for our last night. I chose our room. It had frosted green glass windows which overlooked the banana palms. The walls were painted deep orange with small alcoves like little shrines and the bathroom was tiled in pretty pink. There was no ac and we lay on the bed coated in sweat. We fell asleep in the afternoon with the door open because of the heat.

I was woken by the sound of someone saying, 'Hello hello,' and knocking on the door. I stayed half asleep and let Anthony get up. 'Monkeys,' a man said. A little boy was holding my tablet, my dearly beloved tablet, the device I do everything on, in its bright pink and white polka dot bag. They stood by the door, me still in bed. Confused, Anthony said, 'You left it somewhere.'

'No, it was just here,' I said, pointing to the low coffee table in the centre of the room.

'Monkeys,' the man said. 'Keep door shut.'

Our room was on the first floor and the monkey troupe jumped along the rooftops, looking for food. I kept my tablet in a zip up plastic toiletry type bag; apparently monkeys take bags in case there is food inside. People in the rooftop cafe opposite saw the monkeys take and drop the bag and the boy walking below had picked it up and brought it back. I was very lucky that it didn't break.

I was half asleep and bewildered at the time and afterwards I searched for something to give to say thank you to the little boy. I had brought lots of new gel pens from the UK, the special kind I like as well as some new pencils and an eraser thinking I might do some sketching. I gathered some of the pens and all of the pencils and the eraser and bound them in some new hair elastics also brought from home. I thought I'd missed the boy and his father and wasn't sure how to find them.

I asked around and took the presents out with me, hoping I would bump into them. We visited the main temple again where all the monkeys were, this time it was dusk. In the open courtyard were groups of people and lots of families sitting with tea and food. We watched monkeys including tiny babies climbing up the walls and the arches at the entrance. I couldn't imagine anywhere more wonderful.

Later, on the short walk from the room to the Chillout an Indian man with a moustache smiled at me. I recognised him, but I wasn't sure. 'Monkeys,' he said, pointing upstairs to my room.

'Oh, that was you! Can I come and say thank you?' I followed the man downstairs, it turned out they lived in the apartment below. The man's wife and young daughter were there. He spoke to his wife. 'He sleeping,' he said. 'We can give.'

'For my brother?' the daughter said, as I went to hand over the presents. Hurriedly I split the pack into two bundles, chastising myself for my thoughtlessness.

'Oh but of course, you can share;' I gave her the presents, the family standing around politely just inside their doorway. I was so grateful that I had bumped into the boy's father, and was able to say a heartfelt thank you, clumsily saying thank you in Hindi, me much more excited and overwhelmed than any of them.

I did this by myself and then went to join Anthony and Jude in the Chillout. They were sitting at a low table in the lounging area. The staff were super friendly and the food was great. We ate homemade spicy vegeburgers with thin homemade chips, with fresh fruit juices. A beautiful cow walked right into the restaurant. One of the staff led the cow outside using a piece of bread. I sat quietly on the floor cushions. I didn't know at first what the feeling was but it was so strong that after a while I took out my tablet and went on WordPress because otherwise I might have properly started crying. That feeling, of course, was love: emotional, spiritual and sensory overwhelm. I read one of my favourite blogger's latest post: she mentioned Siddhartha. Three weeks in, after the initial challenges of Delhi and being sick, I had fallen in love with India.

***

Jude decided to stay on in Hampi for a few days. Although he was only eighteen, almost nineteen he was used to travelling in Europe and very independent. We thought it would be a good experience for him to have a few days in Hampi by himself and to travel back by himself. Anaconda said he would make sure he got the coach okay.

The next morning Anthony and I left at five-thirty am. It was still dark and we saw people waking up and starting their day. We drove past carts pulled by oxen, including a convoy, and another overtaking on a bend in the dark. Luckily our driver was very good and braked in time. 'Crazy driving,' he said to us with a smile, not even annoyed. We drove past all kinds of temples and shrines, feeling the cool night air through the open sides of the auto. We saw the dawn break. It was a magical journey. If the night before I had fallen in love with India, then that morning I felt like I had finally arrived.

***

The disadvantage of booking online is that you don't really know what the area is going to be like until you get there. Our guest house in Anjuna was down an empty road with nothing much else around. We walked down to the beach that evening to eat; all along the beach were touristy bars and restaurants, all garishly lit and playing loud competing music. It was the complete opposite to Agonda. We chose somewhere at random and ordered vegetable spring rolls and had a word with ourselves. We reminded each other that the point of coming to India wasn't simply to visit pretty places, it was to have an experience and the experience of Anjuna was just as valid as that of Hampi.

As we walked back to the guesthouse street dogs barked at us, standing guard outside and blocking our path. We were intimidated, the dogs in Agonda had been mostly friendly so we were a bit taken aback, and got ready with a bag and a water bottle, all we had to defend ourselves. We told ourselves we would have heard about it if tourists got regularly attacked by dogs in Anjuna.

That evening we walked into Anjuna town. It was actually a nice walk and we saw some cool looking places; if we'd booked to stay there instead it probably wouldn't have seemed so bad.

We stopped to talk to some young local guys sitting on a bench who offered to share their cigarettes and drinks with us, happy to meet and talk to us. One was a petrochemical engineer doing an internship and about to have a job interview for Shell. 'But today we are happy hippies,' they said, and invited us out to party with them that night.

Later on we walked past two men standing by a scooter. One asked Anthony if he wanted to buy any weed, he said yes and off we all went. 'We also have MDMA and cocaine,' the man said. I wasn't at all comfortable about going off with these men, especially when they took us into a residential area and it was completely dark, down lots of lefts and rights and paths and alleys; I would have had no idea how to get back. I didn't want to be there but I didn't want to leave Anthony there either.

We arrived at a house, there was a woman outside smoking, a Westerner and I was momentarily reassured. I had hoped to stay outside and chat to her but we were ushered inside into a bare room with just a single bed and a floor mat. I got more and more anxious as one, two, then three men appeared in the small room but Anthony seemed completely relaxed.

We didn't have enough money on us to get everything. The main guy said that was no problem, he would take Anthony back on his scooter and I could stay there. Another man said he would make me Lebanese tea. I am sure I would have been fine but all I could think of was what idiots we'd look if something went wrong. It had nothing to do with being in India, I wouldn't have done that in England, and anyway Anthony wouldn't have left me like that anywhere.

We went back to the guesthouse in a taxi to get the bank cards, then onto the ATM and then back into town, with me feeling anxious and panicky throughout. We met the men back in town and I relaxed. While Anthony was walking up the road with the main guy, paying him the other one said to me, 'When we saw you two I said to him, 'Shall we ask them if they want anything to smoke?' and he said, 'No they're too old!'' We laughed and then we chatted about his family and kids and I felt a bit bad that I had been so anxious and afraid earlier on.

Afterwards we were both high with excitement and me with relief. We walked around for ages buying cigarettes, trying unsuccessfully to remember what Jude had taught us about how to tell if they were fakes or not. When our feet started to hurt we went back to the restaurant near our guesthouse to eat dinner.

We'd been there for lunch and I'd had huge spring rolls, overstuffed and delicious like the ones in Hampi. Anthony had ordered noodles and stir fried vegetables which were also very good. At lunch I'd said, 'I'm going to come back tonight and have this, and this, and this,' but at ten pm, high on adrenaline I couldn't eat much. We were very happy, eating dinner by the sea, sharing the adventure.

Feeling better, I shared my insecurities. In Hampi we were waiting on our side of the river for the ferry when a young woman arrived with a big backpack and wearing a short strappy sundress. Seeing every man's gaze fall upon this beautiful creature, even if it's all just animal biology, forced me to confront it: *The only time this stuff matters, is when it does.* Just when I had convinced myself that it doesn't matter what I look like, we meet someone who is so luminously young and beautiful, dressed in a skimpy dress and it kind of feels, *Well that's not fair.* It's not fair that I dress all modestly and you don't. Plus of course I am much older and even in my youth was never amazingly beautiful.

It was very hard for me to even talk to her (although I did) which is a terrible thing to admit. So not only are beautiful young women underestimated in terms of their depth and abilities by both men and women but men and women find it hard to talk to them because they look so good. Like how I was surprised when I saw photographs of one of my favourite bloggers after reading her for a long time first. She writes with so much wisdom and insight and is one of the few who I feel I can relate to. She looked so young and yes so beautiful and makeup-y and fashion-y and wasn't what I expected. I wondered how often she is underestimated or people are distracted by her youth and beauty, expecting wisdom to only come from older people.

I reminded myself that the people who are there in front of us are there to teach us something about ourselves, it's not about them. Above all, as ever, judge against myself not others. I would probably feel better if I did a proper yoga practice or an intensive course or lost weight but in the meantime try and do some yoga and some exercise every day, eat less and lighten up on the dress code especially in tourist areas and when I'm with Anthony.

But it was really nothing to do with her or my weight or my clothes, it was to do with me and my mood. If I'd been feeling better, I would have been okay. *Surrender gracefully the things of youth,* I know.

'It's their time,' Anthony said. 'For them to shine, and they have disadvantages, being unsure of themselves, worried about their future, and age has its advantages. And anyway it's not about the other people, the hippies who don't say hi, the young hot people.'

'We (older people) have no help, only un-help (advertising, insecurity).' I said.

'Well you have older people, showing you the way,' Anthony said. Yes, that's what I need to be! It was good, talking together, being happy and afterwards we walked assertively past the barking dogs with (almost) no fear.

The next day I was sitting on the floor when Anthony said calmly, 'You may want to move.' I knew what that meant: a spider. Anthony asked me to get the jug from the bathroom. The spider wasn't that big so I thought I'd be brave for once and try to help. As the spider began to run over to my side of the room I rushed out of the bathroom forgetting all about the wet tile floor and how slippery those floors are. I fell over the bathroom step and landed, luckily not too hard on my coccyx. Anthony rushed over to me and put his arm around my back. Even though I was saying, 'I'm fine, get the spider,' his face was so full of concern that I realised he was really frightened, (of me hurting myself, not of the spider). I expected to ache for a few days but I got off lightly and took it as a warning.

According to the internet Arambol was, 'Where the hippies go now that Anjuna has become too overdeveloped, but normal people go there too.' I found a page with a description and photographs and sent it to Jude. He emailed back saying it sounded perfect.

***

The guesthouse was up high above the beach and painted bright green which made it easy to orientate to. A big shared balcony outside the rooms looked out onto the sea and the long sandy beach. We booked in for a week and booked a room a couple of doors down for Jude who was coming back the next day.

Anthony and I had a night to ourselves. We took a bit of the MDMA, not enough to feel awful the next day as Jude was coming back early, and reconnected, topping each other up with compliments and romantic reminiscing. When we feel close I never feel insecure.

The next day I went shopping and bought a flouncy black dress, just above the knee, okay for Goa and can be worn on top of trousers for more conservative areas. I said to Anthony. 'It's like I've rediscovered myself as a sexual being.'

Jude arrived back safe and sound. We'd booked him into an ac room in Hampi, having realised that non ac was unbearable. Jude had met a group of girls on the coach and they had been messaging each other; the girls were in non ac and said they were dying and so they all ended up sleeping in Jude's room.

I bought my new dress from Lakshmi's stall. Anthony had walked past her shop on the day we arrived and made friends, promising to come back with me. Lakshmi was petite, absolutely beautiful and so friendly and chatty that it took ages to be able to look around, by which time I was never getting out of there without buying something.

She told me her story: she came from a poor uneducated family in Hampi, with no education and no work. She came to Goa at the age of six and worked as a beach seller with her auntie, for four years with no wages and two years with wages. She told me the other beach sellers compete against newcomers and call the police who chase them off. She learned English from an Israeli hippie with dreadlocks who had an Indian boyfriend and in return Lakshmi taught her Hindi. The rest of Lakshmi's family moved to Goa and they all worked in construction, carrying rocks.

We saw so much construction going on in Goa, the sight of women carrying cement, women and men carrying bowls of rocks and laying out in the heat of the day absolutely exhausted was a common sight.

The adults carried bags of cement and Lakshmi had smaller jobs as she was only ten years old. Finally she got work in the shop we were standing in. Of course, I bought more than I wanted to and spent more too but I didn't mind.

Our room, painted green with our clothes hung up on a few nails and a table with all our stuff: chargers, tablets, snacks, water bottles and toiletries, was the definition of messy minimalism. We had everything we needed but it wasn't artfully arranged or styled in any way. Outside each room there were seats and a small table. The Wi-Fi was a bit patchy so we all spent a lot of time in the restaurant bar downstairs.

As well as patchy Wi-Fi we had water shortages, although they didn't last longer than a few hours. The shower looked to my UK eyes like it was dangerous, with bare flex and a plug in the wall right near the water. I hesitated for a moment before using it for the first time, then thought, 'When in Rome...' A lot of the shops sold petrol for mopeds in clear plastic bottles, like lemonade bottles which sat outside the shops in the full glare of the blazing sun. There's just a different attitude to health and safety.

I got into bad habits smoking Jude's cigarettes and drinking Kingfisher in the restaurant bar; embracing the smoking, drink anytime and lack of routine until I realised that having some kind of basic routine around exercise and writing works better for me.

Our love affair with spring rolls had begun in Hampi, continued in Anjuna and then reached its peak in Anjuna at The Eyes of Buddha where they were huge, filled with vegetables and served with little pots of chilli tomato sauce. The Eyes of Buddha didn't have Wi-Fi so the three of us talked and played cards and afterwards continued playing cards back on the balcony.

Anthony and I got on well and I was conscious of setting a good example to Jude about relationships, speaking out loud about never minding about jokes or sarcasm and letting people off who love you. Realising at last that Anthony would never do anything to hurt me intentionally and that if I act like he has, that hurts him a lot, as it does the other way around.

At the end of April I wrote: 'One month since we left the boat. Yesterday was the first day that I thought: I think my tummy is okay now. The first day I haven't got up in the night or before dawn with diarrhoea.'

A couple of days later, on my forty-eighth birthday I got up early, did some yoga then went for a long walk. Starting that day I decided to start posting the blog on the same day every week to help me create a writing routine. As I thought this I realised I honestly did not know what day it was. Not in the, I don't know what day it is, think for a second then you do type of way. I mean I really didn't know what day it was. I had to remember the last time I knew and work it out from there. I could not remember the last time I had so completely forgotten what day it was.

Having no routine and drinking and smoking anytime was sort of fun but it's easy to cop out of getting anything done under those conditions. Walking on the beach that day, I realised: How lucky am I, or rather, what a gift I have given to myself, to have a whole year in which I can create a routine around writing? Or, to be on the more negative side; I chucked away my job and my three bedroom house, all that better had been worth it. Of course, unhealthy habits and general lack of confidence can follow us almost everywhere. I am fully aware that whatever it was about me that had got in the way of me taking my writing seriously in England could still get in the way in India.

As I walked back along the beach a man asked if I wanted to buy any weed. I politely declined but I was pleased to be asked- I wasn't too old after all! Two other men on the beach asked to take a selfie with me. The previous day a whole Indian family had asked me to be in a family photo with them and one of the women had asked to have a selfie with just me. Jude had been in a family photo too, he had come back laughing about it, 'They just put a toddler in my lap!'

Anthony bought me a ring with a blue turquoise stone for my birthday. It was Jude's birthday two days before mine and we bought him a massage. I walked there with him and stayed and chatted to Meera who ran the place. She said she was watching television, 'Kerala,' she said, 'Many elephants, do you want to see?' so I followed her inside.

The room was functionally furnished with two single beds and a plastic chair. There were only a few items, pieces of paperwork and a handful of decorative and personal items. On the wall were wedding posters- colour photographs of the couple and the date of the wedding and framed pictures of Jesus. It was a kind of functional, practical minimalism. Meera and her brother spent nine months out of twelve in Goa, they had rented the same house for the last fourteen years. During the off season she went back home to Kerala.

Meera told me to sit on the chair and she sat on the bed. She offered me a glass of sweet black tea which she poured from a metal teapot on the sideboard. It was the first time I had been invited into someone's home in India.

On the television was Thrissur Pooram, an annual event involving lots of elephants from two temples. The two groups of elephants stood in a row facing each other across an empty open space. The elephants were ornately decorated with their handlers draped in white. Beautiful coloured parasols were held above them. Every few minutes the parasols were changed over to a new colour. Teams of helpers on the ground helped with taking the old ones down and passed up the new parasols so that the whole row changed colour almost simultaneously. Pink, green, gold, purple, silver, red, the colours went on and on.

I felt very honoured and pleased to have been invited to sit and watch with her and the easy, relaxed atmosphere reminded me of the cosy, slightly soporific experience of watching the Olympics late at night as a child with my grandmother. Female company, no responsibility, nothing to do except ooh and ahh at each change of the parasols; sixty changes and sixty different colours for each of the two temples. Meera told me it takes six months of stitching to make the parasols.

I had imagined the elephants would walk towards each other across the open space but suddenly the crowds began pouring into the space, hundreds and hundreds of people. There were a lot of police to control the crowds. So many people; to me it looked almost dangerous but Meera seemed unperturbed. The crowds were men only. I asked Meera where the women were, she told me that women and children are in a separate area, 'Safer,' she said. The camera shots were all of the elephants and the parasols and the general crowd, no close ups of individual people. It was very different to UK filming of events where the camera picks out and closes in on pretty women, cute kids or people in fancy dress.

The commentator mentioned a long list of countries which I took to mean and Meera seemed to confirm, where Kerala people living overseas were watching. The commentary was in Malayalam, the language of Kerala although it was also available in Hindi or English. Meera told me she spoke Malayalam, Hindi, English and Tamil. I was shamefaced to admit I could only speak English.

I had looked up things to do in Arambol and one of them was a famous Banyan tree with an art installation nearby, a ceramic bowl with 'Give if you can, Take if you have to,' written on it. To get there we had to walk along the beach, across a little bay and then into the woods up a steep path. It was hot and the wood was full of mosquitoes, we hadn't brought any spray out as it was daytime.

One of the street dogs followed us all the way. The dogs in Arambol were all of similar type, medium sized and friendly. Sometimes we would be walking along the path and a dog would just pop out and start following us. Or a dog would be sitting at our feet at a restaurant, a person would walk by and the dog would just get up and follow them instead without any encouragement from either party.

I saw a Banyan tree and thought maybe that was the one although I didn't see the art installation. Further up there was another tree decorated with prayer flags and with smoke coming from a fire. Jude and I went to look. A Western hippy man was there with a young child and an Indian man. They were making tea and we felt like we were intruding onto their camp. The Indian man said they were meditating and invited us to sit but we were too shy and left.

Later on I found out that a Baba (a holy man) lives up there. The internet had pictures of hippies smoking in a circle and mentioned bringing gifts so I was relieved we hadn't stayed as we hadn't brought anything.

I considered going back to see the Baba but really, I didn't want to. Even after giving a group of Russian tourists directions from our restaurant I still didn't want to go. What was I looking for? If it happened spontaneously, like Jude getting a blessing at the temple in Hampi and again at the top of the boulder climb, that's one thing, but I won't search. That is probably the wrong attitude if I am meant to be writing a book but in all honesty I was moved enough by Meera inviting me into her house to watch Thrissur Pooram and even more by the boy and his dad rescuing my tablet for me from the monkeys in Hampi.

On our last night Jude took us out for dinner at a restaurant on the beach; fresh and tasty peanut masala, cashew nut chilli, soft aubergine, eaten with our feet in the sand and the sound of good music and the red glow of lights from inside the restaurant.

***

In the taxi from Arambol to Panaji: I'm trying to write down the colours of the houses we pass but before I can think of the word for the colours of one house we're onto another and another, moving from one scene to another faster than my fingers can scribble it all down. My notebook looks like a list of paint chart colours: olive, yellow, emerald, lemon, sunflower, mustard, ochre, mauve, turquoise, pistachio and avocado. Combinations: turquoise and maroon, orange and yellow, peach and leaf green, dull orange and dark pine green, royal-navy blue and white, terracotta and cream, powder blue and sea blue. An orange house with blue window frames. A house with the upper and lower floors painted different colours. Some houses were faded, some abandoned and derelict looking. Metal balconies. Fuchsia paint matching the earth and the flowers.

The earth where it is uncovered is pinky red and pink blossoms are everywhere, in the trees and on the ground. Rubbish at the side of the road covered in a layer of grey dust, piles of stones, everything gently sprinkled with pink blossom. A family on a moped, no helmets, the man driving, the woman side saddle, a thick gold sash across her back, the little girl in a yellow-gold party dress.

Green everywhere, India is so green, in spite of it being so dry and hot. A bright orange temple with stalls outside selling bright yellow flower garlands. A yellow building with big outside pipes, each pipe painted a different colour. A temple painted burnt orange, red and gold set into lush deep green hills. There's probably not enough colours in the English language to adequately describe the beauty of India.

The visuals create emotions, spark ideas, lines, all this exacerbated by moving. Feeling totally blissed out, from the sweet visual sensory overload and my thoughts. Realisations about writing:

use the senses, use the emotions. Draw on every book I've read, every class I've been to. My spiritual journey before I left; all that meditation, chanting, religions, reading, thinking, discussions. All that, got me here. Here! To beautiful, beautiful India!

Coming up to the guesthouse the area looked a little run down and we were momentarily concerned about what it would be like but when we got to the guesthouse I saw, No, it's okay. It was painted pink with a dark pink trim, the same as the first house I had noticed on the journey.

As it was only for one night we had booked one room for the three of us. Our room was big and painted a clean bright white with a large wet room. There was also another little room with a sink and a mirror in it, plenty big enough to get dressed in and even to do a bit of yoga in. There were three single beds and some fold out foam mattresses that we used as seats and also added one to Anthony's bed which was very uncomfortable.

The shower in Arambol was a trickle even when the water was on. It had run out that morning and we had arrived in Panaji hot, sweaty and dirty. This was a power shower, with hot water too if we wanted. It was such a pleasure, the best shower by far since arriving.

And it had ac! We hadn't booked this, it just did. Except for taking pity on Jude in Hampi, we are not doing ac on the trip. The manager laughed when I got excited about this, 'It's the first time I've had ac!' I told him. In Arambol we had felt fine in temperatures of 35-38°C but we were at the beach and there was a strong sea breeze a lot of the time. Here we were not on the beach and it felt considerably hotter.

We went into town to eat and to use the Wi-Fi to get Jude checked in for his flight home. We noticed the kitchen staff staring at me through the hatch. A whole family asking for money, waited for us outside a shop. We were followed down the street and through the park by people trying to sell us stickers and scarves.

In the evening we got a taxi to the beach and walked back. We passed Banyan trees whose branches trailed downwards, becoming roots and other huge trees that took up the whole pavement and reached all the way across the road, their branches becoming one. I hugged them, their huge trunks still warm to the touch even well into the evening.

We walked past a big group of pavement dwellers. There were a few smart shops and then the area became very run down looking and the roads and pavements became rough and uneven. We passed broken looking residential buildings, yet even here, in a rundown area a colourful mosaic decorated the pavement around a lamp post. There were several local shops, cafes and hairdressers. Closer to our guesthouse, the pavement disappeared. Several guard dogs ran out from outside houses and scared us. Not far from the scary dogs was a big wall, each section painted a different colour.

In the morning Anthony and I went back to one of the cafes. Anthony said it was the Indian equivalent of a working men's cafe, functional looking with stainless steel tables. We sat upstairs and ordered what the young guys sitting across from us ordered- paratha bhaji, puffy fried bread with curry and sweet black tea which came with lime. It was one of the nicest meals we'd had.

Although it felt ever so slightly edgy, it felt good to be in a real place with real facilities and to use them and interact with the place. We felt we were visitors to an actual town that existed by itself, as opposed to Arambol and Agonda where people have come from all over India just to serve the tourists. It's easy, everything is sanitised and safe. As well as the early morning beach cleaning of rubbish and cow dung in Agonda we had seen a policeman with sticks threatening a woman on the beach who had been asking tourists for money, as if the tourists couldn't possibly see anything that might spoil their paradise holiday. Even the street dogs in Agonda looked okay, whereas in Panaji some of them didn't look so good.

Next door to the guesthouse was a mosque and we heard the call to prayer each day. On one side of the balcony was the mosque, on the other some run down residential buildings. On the balcony itself the red and pink sunlit colours, on the ground below an emaciated white cow and in the centre an explosion of lush green forest. It was as if there was too much packed into the scene, as if one thing would have been enough, the mosque or the forest or the buildings or the cow or even the sunlit painted balcony. That is how it feels a lot in India, as if there's just too much to take in, too much packed into the scene. In the UK there'd be one, at most two things. But in India, there's everything in one picture. 'It's as if everything's been compressed,' Jude said.

It came to the end of Jude's time with us. He'd been with us for almost five weeks. We were all silent on the way to the airport. In the dark I saw a house lit up, every alcove painted a different colour. My heart filled up. 'I want to say I love you.' But like at the beginning of a relationship, where all you see is the good and the bright and the shiny and the fun, I've barely been outside of Goa, we've used taxis and booked ac sleeper trains and buses. I've had it easy. So it's too early to say those words just yet.

***

It was our last opportunity to take the MDMA we had bought in Anjuna. We couldn't take it on the plane to Kerala the next day. We had banana and walnut cake and iced tea in a little cafe by the beach and took it there. We walked on the beach, watching the little Indian owls flying about and then walked back to the room.

In Arambol we had just had a little and reconnected, in Panaji we had a lot. My experience was mixed: great sex, crazy spiritual experiences. Seeing pictures on the bathroom wall of two figures seated in meditation, with bars of light crisscrossing their heads: Us, enlightened; I called Anthony but he was not really interested in all this. Overshadowed by intrusive thoughts and anxiety, I got locked in a loop, loops, some of them really horrible. It probably didn't help that we were essentially marooned in a white room with no Wi-Fi so limited ability to entertain or distract ourselves.

The next morning the alarm went off at eight thirty am. The idea of getting up seemed horrific. Soon afterwards the manager came in asking when we were checking out. Still in bed, we managed to negotiate a later check out. But ultimately we had to get up, get packed and get to the airport, all while feeling extremely fragile.

I stand by myself and I am not afraid: Varkala, India

We arrived in Kerala both feeling flat from Jude going and hungover after our MDMA drug binge in Panaji. I struggled with the practical application; with bringing any of the drug insights into our daily lives. When we were getting to know each other, falling in love, exploring spirituality, me in the midst of awakening, yes, then it was special and a really important part of our lives. Later, it became a bit like, for what? And this time, it's got no relevance, to this life, my best life, nothing left to teach me. I'm not looking to escape. It took a few days to recover physically and emotionally. It felt like a loss and at the same time an acceptance of things changing.

***

Arriving in Kerala the buildings looked very different, more rectangular looking, some with pillars and some painted in shades of yellow or pink. One pink house had the lights on and the door open, inside it was painted jade green. Some of the outside walls of the houses looked like they had wallpaper on but were actually tiles or shiny rocks like a chunky mosaic or a classy pebble dash. Many houses had decorative metalwork gates finished in copper or gold and black. 'Very clean,' our taxi driver said.

We passed big bright white churches, lit up with modern stained glass windows and statues in big glass cases outside. At a Christian service, lots of people in beautiful clothes, lots of white, little girls in what looked like party dresses and lots of music. We saw a Mosque, outside a group of men, on the other side of the road a group of women all dressed in white with white head scarves, again, lots of people and lots of music. A little further down the same road we heard more sound, music or chanting, this time coming from a Hindu temple. Three religions in the space of a couple of miles, coexisting in harmony.

We drove past local shops, general stores and poorer looking buildings. The men were much more in traditional dress, wearing lungis- pieces of material, kind of like thick sarongs, worn long or short. It was nice for us to see as most of the Indian men in Goa had been in more Westernised clothes.

The place where we were staying turned out not to be in the actual town of Varkala itself but in a resort area near the beach called North Cliff, with hut style bungalows around a central courtyard. Everything was wildly painted like something out of The Magic Roundabout.

All around were ayevedic and yoga resorts, mostly closed as it was out of season. We had breakfast at a backpackers cafe overlooking the sea, puttu- steamed rice and coconut turned out from a bowl with a banana and a poppadom on the side. We found another restaurant, family owned, right near our guesthouse, it was cheap and we ate breakfasts there after that, masala dosas, black tea and juices.

***

Along the cliff top white-headed eagles flew level with the top of the cliff. In the distance the cliff top was thick with the deep green of coconut palms and the sea was a huge expanse of blue. Towards the end of the day the sea changed colour from blue to green.

On around day two we fell asleep and woke up after dark with the local family restaurant closed. The guesthouse staff directed us somewhere else, along the top of the cliff in the other direction. Suddenly there was a very touristy strip; clothes stalls similar to the ones in Goa but with more silk, more Ayevedic resorts, and restaurants playing loud Western music. We were disappointed to find this place but we were also hungry so we went and ate at one of the restaurants. We sat outside and ate good food, Kerala potato and coconut curry and thoran- shredded vegetables fried with rice, roti and fresh orange juice.

Anthony found another guesthouse online and we went to check it out, it was near the main local temple and looked as if it was maybe in a less resort-y area. We walked there along the cliff, beyond the tourist strip. The path led down towards another beach, one we hadn't been to before. We turned a corner and everything was different. The area was buzzing with Indian tourists only, families, stalls on the beach and little shops and stalls selling drinks and ice cream.

We never made it as far as the place we had seen online because all of a sudden we saw a photograph of Osho and found ourselves outside the Osho guesthouse. We asked if we could look at a room; a young man named Raul showed us around. A little stone courtyard with lots of pots of green plants led into a stone indoor area painted red and yellow. Two hammock swing chairs hung from the ceiling. There were a few small shelves of books.

I once wrote an utterly heartfelt review on Amazon for *Eat, Pray, Love*. I had read that book seven times, written notes in it, folded over almost every page. I knew I was genuine, so when someone commented, *'This review is as pretentious as the book itself,'* it only made me laugh rather than hurt my feelings. So when I looked on the bookshelf at Osho's and saw a copy of *Eat, Pray, Love*, a new bright red edition that I hadn't seen before, I took it as a sign that we were in a good place.

Raul asked us if we wanted up or down. 'Wherever's coolest,' we both said at the same time. He showed us to a room at the back of the foyer. Even with the fan off it was cooler than our bungalow which felt like an oven during the day. I knew Anthony must have been tired as he was able to sleep during the afternoons in there while I could barely stand to be in there for more than a few moments. This was heaven. A mosquito net hung from the ceiling, the kind you roll and hook up during the day and undo and tuck around the bed at night; up until then we had relied on plug in vaporisers. Raul asked us to pay him one night to secure the booking. Anthony asked if we were getting a receipt. 'Don't you trust me?' Raul asked. It was the start of a nice little friendship.

We left feeling excited about finding our own place in person, booking in spontaneously and having made a decision having not been sure what to do. We bought coconuts from a street stall and walked back to North Cliff. It was dark and we could see the white lights of boats out to sea. As we came up to the top of the cliff we could see more and more lights until it looked like a city of white lights out at sea.

It was always our intention to see out most of the monsoon in one place and we were looking forward to the experience, to finding out what the rain would actually be like. Although it was the pre rains rather than the official monsoon, before we left North Cliff it rained for the first time. I stood out in it and thoroughly enjoyed getting soaked to the skin in the thick, warm rain, and waving to people from the nearby guesthouse who were also out in the rain and laughing. The next morning there were puddles everywhere. The smell was delicious; fresh and peaty and the rain had made new and different flowers come out. It rained most nights after that with big storms in the evenings.

Our plan was to stay in Kerala for the monsoon, avoiding the worst of the heat elsewhere in India before travelling and ending up in Chennai in Tamil Nadu for our flight to Thailand. We were meeting Anthony's daughter Maeve in Thailand, and our six months would be up for our visa. We weren't sure what route to take or how easy it would be to travel during the monsoon. The internet makes it very easy to research information but it can't tell you what to do. We had decided to just get to Kerala and ask someone, a local with good English, what to do. Until I wrote that down, I had forgotten that we said that.

Arriving at Osho's, Anthony went to look around and at the rooftop yoga space he met Yogesh, a very friendly Indian man who spoke perfect English, who comes to Kerala all the time and who lives in Chennai. Within a few minutes he had sorted out all our travel plans and given us lots of advice and tips. Yogesh was going back to Chennai the next day so Anthony seized the moment and invited him out for dinner with us that evening. Evening came, Yogesh said, I've invited Robert, is that okay? *The more the merrier,* we said and off the four of us went for dinner.

Sometimes at home, after a couple of glasses of wine I used to try and share my ideas. Sometimes it would seem promising, then I'd say something and everyone would go a bit quiet. 'I've gone too far again haven't I,' I'd say to Anthony, and everyone would laugh. It was only really the two of us for a long time. And then spontaneously we move into Osho's guesthouse, probably only because of the Netflix documentary we'd started watching when we first got to Varkala, and meet Yogesh.

Yogesh wasn't even supposed to be there, he'd come there on a whim, he was supposed to be in Bangalore. Yogesh had met Robert from Switzerland who was also staying at Osho's. The four of us spent five hours in a restaurant, no drugs, no alcohol, discussing all this stuff, sharing our experiences. *Recognising each other.* All with tales to tell, and all listened to wholly. A community. Understood.

It didn't feel as exciting as it was. It didn't feel 'Boom!' or strange or weird, even though it was all of those things. It felt easy and peaceful. It was more a kind of peaceful awakening, rather than the breathless, rather tiring conversations I sometimes have when I meet someone new and get over excited.

To prove to himself that this stuff works- the mystical theories, law of attraction, trusting the universe- and that all the fear conditioning, everything he had been told, was a lie, as a young man Robert had travelled with no money, deliberately going to countries where he didn't speak the language. He went off into the desert without water, prepared to die unless something happened to help him. He crossed a city in Australia (Darwin) without pausing for traffic and without getting run over, sensing patterns and the flow of the traffic. Before he did it he bet some locals so that they gave him money/food. He arrives at a railway station in a strange country and he trusts that the right person will arrive to help him. He still feels fear, but he understands that it is made or caused by thoughts and/or pictures and he simply fuzzes the fear thoughts and pictures out. Robert is alone, no family, 'It's easier, it's too difficult to have contact,' he said.

Robert served as a powerful reminder of what is possible. He told us about being born, 'Don't drink all the liquid, maybe just a tenth or a fifth of it, it makes you forget. I can remember everything.' He knows what he is for, not to work, he doesn't need to work at a job. Robert sees patterns and can sense all the possibilities in the air of a new place.

Yogesh told us that one night he was out at a celebration, a Shiva festival, he and the people he was with were all stoned. As he walked along with a girl she said, 'You are Shiva.'

'And are you?' Anthony asked. 'Maybe a little,' Yogesh said, 'But I don't want to lead.'

People believing in me, saying, 'You are a writer, you must write your book.'

What is my desert-without-water? I wondered the next morning on my walk. Should I go in an auto by myself to the non English speaking cafe we went to in town, but what for? What would actually be useful? At the end of my walk was a little bay. The sand at the water's edge was sprinkled with a layer of shell, like rough crushed mother-of-pearl or multi-coloured pebble dash. It reminded me of the flooring in hotel bathrooms, beige with tiny coloured pearly bits, plain at first glance but beautiful if examined more closely. I used to stay in Premier Inns a lot with work; the experience of travelling and doing work projects was challenging and a key part of my personal development. I used to notice the beauty, my red notebook and my silver bangles on the night table, a walk by a canal, a pond in the middle of an industrial estate. A sign saying *Electric Avenue.* The bathroom floors. This is a louder, more beautiful version of it of course.

Write the book. Have the confidence to do so. *You can have whatever you want as long as you believe it.* Start with things you can believe, start small, you don't have to believe everything all at once, work up to it slowly. Actions are absolutely just as important as beliefs. You've got to *want* to do it. You've got to *believe* you can do it. And you've got to *take steps practically. Believing in myself.* That's the real impact of that night. That is my desert-without-water.

'Every enlightenment has its own melody.' Robert said. Remember or find out who we are, what we are capable of, what we believe we can do. No labels, it's an ongoing process, always changing. All the Gods we learned about, they were all sure of themselves, they didn't have identity crises or crises of confidence. But maybe we forgot? That's one theory I have believed in; that we are Gods who have forgotten that they are Gods. Immortal beings who have created this for something to do, just to pass the time and have taken a potion to make them forget in order to make the experience richer.

I felt a lightness afterwards, the sense of possibility. It's important to notice and to follow through on any actions which can be taken as a result of being inspired, any practical application. It's easy to have insights and not act on them; it's the follow up that's important.

I won't be going off into the desert without water but what can I do? What experiments can I conduct on myself to help me realise who I am, realise my potential, break free of my conditioning and break on through to the other side in terms of my understanding of what all this is? Most of the things I believe in have been theory only, not tested in real life. I've noticed little things, small things appearing when I need them, a bundle of staples, a loo roll, low-level Law of Attraction type stuff. But I haven't really tested it, this stuff I believe in. Not like Robert, conjuring, trust falling, creating, moving, understanding, seeing patterns, the whole picture.

I went up to the rooftop yoga space to do yoga. The space was reached via some chunky whitewashed stairs at the back of the stone communal area. The floor of the space was concrete painted a faded blue. A sign on the wall, written in chalk asked people to remove their shoes. The roof was made of sheets of corrugated aluminium, the sides were open. On two sides were the guesthouse, Robert's rooftop room and balcony, neighbouring buildings and the street. On the other two sides were lush dense vegetation, palm trees and thick stems of bamboo. I saw that Robert was out on his balcony, watching something on his laptop. I walked past to the back corner furthest away so as to be out of each other's eye lines, and spread out my mat. I heard the faint noise of whatever he was watching.

I heard the song *What's going on?* by 4 Non Blondes, the song I often listened to at home during yoga or when I was getting ready for work. I realised that he was watching *Sense8*. Yogesh, Anthony and I had recommended it to him at dinner. I had got all excited about that being kind of like what the four of us were. Obviously television has to exaggerate things to make them exciting; they couldn't just have us, middle aged, chatting over dinner, going for walks and writing; it's a metaphor. Although Robert's early life has some good tales, and now, still travelling, and us too.

A thrill went through me. I listened, I remembered the words from that scene: *'I see you, I believe in you, and as long as we're together, there's nothing we can't do.'*

I did the tree pose; standing on one leg, the other leg bent outwards with its foot resting on the opposite inner thigh, arms stretched towards the sky. I had never felt so still. At the end I stood in tadasana; standing still like a pencil balanced on its end, looking out onto the trees and the deep, thick green foliage. A burst of energy went through me. I realised: *This is my temple.*

About a year previously I had taken ketamine for the first time, enough to go to the K hole and to experience the falling away of everything: no wood burner, no thick red carpet, no sofa, just me and Anthony huddled side by side in the foetal position. Nothing left, only feelings. 'This is what love feels like,' I'd said. I experienced myself as being like one little bubble in a sheet of bubble wrap. Later we lay on the floor and I experienced astral travel, (at least in my imagination, but where else?) I found myself in the desert plains of

Africa, then in a ruined temple in India, green walls, open to the sides so that I could feel the breeze.

The rooftop yoga space wasn't fancy. I could see the road and the backs of buildings. Sometimes there was building work nearby. But at some point there'd always be a crow perched on the wall. Robert was just across the way, our room was downstairs, Raul and Anthony were usually in the communal area playing carrom. What kind of temple would I want anyway?

***

Like when you've promised to send postcards and then you get there and find it's such a lot of effort to buy, to write, to post, I felt the same about keeping in touch with my family. During the first five weeks I had sent a few emails, done one video call and one phone call to my son and replied to my mum's texts. I mean that's as much or more than if I was at home. I sold my house and left my job. I came to India to be free and yet I still feel guilty and responsible. They don't know that I am writing a book, that I have an interior life.

So I sent my son an email saying I was going to be out of communication for the next two months in order to immerse myself in the India experience and asked him to tell my mum. It helped that we were at Osho's, I had mentioned yoga and meditation; maybe they thought we had joined a cult.

I wasn't brought up with social media so for me it feels like it gets in the way to have to be keeping too much in touch with home while travelling. I just don't see how you can fully do both; well I can't anyway. My mum went travelling in the 1960s and all her mum would have got was the occasional airmail letter and been out of contact for weeks at a time. It helped that my son and I had spoken only two days previously and all was well.

I wanted a break from worry and responsibility. *Just let me go.* My whole life has been dominated by one or both and I just want to... abdicate. *I want to abdicate.* I don't want to do it anymore. I want to be in India. 'I don't even know what it is that I am, or who I am.' I said to my husband after the dinner with Robert and Yogesh. 'Well then it's about time you gave yourself the space and time to find out,' he said.

I didn't last the whole two months but when I did email my son again, all was going great for him and he hadn't seemed to mind. As always, I'd brought the whole situation on myself. In the last days in the UK we'd all gone out, it had felt nice and close. I'd probably been anxious and guilty and needing things to be okay before I left and we'd set up Skype, talked about video calls, setting up expectations. But like with the postcards, I hadn't known that once you're out, you just want to be out, the experience is enough and having things to do for back home doesn't always fit.

After the dinner with Robert and Yogesh, as is my wont, I wondered, what's next? Ships in the night, or some kind of Sense8 thing? We had felt like such a community that night. We saw Robert around a few times afterwards, at the guesthouse and out at coffee shops. Sometimes at the guesthouse I was busy writing and at the coffee shops he was talking with others or looked as if he wanted to be alone.

He read my Green Mist Theory blog post which I'd mentioned at dinner, my spiritual revelation/unifying theory that had come to me fully realised in a dream: we're all green mist; we created these bodies because without bodies we can't pick up a pen and write poetry or kiss each other. But the kissing and the poetry are so distracting that we forgot that we're green mist come down for a human experience. Robert said he'd never heard anyone explain or understand it like that before.

One day we saw him at a cafe and I asked him to sit with us, he said, 'No, I want to sit here.' It was good, to be direct like that. Another day we all three found ourselves at the same coffee shop, 'Today I want to be sociable,' he said. He spoke about his plans to be a shaman, a kundalini doctor. 'I have always been connected to a fine line of confidence,' he said. 'I want what I need,' he said, on conjuring things on the internet.

He said he had seen a photograph of us together on Facebook. 'I felt jealous,' he said. 'You two are together.' He gave us advice, 'You can use sex to become enlightened. You are together, you can use it to increase awareness. Have the sex,' he said, 'No problem.' He had the same attitude about drugs; that they made no difference and in fact taking psychedelic drugs was an essential part of the process. Whereas we, as part of experiments to raise our frequencies and awareness, had been experimenting with control around alcohol, drugs and particularly sex and orgasms for the best part of a year.

We went back to the guesthouse and had sex. I felt as if I were clinging onto roots and clumps of grass, losing my mind. Later I did healing on Anthony's foot, he felt it 'pressing down' and healing energy shooting through his body.

Robert said that we, 'The creators,' put people on the road to help us, to give us information but not to keep in touch. 'Once we have talked and imparted the information, that's it,' he said. Although he and Anthony connected on Facebook, he made it clear it was a ships in the night thing. I was disappointed but Anthony said to me, 'We're all on our own individual journeys, we can't spend too much time sharing a reality as we have to do our own things, except if we've decided to pair up, to do this as a couple or with a best friend.' With Yogesh it was different though, we kept in touch, maybe because he was still a seeker, whereas Robert seemed to know everything already.

When the four of us were out at dinner Robert did a shamanistic ritual on Yogesh, cutting the ties from the umbilical to his mother, 'The ties that makes him look for love in all others, rather than inside himself.' So of course I asked him to do the same for me.

To make it serious and meaningful, we set a day and a time, I gave him money and some small offerings, fruit juice and crisps and I brought along a black crow's feather. The three of us met up on the yoga space, he wanted Anthony there too. Robert directed me to sit on the mat on the floor in the centre of the space. He lit some incense.

He said that the purpose of the mother is to, 'Give the baby the bliss,' and then when the baby grows up it, 'Takes the bliss and is set free.' Free to become its destiny. He gave me a 'Scarf of Freedom,' one of the small white cotton scarves people wore, wrapping it once around my neck. 'Now you buy one, you send it with the crow's feather to your son, you set him free to become a great artist, and perhaps he can start a new family tradition.' He gave me the incense stub to keep. We sat for a little while on the roof top yoga space. Of course there was a crow there too.

Later that day Anthony and I went to Cafe del Mar, our favourite cafe on the cliff. I had a funny turn, a few moments where I felt weird all over and with a loud ringing in my left ear. I went to the post shop by myself with the new Scarf of Freedom and the crow's feather. I wrote down my son's address and watched as the post shop man meticulously copied it out into his book and then wrapped and taped and wrapped and taped the parcel so thoroughly as if he were performing a ritual before my eyes. He wrote the address on and put on the stamps. I paid him, and it was done. This all happened during the time off contact; my son seemed to like it, and it seemed to work. And for me, my freedom ritual, well, I wrote my book.

***

Each night we had a bedroom routine, unravelling the mosquito net and tucking it in around us. It was quite small and I found it a bit claustrophobic to feel its edges up against me and once we accidentally shut a flying beetle inside by mistake which was a bit scary. At night we had the sound of the pre monsoon rain, cicadas or their Indian counterparts and the howling of the dog over the road which started up around eleven pm each night.

There were lots of stray or semi stray dogs, some were adopted and fed by cafes or shops. They seemed to have a pretty good life hanging out together as a pack rather than shut up alone in a house all day, always trotting off to take a look or bark at an intruding dog, sitting under restaurant tables, getting fed or adopted by tourists and sleeping on the warm sand of the beach at night. I realise there are downsides, but their complete freedom maybe makes up for that? No one seems to mind them barking, and no one seems to mind the dog over the road howling all night. 'That's what dogs do,' a man said to Anthony when he mentioned the nightly howling.

Osho's was near Papanasam Beach, a Hindu pilgrimage site, 'The Benares (Varanasi) of the South,' according to the internet, where people come to do pooja for loved ones who have died. The Hindu temple was just up the road. At the weekends minibuses and brightly decorated coaches- like the Kenyan bus in Sense8- rolled in along the beach road, full of Indian pilgrims and tourists. A priest handed out business cards offering pooja, he had a beautiful cream auto with flowers painted on. On Sunday mornings the beach was busy even at eight am.

The holy men set up with big striped sun umbrellas on mounds of sand that looked like graves and boxes and cupboards with their necessary items in: bananas, banana leaves, rice and flowers. Families have a ceremony with the holy man then walk down to the sea with the banana leaf and flowers held above their heads. The flowers and items belonging to their loved one are put into the sea. Banana leaves full of cooked rice are left out near the holy men; there were always lots of crows and pigeons eating the rice, as well as the beach dogs. All of this goes on alongside the rest of the life of the beach, no one stares or takes any notice. Walking on the beach it was common to see items washed up: photographs, framed pictures and strings of beads as well as the bright yellow petals of the flower garlands.

The cliffs of Papanasam beach were deep red sand. One day we saw a pod of dolphins. All along the path beside the beach were little white threads which looked like dental floss but were the threads from the raw edged cotton scarves which so many people wore or carried to keep off the sun, to wipe off sweat, the same as my Scarf of Freedom.

There were only a handful of other foreign tourists in that area; the rest tended to stay in the tourist strip on the top of the cliff. The Indian tourists were interested in us, shyly saying hello and asking to take photographs with us. Groups of Indian families came down to look at the sea, standing in groups and just unselfconsciously staring at the sea, without doing anything. 'Instead of clubs and concerts,' Yogesh said when we mentioned this to him.

One evening during a little walk and a look at the sea after dinner, a man came up to us. He appeared ordinary, well dressed and was with friends. He said hello and then said: 'Look at the sea, close your eyes, breathe into your chest, hold, hear only the sea, my voice... There, you feel comfort?' I love that about India, that this kind of thing can happen.

At the veg cafe over the road from Osho's I ate channa masala for the first time since being sick after eating it in Delhi in March; it had taken until well into May for me to face it again. Anthony's nemesis dish was vegetable noodles for the same reason, he couldn't even talk about it for months. We had fresh coconuts and packets of spicy roasted chickpeas for snacks. For lunch we had beans on toast, either regular or Indian style- spicy with chopped green peppers- and from the tourist strip tofu wraps and vegeburgers, delicious soya milk smoothies and fresh juices; no wonder it was seemingly impossible to stay on budget or to lose weight.

We had changed our initial views of the tourist strip, the food was varied and good, and when we'd out gone out for dinner with Yogesh and Robert we had gone there. The day after the dinner, before he got his bus back to Chennai we went out for breakfast with Yogesh to one of the very basic locals' cafes. He ordered for us, we had idli (steamed rice pancakes) for the first time; it was so easy being out with someone who knew all the food and could speak the language fluently.

Eating dinner on the cliff, at the restaurant where we ate our first meal of thoran, we saw a storm come in. The sky was lit with green light and we watched a wall of rain come in from the sea. At the beach near Osho's at the edge of the sea there was a convenient shelf of sand to sit on and several times in the evenings we watched the sky light up pink and white with huge forks of lightning. The waves were big but arrived in slow motion, the sea getting rougher with the approaching monsoon.

One evening returning back to the room Anthony said in a steady voice, 'Don't look just go straight into the room.' I knew what that meant: a spider. He was calm but sounded a bit freaked out and I knew it must be very big. We blocked up the gaps under the door, sprayed DEET around the door frame and got under the mosquito net. It was hard to stay calm and to sleep. When I woke the next morning, I looked around the room, it was fine but there was no way I could go outside where it was. I usually went for a walk early when I woke up. Instead I put a YouTube yoga class on quietly. Anthony woke up to the sound of a woman speaking and was momentarily confused.

I couldn't go out alone and I couldn't stay in the room alone. I sat in Cafe Del Mar losing my mind, trying to get a hold of myself, wanting to get back to being happy like the day before. It was awful how things could go from happy, really happy, to total terror. I was scared I'd have to fly home while at the same time knowing I wasn't going to do that. When Anthony and an old girlfriend were on holiday in an undeveloped bit of Thailand many years before they had seen so many big spiders that they had seriously considered that they'd have to go home, before they realised that the trick is to stop looking for them.

My anxiety was through the roof. This is the problem of misinterpreting the Law of Attraction. It's more about keeping your frequency high, which you do via general wellbeing, rather than a 'Don't think of a pink elephant' loop; that way madness lies, trust me, I know. Back in April of the year before, just as we'd begun to start recharging our dreams and reality, I'd spent a week at my mum's looking after her dog while she was on holiday. I'd been thinking and talking a lot about how 'watch your thoughts because your thoughts create your reality' and I couldn't stop thinking about spiders, worrying I might see one. I saw a medium small one, no problem but it scared me that I'd drawn it.

Usually I would work on my blog at the guesthouse but as I couldn't be there I stayed at the cafe to do it. Anthony went off to the shop. His phone rang. It was a group video call from his sister in London and someone I didn't know. I didn't know how to answer it. I ignored it for a bit then tried, while eating lunch- an incredibly messy tofu wrap- but I missed it, I couldn't do it, I tried to call them back, no answer. I went cold all over with anxiety. I am such an idiot. Why didn't I just leave it? You can't even work a smart phone, then, Oh my God, what if it did answer, while I was eating over it! I thought about how awful it looks when I accidentally press a button on Instagram and see myself as a picture ready to take and upload; multiply that by about a thousand. Anthony came back. 'So what if you can't work a smartphone, so what if you're eating, everyone eats, it's only my sister.'

I asked Robert from Switzerland about fear of spiders, I thought he'd somehow be above all that and have some amazing solution for me but he was terrified of spiders too. 'Now I can't stop thinking it might come into *my* room!' he said, shivering.

I worked really hard on cultivating calm acceptance; thinking, like life, most of the time it's good but sometimes there'll be something bad that will cause a bad feeling but it won't last forever. A few days later I saw it. Raul, Anthony and I were all sitting in the foyer, relaxed; they were playing carrom. It wasn't as bad as I had imagined, it wasn't as big and I was okay. I mean, not okay to go near it, but not freaking out.

I considered adjusting, accepting, letting it live outside our door, but then I thought, *I don't have to do that.* I asked Raul to move it, 'It's not dangerous. It not eat you! Or maybe it get very hungry, it eat you!' he said, laughing. I had asked Raul to move it but he just got a broom and killed it. When you ask someone to do something, they do it their way and I couldn't have moved it as I couldn't have gone near it. I put my mental wellbeing above the spider's right to life.

Coming just days after the contact break email to my family, the shaman freedom pooja and the Scarf of Freedom parcel sending, the killing of the spider felt like a metaphor: *I killed the person I was yesterday and I didn't even feel guilty about it.* The White Tiger by Aravind Adiga which I read while we were at Osho's is a very extreme example of breaking away from one's family and putting one's own life first, which I took as another metaphor for me. What we had to do to execute this trip was let go of our *'Attachments to Things, Places, Pets and Ideas,'* to quote one of my favourite articles from university, or I would never have been able to do this. There's a method and a price, and it's this.

People say we are 'Living the dream.' What does that mean? Out on the other side, what does that feel like? What life is like now: no cooking, no housework, the most is sweeping, a tidy, asking for new sheets, washing down the wet room with the bum gun or a bucket of soapy water, shopping for items we need- food, toiletries, doing the most basic admin, the odd email. My only possessions the contents of one small backpack and a handbag, living in one room. Together 24/7, although we use outdoor space such as balconies, in the UK one of us was often at work for eight hours. What does living the dream mean exactly? What do you do to keep growing? How do you have experiences without spending much money? What about mood and mental health? And what do you do all day?

***

We went to Kovalam, just along the coast for two nights. At the train station at Varkala there was a big canteen style diner. It was very busy. We stood in the busy noise for a moment, unsure of what to do. An Indian man, a customer came up to us asked us if we needed help. 'Yes,' we said. He showed us where to order and pay and explained we had to hand the ticket to the servers. We ordered masala dosas and chai. A little later the man came to check that we had got our food. 'There's always someone who will help you,' Anthony said.

We went by local train, second class non ac with fans and open windows. The train was crowded and we stood in the corridor by the door. It was hot but not unbearable and it was only for one hour. Sweat trickled down my legs. I daydreamed of a shower, white towels. Actually I don't care what colour, I thought, please just let there be towels and if there aren't any I'll ask.

We got an auto from the station which dropped us by the beach near the hotel. It was a shock to be in a super touristy area again, with Goa levels of hassle all along the prom; shawl sellers following us like in Panaji, after the absence of it near Osho's. Even on the cliff the hassle at Varkala had been lack lustre, end of season, they knew us and we knew them. Here there were other Westerners; apparently it used to be the place to go before it got over-developed and people switched to Varkala. Arriving here I felt like we were fresh meat, all the restaurants offering friendly invites; maybe it felt more intense because we didn't know them.

The hotel we'd booked online was closed for the end of the season. We found another easily, white with verandas, a large white room. There were towels on the bed! I meant to ask for a top sheet and forgot.

There was no obvious local or authentic place so we ate lunch on the front, masala and rice. A man walked past carrying trays of eggs stacked on his head. Outside there were women selling fruit in big baskets, waiting for us to come out. The food wasn't that great and I ate too much. As well as trying to budget better we'd been trying to eat normally, eat until full not overfull, which seems to be hard for us.

For dinner we found a veg only restaurant, it was nice and quiet. I had a veg sandwich; toasted bread with onion, tomatoes, cucumber, carrots, salt and garam masala. We ate there all the time after that, veg noodles, veg with pasta and beans, real beans like we'd eat at home and which were scarce in meals in India. Baked beans on toast were sold in some tourist areas and there was an Indian dish which contained a few kidney beans but that was about it.

After dinner we walked to the non-tourist area, up a hill, past tiny shops. One was like a cupboard, it was so small but stacked totally full of fruit, drinks and biscuits.

Returning home, sitting in bed at nine-thirty pm, there was a knock at the door. A man had brought us a top sheet and I hadn't even asked or not out loud anyway. For me it was small Law of Attraction miracle, like getting beans on toast at Cafe del Mar outside of breakfast time, 'Watch me get it,' I had said, and been so pleased when I had. It's the little things, for me.

***

I had learned a lot about mine and Anthony's relationship in Goa. In the early days of our relationship and my spiritual awakening I read *The Tibetan Book of Living and Dying.* It said that the student sometimes sees the face of Buddha on his master's face.

One night in the house in Harleston we took a lot of MDMA and had sex on the sofa and suddenly during sex I had the realisation that Anthony was Jesus. I had almost bought him a pot of Frankincense face cream for £50, almost but not quite, so my mind was pretty blown. I remembered that I had thought this before, when we first met. Oh no, I thought, I lost faith, I forgot. However much I used to push this idea, Anthony always resisted. I used to think this was a test of faith, 'Believe it even though he's telling you not to.' This occurred on drugs mainly.

In Panaji, on MDMA I had those same feelings again; convinced that Anthony was 'Golden Light Baba' and that all I had to do to have my faith rewarded was to have faith that I didn't need to breathe and to not breathe. In Kovalam, I brought up the Panaji Golden Light Baba experience. Anthony said firmly, 'But that isn't what I want, I've been telling you that ever since we met. I'm not the Messiah, I'm just a very naughty boy!' And at last, I was able to let that go. It was also when I began, at last, to believe in myself.

I was trained as an occupational therapist and then worked as one for twenty years, building on a natural urge to problem solve and to do activities. Someone telling me that they were bored was like a red rag to a bull; Anthony used to say to his kids when we first met, 'Go and tell Rachel that you are bored,' and I would spring into action. Solving other people's problems, providing other people with activities that were just right for them, while distracting or overloading myself with too many or not the right activities.

I did it to Anthony too, I was always trying to encourage Anthony to do more; I thought he wanted to. Sometimes he'd mention that he didn't have any hobbies or he'd express an interest in something particular and I'd jump into action. Also, I'd see all this untapped potential but he was and is happy how he is.

'I don't want you to be disappointed in me, I've always felt that you've had such high expectations of me.' Whereas I have never felt that from him, he's always loved me whatever I've been doing, and me the same; I don't love him any more or less if he is or isn't doing something. I don't want him to do something he doesn't want to do.

It's me. Imagine if he'd been unscrupulous, he could have had me do anything. Instead he refused and at last, almost nine years later, I have finally let him be who he is, a man, my husband, let us just be a man and a woman, and me become who I was meant to be all along, what I wanted and what I was interested in as a child. Right under my nose, so simple, so obvious. My old primary teacher said to me a few years ago, 'What happened to the writing?' My friend Molly said to me recently, 'It is your vocation.'

India is a relaxed country so perhaps here I can learn to relax. In Goa I rediscovered myself as a sexual being. In Varkala I rediscovered my spirituality. In Kovalam I reset myself as a writer? Is all India about rediscovery?

'This trip is far more about you writing a book than about me doing anything. I think I know what my role is, it is to support you in writing the book, by supporting the trip, planning, booking trains, booking rooms.' Anthony has kind of fallen into that role and he quite likes it. He's happy to be the one who gets an auto into town to go to the ATM or sort out train tickets while I stay and have some alone time and write. He's happy to do the budget and organise the money and pay for things and work out tips. I was thinking I should do more of that stuff but I don't really want to and he said, 'I have to do something.' He's used to working, going out of the house, he gets restless.

Of course we also talk about stuff; he has insights which I write down, I expand and clarify things by speaking to him. As always he contains and reassures me, acts as a sounding board, a stabiliser and spiritual advisor.

The question from the evening with Robert and Yogesh: 'Remember who you are, what your purpose is.' Could it just be this? I've found it so hard to do and yet here I am, a year off, no job and a companion to love me and look after me. It is hot so plenty of time indoors; everyone does it, stays indoors and rests during the afternoon. A relaxed country, no 'cult of busy,' anything goes here, what better time? And a sensory experience to write about. I love it here, but my main thing is the year off and space and permission to write.

I thought we were in India for Anthony, to be honest. I mean it was his dream to go back there, and to travel. I didn't really have such a desire as I'd never done it. I had the urge to escape and to see what happened, to experiment with chucking it all up and trust falling into the universe, all that stuff, rather than India or travel per se. But I might never have got the confidence and realisation to reset myself as a writer had we not escaped the matrix and all the other conditioning. Work made it hard, hard to believe. Here, with no family, no one who could doubt me, no one who will be surprised if I say I am writing a book, I can do it. Plus it's a great backdrop obviously, both to write about and to develop within.

Looking back to my anxieties about Anthony's ex, which I found so hard in Delhi- he had gone to India twenty years ago with his ex- all that seems so irrelevant now. Realising how far away that seems, how little it matters. It was a trip down memory lane for Anthony, not about his ex but about India, staying in the same hotel, wanting it to still be the same; and we had Jude with us, Anthony was sharing some of his parents' history with him. If Anthony hadn't gone to India before he wouldn't have wanted to come back and I wouldn't have ended up in somewhere so culturally different, so supportive and so far away. I wouldn't have left my job, I wouldn't have got out of Norfolk, I wouldn't have fulfilled my life. As I said that night with Robert and Yogesh, if I die without completing this book, I will be very disappointed in myself.

We're both special. All this means that we can just enjoy each other and I can focus on my creative powers. *I can be happy.* As Anthony said, 'It took a while for this trip to become ours.'

In Kovalam Anthony was reading about positive nihilism: 'There is no meaning, save what you ascribe or subscribe to yourself.' Religious people pick religion. Anthony is just concerned with getting from birth to death whatever way. To make it fun and interesting you can do stuff, explore ideas, read, get to know yourself, observe yourself doing. Can choose not to do stuff or to opt out: Robert from Switzerland opting out of working, Renton in Trainspotting opting out of the trappings of a conventional life. It felt quite freeing, talking about this, standing on the black sand of the beach. 'Nothing matters, we're all going to die and everything we've done will be forgotten.'

This is a simulation, we're here once, nothing is real; those beliefs got me to disentangle from mum and son, sell house, leave job and get to India. Before we left, during all the stress on the boat, I wrote: Is it helpful in times of trouble to return to the original theories and ideas that got us here? This is all an illusion. There are others, but the one that works in all situations is: 'It is an illusion'. Why don't people talk about this? Okay so people do sometimes when they're stoned, and sometimes when with friends someone might casually quote Bill Hicks or say 'Everything is a creation of our thoughts,' but no one actually discusses it in a serious way. No one I know anyway, and certainly it's a long way from being talked about in a national newspaper, for example. Is this because we live in a Christian country?

But it's not exactly atheism either, they don't believe in anything, whereas 'It's all an illusion' is a belief system of sorts. It's certainly something you could discuss with others around a dinner table, working out what it means, how to live in this world while at the same time holding that belief. Anthony and I talk about and explore this idea fairly regularly. That some people are conscious, some are potentially conscious but asleep, and some are just asleep.

One night in a Travelodge in London, just the two of us, stoned: Just us, and us just consciousness. Two clumps of consciousness or one that split into two, male and female. I got scared about it just being the two of us, or that it was just me, all alone. Anthony said if you really believed it you wouldn't be scared, it would just be how things were. I got scared at the idea that I'm just consciousness with no body, none of the scenery being real. Why is that so scary? Am I afraid that it would send me mad? On the edge of the cliff, 'I choose to step back and run away.' 'So do most people,' Anthony said.

After beauty, spirituality, after spirituality, awareness, after that, nothing. Pointless, joy, everything pointless. Choose something, art, writing. Choose writing. CHOOSE WRITING.

I've often thought about the writer Iris Murdoch and her husband John Bayley's toilet (apparently neither of them cared about housework and supposedly their toilet was filthy) and later about Kim Gordon (I read her autobiography, *Girl in a Band,* while we were at Osho's.) It goes to show how deep women's conditioning is that even someone as cool as Kim Gordon can feel bad about not being able to bake or sew; I mean really, a super cool artist from the band Sonic Youth! If even super cool Kim feels like that, it's not surprising that I do too, but we can't do everything, we aren't meant to do everything, we can't all care about sewing, baking and toilets. It's okay to specialise, I tell myself.

Soaked in colour, bathed in love: Varkala, India

The monsoon proper began one Friday night and rained all through the night and into Saturday morning. Lying in bed listening at four in the morning it sounded like there were layers and layers of rain. The rain was like music, loud and all around like the surround sound in a cinema.

'They say that even a plant that has died can come back to life in the rains,' Umesh, the owner of one of the restaurants said.

During the monsoon we often ate dinner at the veg cafe over the road, Gobi Manchurian: an only-in-India 'Chinese' dish, made of small florets of cauliflower either 'dry' or 'wet,' deep fried or soft in a tasty brown gravy, and Channa Batura, a small dish of chick pea masala with three slightly puffy, chewy deep fried breads. I was in awe of the different 'breads,' as well as chapatti, roti, dosa there was idli -steamed rice cakes and poori -deep fried, puffy like batura but less chewy.

We got provisions to make food if it was raining too much for us to want to go out. Although it wasn't far to the cafe sometimes we just didn't want to get another set of clothes soaked, especially when it was so hard to get stuff dry. I enjoyed cooking for us again, even if it was only making porridge in the guesthouse kitchen. We bought bananas from stalls near the temple and dried fruit and soya milk from the cliff to and crisps and nuts to have in the room, 'I had to use nail clippers to get into the almonds,' Anthony said; impenetrable packaging was another phenomenon we noticed about India.

When it rained hard in the evenings water came into the guesthouse and covered the floor of the communal area, Raul pushed it out with a big mop. Drain holes in the bottom of the walls let the water out, and in. One evening a big puffed up frog and a snake came in, the snake trying to eat the frog before being shooed out by Raul. Coming out of the kitchen with porridge one evening I saw another snake outside the kitchen. I told Raul but before he could get it out it went under the door of another guest, a holy man who worked at the temple and lived at Osho's full time. Raul banged on his door over and over; after ages the holy man came out, taking out his headphones, looking surprised. Raul spoke to him in Malayalam, the man looked at Anthony and me, 'Yes,' we said, and mimed, 'Snake went under your door.' It had gone under the bed; we left them to it.

When it rained we could look out onto the street through gaps between the metal roof and the wall of the communal area, watching sheets of rain. It was like when we'd watched footage of monsoon rain on YouTube before we came, trying to get a sense of what it would be like. People in autos or walking with umbrellas, men walking, no tops on, with simple pieces of white cotton fabric wrapped around their waists, which made sense, small and easy to dry. One afternoon it rained for four hours and we stayed in and watched a film, it was like a wet Sunday afternoon feeling. The temperature got cooler; it felt cold in the evenings in the room a few times and I rued the loss of my nice grey jumper, comfy yoga pants and soft cosy socks left behind in Delhi in blazing hot end of March.

The sound of hard green fruit falling on the tin roof was a constant sound and quite loud. The green fruits and big leaves fell on the steps leading up to the yoga space. Rainwater pooled in the centre of each step where people's feet had worn little wells.

We washed our clothes in the bucket with shampoo or soap and hung them to dry indoors or outside during gaps in the rain. Even when dried outside they still had a mildew smell. Sometimes we handed them over to be laundered by Raul, they smelled better, but we had to wait for them, and I liked the simple activity of washing my own clothes. We both separately slipped and fell heavily on the wet floor outside the bathroom, coming crashing down on the hard floor, fortunately not injuring ourselves. It was surprising to realise that the slippery tile or marble floors turned out to be the most dangerous thing about India for us.

Some foreigners talk about carrying loo paper and complain about the squat toilets. But actually we found there were hardly any squat toilets, only in very non touristy cafes, or on trains and train stations and even then there was usually a Western option. At a cafe in Kolam, a nearby town, I asked for the loo, the man asked me 'Urine?' and directed me to one with a slope and a small hole only! I love the no shame, it's good for me. Instead of toilet paper, most toilets had bum guns, like a mini jet wash, a wonderful invention. If not there was a usually a smaller jug and a low tap near the toilet. Outside, people use a bottle of water.

***

The beach changed every day during the monsoon. The channels down to the sea got wider and deeper and the beach itself got narrower. The edge of the channels formed a big shelf of sand, cake like. Once I sat on the edge of a channel and it collapsed underneath me and I fell into the sand. When paddling in the evening, it felt strange that the water was cold and the sand was warm.

After dark the beach was beautiful, flood lit with one big light. Beach dogs slept on the beach in holes they had dug or on top of the priests' pooja stall mounds. One night after dinner a group of women appeared out of the dark in sarees of yellows and golds and different colours yet all coordinated, a vision of complete and total beauty.

At the height of the monsoon when the sea was at its roughest, the lifeguards blew their whistles if anyone so much as paddled. Some days the fishing boats were told not to go out. Once I watched the lifeguards shouting and shouting and blowing their whistles as a little boat went out. It took ages for the boat to get over the waves at the shore. I watched as the boat eventually got out from the shore. After a while it disappeared into the distance, the lifeguards still shouting and blowing their whistles.

One day I walked along the cliff to a different beach by myself. There were crushed shells under my feet. There was rubbish too, on the beach itself and nearby in smelly rubbish dumps but crushed shells nonetheless. Catching the beauty of it, I thought about the Osho poster in the guesthouse: '*You see your master everywhere.*' Yes, in the crushed shells, in the sarees and the red cliffs of Papanasanam beach. Is the answer there, in the beauty; shells, crows, stillness, that spiritual sense of wonder when looking at leaves as if seeing them for the first time?

When we see beauty, shells, as if for the first time, is that arrival, is that us arriving in the present moment? But I've also gone for a walk and looked at flowers and thought, we made those. In the room at Osho's we watched the film *Her* about AI. Maybe we are the AI that built the bodies. Maybe we are the aliens that came down into these bodies. Once you found it though, that'd be it which is why we don't try that hard to find it and why we forget and why it's so hard to remember. That's why finding one's purpose is so hard, and so hidden... 'The meaning of life,' otherwise we'd all exit too early.

This 'spiritual experience/working out' takes a lot of time, sometimes several hours a day with thinking and talking. It's one of the things I do, like writing or yoga. Feeling at ease with myself, relaxing, doing nothing, writing, having a flexible routine. Knowing what's good or not, or just accepting myself how I am and how I do things; one day this, another day that. Those little moments of ease, of awareness, looking down, through my eyes, not comparing self to others; noticing muscles under buttock, red sarong, feet, chipped red nail polish, grey silver anklet. A sense of myself 'arriving;' a sense of my body, a heightened awareness. My nose much better even with no nasal spray. OCD better- in some ways- Anthony does the money so I don't have to take a bag, or even a key.

Anthony and Raul played Carrom often, miming the flicking of fingers and making a ping ping sound to invite each other to play. Towards the end Raul asked us to correct certain pronunciation, or asked us the words for certain things. We taught him the words for parts of the body and he'd rattle these off easily; 'English is easy, so easy!' he'd say, laughing. Raul hadn't been to school 'Not even one day,' he said. He couldn't read or write in Bengali, his own language but he could speak several Indian languages as well as enough English to get by. I showed him how to find English lessons on YouTube, how to search 'learn English in Bengali.' He was from Assam in the North East of India, a three day train journey away. He showed us pictures of his wife and daughter who he saw for three months a year in the off season.

Spending time with Raul made me firstly think I was so grateful for all the education I had, all the information, everything, all the myriad of knowledge and information and learned experience from my occupational therapy degree, from college courses, from book clubs, from so much reading, books as a child... all that information in my head, all those things to think about, to draw upon.

But then I thought, well maybe we're over educated. Imagine if you couldn't read, you'd walk around immune to billboards. Would you be less conditioned (other than religion); if you'd never learned to read, would you be kind of protected? I didn't have the same or as much religious conditioning as Raul, nothing overt, except atheism at home, and some Christian conditioning at school. But all that education I had, all those books I read, all that was conditioning and was it all good or has it left me with more to unpick? Or did some of it set me on this path to unpicking it? Could it have been done another way?

Raul left to go back to his family. With Raul gone, the only people left were us and the holy man. The occasional Indian family came to stay for one night, visiting briefly on pilgrimage to Papanasam Beach and the temple, and now and again groups of Indian men, middle aged and older came to spend the evening and to drink in one of the rooms.

We'd been in Kerala for a month before I even noticed that alcohol was restricted. At the tourist restaurants on the cliff, beer was served in big pottery mugs and the bottles wrapped in newspaper and put under the tables. Otherwise it was sold legally only in liquor shops or licensed bars although we didn't go to either ourselves.

The communal area was open a little at the sides and as the rainy season wore on it became unbearable to spend even a few minutes there due to the mosquitoes which bit Anthony mercilessly. Raul's replacement burned cauldrons of leaves and newspapers, smoking the place out which helped for a short while. Our room was safe, we religiously kept doors closed especially when the lights were on, and the windows were securely covered with mesh. The windows faced over the tree filled swamp and let in limited light and ventilation. As the monsoon wore on the room began to smell damp, our clothes always seemed to be damp and one day I noticed that even my back pack was mouldy.

I knew that in the monsoon there were lots more mosquitoes and therefore viruses and illnesses such as dengue fever. There was also an outbreak of nipah virus in Kerala which killed seventeen people. We monitored the news but stayed put, it was contained an eight hour drive away. We had minor illnesses, I woke up with a very sore throat and went and got antibiotics straight away. Anthony got a bad migraine and spent a day silent under the mosquito net which scared me a little. I got an auto to the pharmacy in Varkala to get some migraine pills for him. Compared with Goa, where I got Jude to come with me to the pharmacy when Anthony hurt his back because I was too scared to go in a taxi alone, I had come a long way. Or a short way anyway, more at ease, less scared of everything.

I woke up at four am the day after Anthony's migraine day and suddenly realised we had to move: it's damp, it's unhealthy, we're in the middle of a swamp, there are mosquitoes everywhere, there's a deadly virus in the news. It was absolutely lovely outside of the height of the monsoon, but not anymore.

I gave myself a day off writing and we went and looked at guesthouses. We were just about to reach the last guesthouse on our list when a man called out and asked us if we wanted a room. He was calling from a very smart guesthouse, obviously out of our price range. He showed us around, the rooms were very smart, big, with big windows and up higher, nearer the sea. We explained we were on a budget and after some very friendly negotiation he gave us a very good deal as it was out of season and we said we would stay for a month. We both felt strangely invigorated. 'Do you think it's because we've had a little bit of change, after not doing much for a while?' Anthony said.

**

Just before we left Osho's we met Renate for the first time. Robert from Switzerland had told us about a woman he had met at a coffee shop down the road between the beach and the temple. A German born US citizen who had moved to India twenty-five years ago, who was now aged seventy six but looked much younger, who had done a lot of yoga, was very poised and with a good firm handshake, 'An amazing woman,' Robert said. We wanted to meet her. A few days later in Cafe del Mar we saw a woman who fitted that description, and made eye contact. The three of us spoke for a while from across our tables before we moved our chairs to her table and carried on talking.

Renate first came to India in 1995 on a three month holiday to Varkala with a girl friend. Renate fell completely in love with Varkala and on the plane home she told her friend that she wanted to go and live there. Her friend said it was impossible, that Renate's husband would hate it and would never in a million years agree. 'If you have a heartfelt wish, the Universe will grant it.' Renate said. Seven days later Renate called her friend. 'It is done, my wish has manifested.'

On her return to the US Renate and her husband had gone out for dinner. After three months away, Renate had expected that there would be things to discuss. But what happened next was that over dinner her husband dropped a bombshell that resulted in the end of their marriage. But Renate wasn't devastated. 'Great, I can move to India,' she said. By the end of the same year she was living in Varkala.

The first thing she did was to set about learning the language, a word each day, asking the waiters, What's the word for this, and this, and writing it down in a notebook. She remembered the moment when she realised she could put together sentences and tenses correctly and say something like, 'The clouds are moving across the sky.' We watched strangers be surprised when she spoke to them in fluent Malayalam.

After that first meeting we saw Renate several times each week, sometimes every day. Over many coffees and a few cigarettes she shared her stories and philosophy. Each year she spent time in an ashram doing yoga and meditation. 'Did you achieve enlightenment? Anthony asked light-heartedly after her most recent spell. 'Well I think that if you do there's no need to go on about it,' she said.

Renate told us she followed her own religion, believing that everything is to be found inside oneself, and maintaining a sense that everything is as it should be. 'I am not attached to outcomes,' was something she often said. Renate had never been a hippy. She told us that in the 1960s, having of course heard of free love and hippies, she had been invited to a hippy party. She put braids in her hair and went along to see what it was all about. She said she watched all the hippies laughing at a man who arrived wearing 'square' clothes. 'You speak of love, and yet you invite this man to laugh at him? This movement is not for me,' she said.

Renate had no smart phone, no home computer, laptop or tablet. She went to the internet cafe once a month to check her bank statements and the rest of her emails, which were, 'Mostly rubbish,' she said. In the evenings she read books or talked on the phone.

Renate had experienced a very tough childhood and had worked very hard even from the age of eight, cleaning flights of steps, fetching coal and weeding the allotment. Later she had a very successful business with her husband. In her career when she was at work, 'I was really at work,' she said. Her friends said she would miss it but she said she never did, 'Especially not the employee issues, the order problems, no, not at all,' she said.

Through Renate we met Lyn from the UK. After multiple near fatal health problems and her husband walking out after thirty years of marriage, she'd thought her life was over. Her daughter who made regular trips to India suggested that Lyn join her family in India for Christmas. Like Renate, Lyn's husband would never have gone to India. Lyn stayed in a guesthouse near the beach. She remembered walking down the steps that led onto Papanasanam beach. On the beach was a group of Indian people, 'Dressed up beautifully, with colourful umbrellas, who swept me up along with them.' She recalled walking along Papanasanam beach and 'Just feeling this feeling of peace.'

Both Lyn and Renate were such great role models. And in India it is not at all unusual for a Western woman to have a much younger Indian boyfriend or husband. I joked that it was my Plan B. But even Renate, poised and beautiful and aware and healthy at seventy-six often said, 'Getting old is not for sissies.'

***

Our new guesthouse was almost certainly meant to have been called Sea Wind but was actually called Sea Win. There were a lot of names like that, almost meaningful but not quite. Our room was spacious and full of light, very clean and smartly painted in green and gold. The floors were done in new looking marble. We had a bathroom (with a bath and occasional hot water!) and a balcony looking out onto palm trees and the sea. Away from the swampy area, up high and nearer the sea, the mosquitoes were much fewer and on the balcony they could be kept at bay with a big stick of incense.

We realised we would probably never again lie on a mattress as wonderful as this. I slept on the side of the bed nearest the window. It was a big window with new mesh, and shutters which we never closed. A few times when it rained and was windy at the same time I felt the spray on me in bed. There were fireflies amongst the palm trees and their lights, the lights of the boats out to sea and the lights of the stars and planets in the sky beyond the trees were almost indistinguishable from one another.

The palm trees were big, and waved seriously in the wind. I had forgotten that monsoon doesn't just mean rain. Awake at night watching fireflies, one came into the balcony, landed on the wall, the ceiling and came right up to the window. It looked almost like an ember, except that it behaved so obviously like a flying thing- the way it moved, landed on the wall and didn't go out. Eventually it settled on the window frame and went to sleep; it stopped moving and its light went out.

Sometimes it didn't rain for two days and it felt hot and sweaty until it rained again. Inside there was the noise of lizards, like the sound of waving a sheet of tinfoil or thin plastic, a kind of shimmering thundery echo. At Osho's we'd had one dog howling, at Sea Win we had a cacophony of high pitched various sounding dogs; one or two started then more and more joined in. The sound was so ridiculous that it made us laugh even if it was late at night and we were trying to sleep.

The crows were ever present and again we fed them cashews on the balcony or the ground below. When we put food out the nearest crow didn't just come and take it, instead they caw cawed for ages until the other crows came too. Sometimes it got very loud on the balcony with crows below and on the roofs nearby, or right onto the balcony itself. Once we accidentally left a packet of nuts out and while we were indoors the crows came, picked up the packet so the nuts dropped all over the floor of the balcony and ate them. 'Those nuts were quite spicy,' I said, 'I hope the crows will be okay.' 'They are Indian crows,' Anthony said.

Another day I saw crows on the balcony. 'They've got something.' I said. 'It's okay, they can have them,' Anthony said, thinking they were just some nuts. Suddenly I realised it wasn't nuts. 'They've got your weed!' I said. We both went outside and watched as, as if in slow motion, a crow flew onto the balcony ledge and then off across the garden carrying a poly pocket with a plastic case inside. Anthony cautiously went downstairs, luckily our landlady was not in the garden and found the case. It was open, the crow must have dropped it from a height so that the catch opened and almost all the weed was gone. Anthony had intended to stop smoking for a while anyway; the crow just brought it forward a bit.

***

I'd wanted to experience living somewhere for an extended period of time. I'd imagined yoga classes and learning to speak the language, maybe teaching English in return. I didn't do any of that. But I developed a writing habit and we had a routine. A friend back in the UK asked me what my writing routine was. 'We go out for breakfast, come home, I write for an hour or two.'

I got my thyroid bloods done. Renate told me about the lab she used; it was quick, easy and cheap. I got my result and phoned my doctor in the UK to check my medication dose. He was from Delhi, and seemed almost as excited to speak to me as I was to him.

At Sea Win I took our rubbish down to the bin area, later, making porridge in the kitchen I saw all our rubbish strewn about; tissues, Dark Fantasy biscuit boxes. 'Dogs' our landlady said. I was glad there hadn't been anything embarrassing in there. What if I were using tampons and sanitary pads instead of cloth sanitary pads and moon cup? When I got worried about my period being late and we bought pregnancy tests, I took the packets and used tests to Cafe Del Mar. 'They have a good bin,' I said which made Anthony laugh, but it was true, they had a bin in the loo and not everywhere did.

***

I wrote in my notebook: Exciting things that have happened this week- my new dress, the room being cleaned, buying my new Om pendant, a few moments of enlightenment.

Writing, of course it had to be writing. I stayed up late writing my blog then woke early at four am and carried on writing. I was tired, spaced out. I did some writing, a lot of organising and moving around. Then I went to have a break with Anthony on the balcony and we had an intense spiritual discussion, carrying on from previous days. I went back inside and immediately wrote up my spiritual insights: *If there is a God, and if God has a plan for me, this is it. If there was another, I wouldn't want it.*

I returned to the book to try and actually produce something as I felt like I hadn't done anything as I hadn't written any new stuff or really altered anything on the book. Words danced, I carried on, I stretched: my eyes blurred, I tried to carry on, then stopped. Words dancing, white. I lay on the bed, my hands over my eyes, then took my t-shirt off and put it over my eyes. Behind my closed eyes was bright white, with dancing shapes, triangles, like a distorted toolbar. Then awareness, peace. 'Neutrality' not love. I have a choice: 'illness or awareness, can't have both. It was like I overdid it and had some kind of episode which reset my brain- wiped it clean.

Now what? What to do. I got up and started trying to ground myself. I ate a banana, and some banana ball cake. I looked outside for five things I could see. I did the yoga tree pose. I put on some music, a song my friend Hayley had sent me, which was normally soothing. Except that before the song there was an ad and that ad was for the Netflix show The end of the f***ing world: *'Sometimes to find your way you have to lose your f***ing mind,'* it said.

Buying the Om pendant was a spur of the moment thing, a marker, a treat and a celebration. Learning about it properly also taught me that it's okay to be in different states; you're just in a different realm or altered state of consciousness.

Enlightenment isn't really a spiritual journey, it's a practical one. It's about stripping away all the things that get in the way, like Michelangelo making David out of a single block of marble 'I just cut away everything that wasn't David.' This creates the conditions for it just to appear to you, or rather for you to realise that it's already there. It's about stripping away the conditioning, distractions and stress that stand between us and get in the way of our own personal peace: illness, pain, overworking, over exercising. Doing things you don't enjoy. Not enjoying the things you're doing because you're hungry, tired or not in the mood. Enjoy what you need to do, that's where mindfulness can help, I've really enjoyed hand washing my clothes in the sink when I've been really present.

***

We went to visit Kanyakumari in the state of Tamil Nadu, situated at the southernmost tip of India. We couldn't find our carriage and asked a group of young Indian men who first of all fell about laughing. After they stopped laughing they said, 'This is India, just sit anywhere.' We met a man on the train who talked to us about Kanyakumari and Hinduism, seamlessly moving from tourist facts to what sounded like mythical stories then said, 'But I'm not that religious.' Yogesh would be the same; he would know everything about the Hindu temple, tell us many Hindu stories but say he wasn't all that religious. It's just a totally different standard to the UK, where people are hardly religious at all in comparison. 'Indian people, we believe in God,' the man on the train said.

We saw a Western man and woman walking down the main street with an Indian man, we heard the Indian man say to them, 'You are in India,' and we looked at each other and laughed. Anthony recounts a story of when he was in India twenty years ago, fighting his way onto a packed train and when he finally got on, hot, sweaty and stressed, he looked up and saw an Indian man dressed all in white stretched calmly out on the luggage rack, who looked down and said 'This is India,' and Anthony laughed and realised, of course, yes.

After the luxury of our room in Varkala the room in Kanyakumari was a bit of a come down. It was generally quite tatty and dirty and although the sheets and pillowcases were clean, where we caught an accidental glimpse of the mattress and pillow underneath they were black with dirt. The first night we struggled to get to sleep imagining bedbugs and cockroaches, but it was fine.

Kanyakumari is a pilgrimage site and the shops and restaurants were for Indians. There was much less English spoken; at the chemist shop I had to make buzzing noises and flap my arms to ask for mosquito cream which made the woman in the shop laugh. On the pavements outside shops were decorative patterns- rangoli- made out of chalk. Stalls sold cheap Indian style clothes. At the side of the road were motorbikes, on the seats were tall piles of t-shirts and lungis for sale. I loved the souvenirs: rough furry coconuts with a hole cut in and an ornamental bird so it looked like a nest, whole stalls selling spices, 'Your name carved into a shell,' mirrors, plant holders and pictures made of shells and wild brightly coloured shell ornaments, plastic wares and rows and rows of fluorescent pink teddies.

At the end of the high street we saw the decorative coloured mouldings of a temple and before we knew it we found ourselves in the temple entrance. A man sold us a big beautiful flower, its petals lush and thick, the flower wet and heavy in my palm, filling my hand. A temple guide took hold of us, directed Anthony to take off his shirt, pointing to a sign on the wall that said men had to take off their shirts to enter.

The whole temple was carved from a single piece of black rock. We passed a statue of Ganesh and a statue of Hanuman, we copied our guide and bowed, and intricate carved writing on the walls, but the tour was conducted at such speed we barely had time to look at anything. We found ourselves at the end and handed over the flowers to a priest. Anthony was given a banana leaf containing red powder and white blossoms. The priest dipped his finger into the red powder and put it on Anthony's forehead, and directed Anthony to do the same to me. A woman pinned a folded string of white blossom into my hair, using one of her own hairgrips to hold it in place. We gave the priest some money then went out to find our shoes, carrying the banana leaf of powder and blossom. We walked down the road with our red forehead blessings, surrounded by the smell of the blossom in my hair, feeling blessed and touristy in equal measure.

There were no Westernised restaurants in Kanyakumari, which was a new experience after where we'd been in Goa and Kerala. We ate masala dosas, chickpea and cashew nut masalas with lemon rice. The food was served on plastic yellow plates. When we had masala dosas the sambar and chutney was ladled onto the plate next to the dosa, with the man coming around to refill halfway through- I love India!

In one of the cafes the tea was served in the metal cups and saucers that we had last seen in the local cafe in Panaji. Then, I didn't know what to do; the cups are so hot that the tea takes ages to cool, and the saucers are deep like bowls. I had wondered whether we were meant to tip the tea out into the saucer but I wasn't sure so I just waited patiently for it to cool.

In the interim between Panaji and Kanyakumari I had read *The White Tiger,* where the narrator from North India arrives in Bangalore and is faced with the metal cup and saucer arrangement for the first time. He looks around to see what everyone else is doing but they are all doing it differently; they are all strangers, newcomers and no one knows what to do. Later in the book the narrator again makes reference to drinking tea from a metal cup and saucer, only this time, he 'knew the proper way to do it.' Except maddeningly he didn't tell us what that was! So I looked up on the internet and my original instincts were right; you transfer the tea from cup to saucer and saucer to cup to cool it down.

In one restaurant a group of men, one wearing a smart-shirt and cowboy hat, asked to take selfies with us. They all laughed at how tall Anthony was. Anthony played up to it, he stood on his tiptoes and then crouched down and everyone laughed.

As well as the big temples that the pilgrims came to there were many smaller ones including an old closed off temple with carvings of the Elephant Lion God at the pillars; all kinds of smaller shrines, and a big white church with a square containing glass cases depicting scenes from Jesus's life. Nearby were two smaller churches, one pretty pastel coloured, another white, as well as several little churches in amongst the houses. We saw the top of a gold temple in the distance and decided to walk there; along past the boats and then inland amongst the houses. The temple was the most beautiful gold, situated near some tumbled down buildings. Inside it was full of brightly coloured statues and beautiful mouldings. In the centre was a floor of sand where some young men were relaxing and the man in charge of the temple was fast asleep on a blanket.

On the way back, outside one of the houses a woman greeted us. She hugged me, taking hold of me so tight and squeezing me almost too hard. She asked us to take a photograph of me and her and send it by post. No one in the family seemed to have a computer or a phone. A little girl wrote down the address, the only one in the group who could write in English.

The houses of Kanyakumari were painted and tiled all different colours; some were tiny and reminded me of dolls houses with wallpaper on the outside, only this was tiles. Inside they were painted different colours; a room painted pink and then an archway to the room beyond it which was painted green. Some houses were painted all crazy colours, stripes and wild combinations, one even had a huge picture of an elephant on the front. Everywhere we looked there was colour. Even beside a dusty grey wall, beyond it there would be a bright pink wall, an orange house.

The people of Kanyakumari were so friendly. 'Welcome' was written in green chalk on the slope from the dhoti factory to the residential area. The women and children we met were friendly. We passed small groups of men sitting playing cards. 'Welcome to our home,' someone said. I was in a state of temporary romantic love with the place, fantasising about moving there. At night my favourite house, the one which looked most like a dolls house with colourful tiles outside and pink and green rooms inside, was draped in multi coloured fairy lights. Even the fishing boats were painted up prettily in all different colours with names and eyes painted on the front.

A few years ago Anthony called out to me to come into the garden and showed me a rainbow that went right over the top of our house. He said that he'd just had the urge to go outside, and there it was. We thought it was a lovely moment, and it was. But in India it's like there's rainbows everywhere. You don't have to look for them. Every scene is packed with so much colour and beauty that it's almost overwhelming. It is like being in a permanent state of bliss or altered state where everything is bright and beautiful.

At the train station we asked a policeman on the platform where to go. He pointed way in the distance- Indian trains are very long- and said, 'B1, by the green tree.' Sure enough, that was exactly where our carriage was, right next to the green tree.

On the train we met Indian people who seemed bemused by all our photographs of houses and our excitement, us struggling to explain why your neighbours in the UK wouldn't like it if you painted your house that way. 'They like everything to be the same,' was the best explanation we could come up with.

***

Along the cliff walk there were coconut palm branches and broken roof tiles, we wondered at times if it was safe to walk there during the monsoon. Buildings began to look tired and a bit tatty. But as the monsoon began to come to an end and the new holiday season drew closer the buildings started getting done up. At the restaurant where we had spent the evening with Robert and Yogesh they took the old roof off and put in new beams and a new roof within days. The roof itself was woven from natural fibres and the beams were hand bound in the corners with rope. The new roof beams were painted. The wall at the front was painted with mandalas. Anthony the waiter explained that they do this every year. The restaurant opened again a few days later, just as Anthony had said it would. Anthony had a side line booking train tickets and got our tickets for Kolkata and Varanasi. He was from Kolkata and told us, 'Any problems, call me, in ten minutes my friends will be there.'

At Sea Win we had accumulated far too many clothes; the hotel caretaker said he could send things to a charity for us. We even had a drawer like you would at home, with old batteries, loads of lighters and miscellaneous items. Towards the end I opened it and a big cockroach slowly crawled out of the drawer, which I took as a sign that it was time to pack up and move on.

I fell in love with you and I cried: Chennai, India

Everywhere we go has its own 'things.' In Fort Kochi it was walls with words; words and moss. I thought of Elizabeth Gilbert who wrote a very big book about an early female botanist who specialised in moss. There was the smell of monsoon damp and mould and moss on the outside walls. A big stretch of once-white wall was covered in a long poem, partially obscured by moss. Another wall outside someone's house spelled out a life philosophy from A to Z. The buildings looked Portuguese, with decorative iron work railings. The auto drivers were pushier than we'd been used to and repeated certain phrases, 'Do me one favour;' offering a cheap starting price then saying, 'If you don't mind I'll show you...' and tried to take us to tourist places or to certain department stores. The people in the shops also had a particular strategy, they called out, 'Do you remember me?' which confused us at first.

The use of the English language in India is slightly different to its use in the UK and can sometimes sound like over and understatements. So on the pizza menu in Kochi it was stated unapologetically, *'Dreams take colour... We invite you to taste the flavour of a dream.'* On the other hand, a road traffic accident with multiple fatalities can be described in the newspaper as a 'mishap.'

The place we were staying at was a home stay; the woman of the house cooked us homemade Indian breakfasts, vellappam (a kind of rice pancake) with mild curry, puttu steamed rice, served in a cylindrical shape, the rice long almost like very short rice noodles with green peas masala, and sweet black tea in black china cups and saucers.

There was a vegetarian restaurant just around the corner. The owner greeted us warmly, chatted with us and put a photo book of Kerala in front of me. It reminded me of being at my Grandmother's and being given a big book of cats to look at. The owner noticed that I had a cold and went out to the pharmacy and came back with little eucalyptus capsules for me. We ate a lovely veg thali, with many different curries including okra and the most amazing new dish, a green kind of mousse made from coconut and coriander, 'Best eaten with this,' the owner said, a yellow sponge cake that was 'In between sweet and savoury,' 'Gujarati idli.' It was made of chickpea flour and was spongy and moist and made a perfect combination with the green 'mousse'. The restaurant was called *Grandma's Kitchen.*

We walked down to the sea. There was a stall selling only umbrellas, opened and displayed at the front of the stall like colourful jellyfish, and sun hats with different coloured ribbons, the perfect combination for the monsoon season. There were lots of people selling fish and little carts sold cut fruit. Stalls sold glass bottles of coloured oils and monkey ornaments carved out of coconuts.

In the harbour were big grey Indian Navy warships and huge red container ships and at the edge on wooden platforms, Chinese fishing nets- big wooden swing like structures that dip into the water like a pelican's beak. The Chinese fishing nets are a tourist attraction and we ended up going onto one of the platforms where the net was operated from, meeting the fisherman, taking photographs and handing over some money. Unusually compared to where we've been so far, there were rubbish bins everywhere. Teams of workers were collecting rubbish in baskets and sorting it into sacks, presumably cleaning up ready for the season. The fisherman told us that the beach had been covered in rubbish, most of it washed up in the monsoon.

The beach dogs were different, strange looking, the size of almost-grown yellow Labradors but with stumpy little legs, as if a Dachshund had ran amok. The cats and dogs were bigger and plumper than their Varkala counterparts, who had begun to look a bit thin. There were lots of goats in Fort Kochi too, white and black and white, a little thin, just wandering around.

The clothes were different: blue cotton summer dresses in delicate pale prints with flowers or polka dots, worn over leggings or jeans. Teenage girls in blue and brown plaid shirts with jeans like the young Indian men wear. Two young women arm in arm, one wearing a bright orange kurti and a white scarf with little pink and blue stars, her friend wearing a bright pink gauze party dress. Even the umbrellas were different; subtle, brown and prettily patterned.

The train left Kochi at around seven in the evening for a fifteen hour journey to Chennai. First to get on after us was a young man who had the bunk above Anthony, he got straight up onto his bunk but the three of us talked for a while. He was a final year engineering student, he said that Indian parents want their children to be engineers or doctors. He said sometimes parents decide when a baby is four months old or even before they are born what they are going to study. His parents were from Kerala but work in the UAE and he was brought up there. He told us UAE is nicknamed Little Kerala as there's so many people from Kerala there. We asked him if he had any pressure to get married, 'Not yet,' he said but he said that his cousin who is a girl does, 'She's same age, at university like me, and wants to be a doctor.' He talked about politics and corruption and the garbage problem. 'As soon as I can, I'm getting out of this country,' he said.

Later a man who had the bunk above me got on. He sat down next to Anthony and we chatted for a bit. He lived in Kerala but was going to Chennai for a one week training course. He said he preferred Kerala for its climate and the nature, and said that Chennai would be hot. I asked him if he minded going, he said, 'No not at all, it's only one week.'

The man went up to his bunk and everyone got ready for bed; for me this just meant undoing my bra- I had put on comfy clothes to sleep in. The ac made it chilly and I folded my blanket double. The bed was firm but not exactly uncomfortable. Someone closed the curtain to our cubicle and the lights were dimmed. It felt cosy, safe and peaceful. I think staff came and shone torches to check on us in the night. There was a guard asleep out near the sinks by the loos. I think it felt okay to be with strangers because we'd chatted. I lay awake for a while, just enjoying the feeling, excited to be on the train. When I went to the loo, I counted the curtained cubicles to find my way back to the correct bunk.

I woke up in the morning and looked out of the window. The houses looked like the ones in Kanyakumari, which is also in Tamil Nadu, even though Kanyakumari and Chennai are far apart as Tamil Nadu is a large state. The train arrived later than expected and the man doing the training course said he had just enough time to get to the course for the starting time. No shower, no breakfast, going straight to a work course after a fifteen hour overnight train journey. He didn't seem to mind at all. I thought about how people in the UK, myself included, would all complain if our employers expected us to do that.

***

Yogesh, our friend from Chennai had told us that Chennai is hot and dry and that where we were staying was busy, 'You are staying in the real India,' he said. Our guesthouse was down a narrow alleyway off a busy main street, hectic with autos and people. We dumped our bags and went for masala dosas at a restaurant just across the main road which the guesthouse staff had directed us to. Many of the shops on the main road near the guesthouse looked like they hadn't been painted since they first opened; money not spent on shop ascetics. The main high street was full of shops for locals rather than tourists, and we didn't see any other tourists out in the street.

We stopped at a juice place and had fresh juice, salted peanuts and ice cold water. It felt good to be back in a dry heat, hotter but less humid, more like Delhi. I washed loads of clothes and hung them in the bathroom and even though we had no proper window, just vents they dried within a few hours and didn't smell.

We went out for dinner at another local non touristy restaurant. Staff stood all around staring at us while we ate. It was a real lesson in overcoming self consciousness, eating rice with my fingers as well as I could, staying in the flow and not getting put off by six people watching us. The food was served on yellow plastic plates again, the same as in Kanyakumari. I had onion oothappam for the first time, a bit like a thick round pancake topped with onions.

The night was warm and felt exciting and I didn't want to go in for the night yet so we went to the little shop on the corner and bought 7Up, biscuits and cigarettes. I wasn't sure if it was okay to smoke there, my UK conditioning. The hotel forecourt faced the alley but there wasn't anywhere to sit so we perched awkwardly on a little concrete step. One of the hotel staff brought us chairs and we sat down and gave the man a couple of cigarettes.

Opposite was a row of parked scooters. Three street dogs were squaring up and barking at each other; they were thick set with faces like Ridgebacks, sturdy, their bodies muscular and well covered. People went past, some said hello, we didn't see any other Westerners. An older Indian man wearing a lungi and a classic Indian shirt, short sleeved with a front pocket, walked past, greeted us and said, 'Welcome to India.'

The wall opposite where we were sitting was a faded paint-peeled orange tinged with blue. An orange cat sat on the wall. The cats in Chennai all seemed to be orange, not bright ginger tom colour but a paler orange. The colour of tiger milk, a drink my grandmother used to make me as a child, milk mixed with orange juice. A few feet below the cat was a little overhang roof of old blue corrugated metal. Beyond the wall the blue sky was tinged with yellow. The colours were warm and dusty, as if they'd been made out of chalk pastels. I gazed at the scene, wanting to remember, absorbing the colours through my pores. 'Look,' I said to Anthony, 'Isn't it amazing how the colours all go together, blue metal roof, orange wall with blue tinge, orange cat, blue-with-yellow-tinge sky.'

'That isn't the sky, that's another building,' he said. I looked again and saw that what I thought was sky was actually the wall of a big building in the background. It didn't matter though.

A man came out of a door near where the cat was; he spoke to the cat as if telling it, 'Get down and wait for me, be a good cat, I'm going to the market to get you some fish,' before walking off. The cat looked at him while he was speaking, stayed still for a few moments, then jumped down onto the blue roof, a parked scooter below, then along from seat to seat the length of the row of scooters, and disappeared from view.

We stayed one night in the first guesthouse then moved to Broadlands Guesthouse which Yogesh had recommended. The guesthouse, set on a dusty side street off the main Triplicane High Road didn't look like much from the outside except for its quirky welcome sign: *WELCOME! NAMASTE TRAVELLER! Pray lodge in this unworthy place. The bath is ready. A peaceful room awaits you. Come in! Come in! Please!*

Stepping inside though was like stepping inside an old French chateau. The guesthouse had around thirty to forty rooms built around a central courtyard with a square balcony. Stone floors, dusty hallways and winding stone staircases led to tucked away rooms and a roof terrace. The rough-surfaced old walls were painted faded white, the paintwork of the banisters of the balcony and the many doors leading off it old baby blue gloss; the same colour as my Goa birthday ring.

In the courtyard below were plants in big old white painted stone plant pots and a big green tree full of crows, its branches growing up above the banisters. On the dusty stone walkway of the balcony there was an orange cat; one of the guests, a woman, was taking care of her. 'She's sick, and pregnant, she needs to drink, she's dehydrated,' the woman said.

Our room was big and spacious with white washed walls, blue doors and a concrete floor. The high ceiling had wood beams painted baby pink, and lots of cobwebs. There were three big windows in the room and one in the bathroom, all fitted with mosquito mesh and blue shutters. At night with the bedroom light off when we opened the double blue doors to the bathroom and put the bathroom light on the bathroom glowed blue like a portal.

From one window we could see the big white mosque next door and a flock of pigeons who lived on the waste ground between us and the mosque. I saw Indian squirrels running about on the abandoned sheds in the waste ground outside our window. It was the first time I'd seen them since Panaji, and before that I'd only seen them in Hampi. From the other window we could see the neat paved grounds and car park of the mosque, nearby houses and flats painted blue, green and peach, and a green tree with red flowers.

From the window in the bathroom there were white buildings with a glimpse of bright yellow house in-between. The balconies at the corner of one of the white buildings made gaps which looked like windows; through the top one I could see the yellow house, through the bottom I saw a green one. I looked again another day, the green had changed colour. I was momentarily confused, that scene had been so strong, had I misremembered? No, there was a sheet or a towel on the balcony, blocking the gap and changing the colour!

In the morning we were woken at a quarter to five by the call to prayer. We were so close to the mosque that it felt almost painful on my ears. I went back to sleep, and despite the early morning wake up we have both loved it each time we've stayed near a mosque; there's something timeless and quite magical about hearing the call to prayer.

The next day I sat on the blue painted wooden threshold between the space outside our room and the balcony walkway. I was writing or should have been writing and having a few moments to myself. Instead of writing I was trying to find a title for my book, the kind of thing writers can waste hours on. Going over and over, searching, trying to come up with something, even though I knew that wasn't how it was going to happen, that a title needs to just come. At least I've set my intention, put it out there that I want to find one, I thought. I wondered if there was an Indian word, like Namaste 'Namaste India', but something less well known, that I could use. I could ask Yogesh, I thought. Yogesh was coming that evening to take us to a temple.

In the courtyard below were three women, part of the housekeeping staff of the hotel standing together in a group. They were wearing everyday cotton sarees, everyday for them but beautiful to me like so many things in India. One red with purple swirls of colour; one an orangey pink with black print, one pale blue, almost matching the gloss work, with a printed pattern of creamy yellow buttermilk, and orange-pink leggings which matched the orange-pink saree of the other woman.

The woman with the red-purple saree was wearing a big gold nose stud which flashed like a light. She was standing with the sun on it in just the right place, or I was sitting in just the right place to see it and looking at just the right moment. The three women standing in a circle or a triangle in the courtyard and the nose stud shining in the sun was like a scene from a film, easily as beautiful as if they had been dressed in Indian wedding finery and as special to me as the orange cat from the night before. Later, I forgot to ask Yogesh but he gave me a title anyway.

I got ready for going to the temple and had a little time to spare, interstitial time, the time in between things when I have nothing to do which is so rare and which I love so much. Anthony was downstairs using the Wi-Fi and talking to Christopher, an African American from Detroit who was staying across the walkway from us. Yogesh was on his way. It was raining, we had been surprised by the rain in Chennai; apparently it doesn't always rain at this time. The mosque and its lights were white in the dark and the mosque's pool of water glittered. I moved the cane chairs with their cushions and our clothes hanging on them away from the windows with their open shutters and sat down, my feet propped up on the other chair. I had only the low light on so as not to attract mosquitoes.

In front of me was a little red table. Spread out to cover the bed were my lungis, purple and green and gold. The light from the mosque shone on the rainwater on the blue painted shutters; they looked as if they had been sprinkled in blue glitter. A fork of lightning flashed in the sky in the gap in between the shutters, one open, one closed. As the wind blew the shutters the light danced over the raindrops and they glittered even more.

Is it okay just to be happy? And what do you have to do to get there? A lot, because of how things are set up in life. I thought of the John Lennon quote: His teacher asked him, *'What do you want to be when you grow up?'* 'Happy.' he said. *'She told me that I didn't understand the question. I told her she didn't understand life.'*

Here, as I was writing this, I got a notification that I had to resign into the Wi-Fi. I went on WordPress for a break and saw, 'For my life to have any meaning, I have to live it for myself.' That's the meaning of life, to live it. To live it for yourself, via escaping conditioning, family, everything that gets in the (your) way.

Yogesh arrived and the three of us got an auto to a completely different part of town. The area around the temple was busy and colourful with stalls selling, 'Everything to do with visiting the temple,' Yogesh explained. 'God clothes,' which I had previously thought were children's clothes; fresh flower garlands, the smell of the blossom sweet and strong, the same as the blossom put in my hair at the temple in Kanyakumari, 'And of course food, for afterwards.'

We walked, clockwise, around the outside areas, non-Hindus are not allowed inside. The rain had pooled in puddles on the stone floor under our bare feet. The outside of the temple was decorated with beautiful coloured mouldings. Coloured electric lights, like fairy lights were placed around, decorating a statue of Ganesh, a juxtaposition of old and new.

There was a stable full of well fed, happy looking cows, some milk white, the others different shades of brown. Keeping cows at the temple was a mixture of cow rescue and to use the milk, Yogesh explained. Yogesh told us Hindu stories and pointed out religious devotional writing on the stone walls. 'It's all like love poetry,' Yogesh said, 'Like, *''I fell in love with you and I cried.''*

I felt myself well up. Even though Yogesh is one of us, we've said anything to each other and the other person there with us was my husband, I choked back the emotion and changed the subject back to the cows. But when Yogesh said I could go and see them, that made me all the more emotional, thinking of how gentle they are, of the street cows left to eat out of garbage and the horrors of the dairy industry.

At the temple there are poojas six times a day; we saw the last one which is longer and bigger as it is the closing ceremony. Everyone stood outside the main temple and looked in. The crowd began to chant, a low, repetitive singing that wrapped itself around us. Clouds of incense filled the temple and the courtyard where we stood. The main statue of the God was being bathed in milk. Lots and lots of milk, poured over like a fountain or a waterfall. Yogesh told us that it's not just milk that is used, it's fruit salad, all kinds of offerings. I was bordering on being overwhelmed. Nothing can beat this, experiencing a Hindu temple with a Hindu and a good friend.

In another temple room, the God's wife was dressed up in a gold and green silk dress. The dresses are changed during every pooja; people bring the dresses hence the stalls outside. At the end the God's feet were carried on a small chariot from his temple to hers where they spend the night, symbolising the God spending the night with his wife. 'Even the gods need sex,' Yogesh said matter of factly.

During the pooja two white people dressed as Hindus went to go inside the temple and the priest stopped them. Yogesh said to us afterwards, 'There's no test, (for Hinduism) they could be more devout than me. The priest stopped them but if they had gone in no one would have done anything.' There's no test, either for Hinduism or enlightenment. Anthony and I talked about how we get something out of it without being religious, going to the temple, being in a religious country but still not religious.

I had wondered what happens to all the milk. Afterwards, walking away I saw cats. 'There's lots of cats,' I said. 'There's a lot of milk!' Yogesh said. He told us that people take some of it, some of it runs off, the cats drink it. 'Rivers of milk, for cats,' I said. There were cats sitting on a low wall just outside the temple and just beyond the wall was a little house. I could see into their downstairs room, there were lots of orange and orange and white cats inside, it looked like a cat cafe.

Later I admitted to having a moment. I told Yogesh about the poetry, about the title for my book, that *'I fell in love with you and I cried,'* could be my title, although I forgot to tell him the bit about me deciding to ask him for it. I told Yogesh about the women in the courtyard, the beautiful scene, the nose stud. He told me that in Kanyakumari, my favourite place in India so far there is a statue of the Goddess Kanyakumari, apparently the nose stud of the statue shone so brightly that sailors thought it was a lighthouse and ended up getting caught on the rocks.

I'd always thought a lighthouse was to warn sailors of rocks, to tell them where not to go, rather than somewhere for them to head to. Discombobulated that I could have totally misunderstood something so everyday I looked it up on Wikipedia. Yes lighthouses were originally built to guide ships into a safe harbour. In more modern times they became warnings about where not to go. From there I came across a surprisingly interesting biography about a famous lighthouse designer and builder, a great story about being gifted opportunities and making the most of them.

Back at the guesthouse the three of us chatted, swapping 'spiritual' experiences we'd had since the last time we'd seen each other. Yogesh told us about returning to Chennai the day after our evening together in Kerala; he'd had a fifteen hour bus ride back to Chennai then gone into work to prepare for teaching.

At work he had loads to do- photocopying and getting ready and only half an hour in which to do it. He felt spaced out, paranoid, thinking he looked stoned, but everyone was smiling at him and offering to help. Yogesh realised he hadn't eaten for fifteen hours. He asked for some water; one of his students poured some Red Bull into a glass, it looked like a potion. He thought of what Robert (who we met at Osho's guesthouse at the same time) had said about drinking the potion when you are born, the potion that causes us to forget who we are. 'Don't drink all of it, then you'll remember,' Robert had told us. Yogesh remembered this, and only drank some of it. He felt a force of energy crackle all up one side and pass all the way though his head and body. Time altered. He felt full of energy. He did all the work, that he had so much of and so little time to do, the work that he'd had only half an hour for but that should have taken even more. He looked at clock, only ten minutes had passed.

***

As always we had quickly created a little world of familiarity. From our guesthouse it was just a short walk, past the big white mosque, on broken pavements or in the road to reach the juice bar and the place we went to for breakfast. My favourite juice was

Mayflower, made of kiwi and lime. In restaurants I ordered sathakudi (sweet lime) juice because I had never heard of it before. For breakfast I had Pongal, again because I had never heard of it before, an almost-impossible to finish dish that felt like eating the creamiest mashed potato although it is actually made from rice. I told Yogesh about it and said I thought it would be the ultimate heartbreak comfort food; he laughed and said at his work they call it the sleeping pill, as it makes the students sleepy. I also had tomato oothappam which looked like a pizza. For dinner we ate Sambar idli a speciality at that restaurant, and Sambar vada (rice cakes with curry) which even came in dear little mini versions.

Where we were in Chennai, as compared to where we were in Varkala some things were not quite so easy. We couldn't just take our devices and chargers to the nice tourist restaurant, plug them in over dinner and use the fast internet to catch up on social media and download something to watch; the local places did not have Wi-Fi or charging points.

A fruit and veg market was a short walk away. Stalls on either side of a narrow street sold tomatoes, piled high and such shiny bright red they were irresistible. Other stalls sold bananas, onions and different kinds of fruit and veg. I saw long green vegetables that I'd never seen before that looked at first glance like enormous runner beans. Some stalls sold only coriander; walking past the smell was wonderful. People sold fruit and vegetables from blankets on the ground. In the midst of it all was a little temple with a God statue surrounded by animals in bright colours and a little shrine with candles.

I handed over a 10 rupee note and pointed to the tomatoes. I got a big amount. I ate a couple and bought a bunch of bananas from another stall. Then we went down the backstreets and fed tomatoes and bananas to the cows. A man gave me advice in sign language: Don't bend down, due to the horns? Throw the food on the ground, or put on hand and put hand out. I misinterpreted his facial expression as gruffness at first. People in Chennai sometimes watched us and even stared but did not seem unfriendly.

It was one of my favourite things to do. Helping people a little by buying things off them, and feeding the cows, some of whom are painfully thin and all of them at risk of obstruction, illness and death from eating the plastic bags that food is thrown away in. The feeling of standing amongst garbage, feeling a cow eating softly out of my hand was spiritual, bittersweet.

One day, late afternoon-early evening we walked to Chennai beach, the same direction as the restaurant where we ate dinner, walking along a very busy main road with no pavements, negotiating our way past autos, scooters and other pedestrians. Past street stalls of food and plastic tat and glass fronted air-conditioned shops selling the most beautiful gowns and long embroidered men's jackets; in my fantasies Anthony and I would dress like that. At the crossroads we turned left, instead of crossing over to the restaurant or turning right at the flower garlands which I used as a marker for the way to the market.

We passed more shops and restaurants, walked past cows eating out of garbage, past banana street sellers and then onto a main road with wide pavements. People were living on the pavements with homemade shelters, cooking equipment, a chicken and possibly an auto or a scooter. In India it's possible to set up home on the pavement and to work, and have a place. In the UK people put in spikes on the pavement to stop people sleeping there and even hose down homeless people in cold water, and people can't work without an address and a bank account. We walked through a subway and came out onto another main road, crossed over and arrived at the beach.

When we see something for the first time, we see it through the filters of our own experience, comparing it to our own familiar versions. Chennai beach was nothing like any beach we had seen before. It was huge: long, wide and flat, it is the longest natural urban beach in the country according to Wikipedia. There were numerous closed up little stalls about the size of a packing crate, covered in tarps. I thought maybe it was because it was out of season but Yogesh told us afterwards that it was only open properly in the evening; we were there too early. There were a couple of plastic roofed stalls with a few chairs and tables selling snacks and drinks with a few customers and only a few other people around. We were the only foreigners. In the distance near the promenade wall was an encampment.

A man went past us on a horse, he made the horse go fast past us as if showing off. Along the main drag of stalls were two men with fairground stalls set up, balloons on a-board with guns. 'Give me a break, give me a break,' the man kept saying to us as we went past. Anthony almost had a go, then stopped, suddenly realising he didn't want to potentially be centre of attention. Something about the atmosphere made us uneasy.

A boy was selling strange ginger coffee from a flask; it was very milky and tasted of ginger but only faintly of coffee. We were on our way back to the road when a child ran out from the encampment towards us. Close up they were absolutely filthy. The child started tugging at my arm. A man from one of the stalls threw a stone in the child's direction and they ran off. A moment later another smaller child came running but by then we were almost at the road. We might have been wrong but we instinctively did not want to hang around or to give money even though the children were a pitiful sight; sometimes conspicuously giving out money can bring unwanted attention. Once Anthony had been completely surrounded at a railway station by children asking for money. On the way home I bought some bananas from a woman with a stall at the side of the road. I said thank you in Tamil, wrongly and she corrected me (Tamil is hard!) and fed the bananas to the cows eating out of garbage. This felt like something good we could do: many things were complicated but this wasn't.

***

Yogesh lived in the top apartment of his landlord's apartment block and we sat up on Yogesh's roof space with his landlord and family enjoying the lovely evening breeze and the views of Chennai. I spoke a lot to the daughter who was nearing the end of High School. She laughed when I told her my dress was made out of a lungi. I talked about psychology, not a huge profession in India, and occupational therapy, also fairly small with posts often staffed by Europeans. We talked about Indian squirrels and how I think they look more like chipmunks, and then everyone talked about Alvin and the Chipmunks, a surprising point of familiarity for all of us.

Indians walk side by side fearlessly even when there's no pavement and Yogesh was the same, walking and talking with us from his home to the restaurant. About crossing the roads Yogesh said: 'In Delhi you put your hand up. In Hyderabad you make eye contact with the driver. In Chennai you just walk out and the driver will make the adjustment.' I was still terrified though. Later Yogesh sent me an article describing how it's no good getting the signals mixed up, if you use the Delhi Stop hand signal in Hyderabad, the drivers will slam on their brakes, potentially causing an accident. After dinner we went back to his again. Yogesh called Broadlands for us as they normally have a ten pm curfew. He spoke with them in Tamil. He told us they'd said, 'It's okay to come back late, Rachel and Anthony can come back anytime.'

Being at Broadlands had provided our first real taste of backpacker sociability. Downstairs outside the office and looking onto a little courtyard there was a seating area where the Wi-Fi worked with an old sofa, two metal folding chairs and a low wall that doubled as a seat. This area was an informal meeting hub, most times there was either someone there or someone came along at some point. Christopher from Detroit said 'I'm not normally very sociable but every time I sit here, I end up chatting to someone… its nice.' Christopher had been in India for six months and had travelled all over setting up links with crafts people wanting to export to the US. Christopher was a Christian and had a beautifully warm and positive attitude towards both his fellow human beings and the way the Universe worked, believing in opportunities and in going with the flow. Christopher said, 'You two, doing it together, going with the flow.' We made a strong connection. We shared our stories; Christopher on his ex wife: 'She had her own problems, but I thought if I could only love her hard enough...' Christopher spoke about experiencing racism in India as an African American; the mother of an Indian friend in a village had been afraid of him until she had realised that he was a Christian. Christopher commented about it being unusual to meet other Black people in India, most travellers and tourists being white Europeans, and that it was a surprise to find four Black people at Broadlands at the same time; Christopher, David and a young couple from France. Finding themselves on the rooftop all together Christopher and David said the four of them had shared a hug.

David, from the US had lived and worked for nine years in Hong Kong before coming to India. He had worked as a chef in the US; long hours and low wages. His girlfriend had got a job in Hong Kong and he ended up getting an interview at the same place. At the interview they asked him if he was prepared to learn Cantonese. 'Sure,' he said, and they offered him the job. During his time in Hong Kong he found a guru, but eventually she said she had taught

David everything she could. At the bottom of the Hong Kong payslips there was some small print which he never paid any attention to, then one day he was out and heard people talking. Apparently ten percent of your income was automatically saved for you. If you were to leave, you could claim it back. He had been earning good money in Hong Kong, and that money was enough for him to go to India; he'd been there two years so far.

David had just spent nine months in an ashram in Varanasi learning Sanskrit. 'It's not like you can order a cup of tea in it, it's not used like that, it's to better understand the mantras; when the meaning is known they are easier to remember.' He was on his way to another ashram, just having a dip into the 'Real life crazy,' to remind himself to get out. 'It's like sleeping in Church,' he said, of being in an ashram. He told us how to tell if it's a real ashram; it will have a plain website- they are meditating, they are not on the internet. David said the Indian students at the ashram laughed at his clothes; he used to wear a lungi and a vest or a t-shirt. He bought Indian shirts, they still laughed at him, but now it was because of his backpack, 'How am I supposed to carry my books?!' he said.

We went out to dinner with David, he took us to a regular place of his. Like Yogesh, David walked fearlessly in the road, striding ahead, tall and in Indian dress he cut a striking figure. Anthony walked beside him, with me following cautiously behind. David recommended his favourite dish, Gobi 65. This was Gobi Manchurian, the deep fried dry kind.

David shared his philosophy. He said it's like when you die you're asked, 'Were you happy?' 'No, maybe I needed to be rich,' 'Okay go round again,' 'No, maybe if I were poor...,' 'Okay go round again.' 'No maybe I need-.' 'Okay, go round again.' You can stop all that by just being happy now. I said something like, is it about seeking understanding, or seeking happiness. He said, it's both, it's like, do you smile because you're happy or are you happy because you smile?' '50% plan 50% let unfold,' he said, 'Mistakes led me here.' 'Try not to think too much. Use mind for arithmetic. Use heart for the rest.'

Anthony had asked David in a quiet moment, 'Why are you in India?' 'I don't always answer that question but you seem pretty cool so... I'm here for self realisation and I'm not leaving until I get it.'

We met another young French couple, a man and a woman, she spoke to Anthony about her experience of Kolkata; seeing lots of people sleeping on the streets had upset her. She'd expected to find backpackers to socialise with but there weren't many around and those that were weren't that friendly, mirroring our experiences in Goa and Hampi. The man talked to me about clothes, about Western versus Indian dress. I told him I covered up. 'But is it for you or for them?' he asked. It's a hard question to answer. 'Both, I suppose, it makes it easier for me, by making it easier for them.'

There was an Italian man next door who had been in India for twenty years, we never found out what doing, or if he'd been back and forth; he was very thin, he said he was unwell, so he was going home for health tests under the free health service. He had spent time in an ashram, he spoke about his master and said, 'You must go there.' He was still very upset about Italian politics, whereas I'd all but forgotten about UK politics after four months.

On the other side of us was a Western woman, a yoga teacher. We got off to a slow start. She told me not to smoke outside my room on the step because the smoke got into her room, which was fair enough and I stopped. After a few days she did chat to us a bit, but didn't have anything good to say about where we'd been- Kerala- 'That's where everyone goes,'- or where we were going- Pondicherry, 'Full of Westerners, it's not really India,' she said. When we came down with our backpacks to go to Pondicherry and she saw our yoga mats she said, 'Do you do yoga?' sounding really surprised.

'People underestimate us, maybe I shouldn't mind, but I do.' Anthony said. Sometimes we feel more vulnerable than others. If I feel people underestimate me or think I'm boring or whatever is it because I think those things about myself?

Invisible steps: Pondicherry, India

We went to Pondicherry for a few days. Just beyond our room was an invisible step in the shiny marble corridor that we had to be mindful of, and beyond that was a little balcony that looked out onto the alleyway.

The 'spiritual journey' can be lonely sometimes. I wrote in my notebook: 'I feel far away... maybe that's part of it, necessary, and that I'll come back, naturally. I could force it, through fear or guilt, but no, wait it out. Who would notice, anyway? My husband is used to me being quiet or chatty and doesn't get unsettled if I am off by myself either emotionally or spiritually.'

I thought about David, completely devoted to the pursuit of self realisation, seemingly sure of his path, with a guru and long periods spent in ashrams, and Christopher, a Christian with faith in God. 'Should I be doing more?' I wondered. Should I be more focussed on 'The Quest' or associated practices, do something more 'formal' rather than this strange and ever changing way of mine? But at the same time, I was also feeling spiritual and sensory overload.

Maybe how it works is, do the underpinning work, have a good day, and then be still, and look at something beautiful. Be still, and notice something beautiful. Be still, and find something beautiful to notice. Be still, and notice something so that it *becomes* beautiful. A state of grace: it can be visual, the orange cat on the wall, the raindrops on the shutters, or physical: a yoga pose, the sensation of lying on the most comfortable mattress in India, a good coffee or a dish of gulab jamun.

Maybe it's all part of the same thing for me. I knew there was a reason I'm walking around wearing a huge Om; it's not for others, it's for me, to remind me about the different levels of consciousness, or rather the different places that our consciousness resides in. Maybe I experience a higher state of consciousness *via* experiencing the world through the five senses? I feel as if I *can't* do any more, but maybe I *don't need* to do any more. *'Every enlightenment has its own melody,'* as Robert from Switzerland said.

To find what you're looking for, call off the search. I don't know if I want to spend my life on a lifelong spiritual quest. Isn't that yet another trap to take away your life, to make you think you're not good enough where you/your life are?

"At some point in life the world's beauty becomes enough. You don't need to photograph, paint or even remember it. It is enough." - Toni Morrison, quoted in *Turtles all the way down* by John Green, which I read in Varkala.

Sitting on the floor of our room in Pondicherry I read a quote from Rumi-

"All your anxiety is because of your desire for harmony. Seek disharmony, accept it all, then you will gain peace." I thought about how when people have babies they have all these hopes and anxieties. Will everything be okay? How will they turn out? Rather than simply accepting everything, this life, as it comes, as it is, as we are, as I am, as I was, as I will be. Whatever I do, whatever I've done or haven't done, whatever I will do or won't do. Be at peace with it all.

The hot windowless room of the guesthouse in Pondicherry was not conducive to writing, or maybe it was my emotional/spiritual state. Plus we didn't feel that well. We'd been eating at different places in Chennai and had also been quite casual about drinking the water off the table even at new places, saying no to the bottles of mineral water often offered to foreigners and drinking the free water like locals; this usually comes from big bottles or is carefully boiled tap water. But if it isn't a regular place you don't always know if it is okay. Maybe we'd been too cavalier. The catchphrase of the Pondicherry trip was us coming out of the toilet and saying, 'Well, *that* wasn't normal!'

I didn't do much actual writing except making notes but I did stay up late reading blogs. WordPress was especially inspiring and I was almost overloaded with things to think about. I read a blog from Des about family influences, about the process of identifying the influences that have come from our parents and then choosing which to keep and which to strip away. I read a blog about not having any friends and then that night I had a dream. In the dream I realised, 'No one likes me. No one likes me, and that's okay,' and really accepting and feeling at peace with this realisation. *"The most terrifying thing of all is to accept oneself completely."* – Jung. The next day I woke up and discovered that it was 'Friendship Day.'

In quiet moments I sat on the invisible step and looked through the railings into the alleyway below. I thought about how I had travelled there, how I had the room, money, a plan for what I was doing next. I thought about creating a little pocket of safety. I thought about should it be more edgy, is it too easy? I thought that if I have that, a safe place to sleep and somewhere to sit and have a quiet moment, I am okay. I thought about how even people in more edgy environments would still have little pockets of stillness like this, a place to sit and at least eat safely, a place to sleep. I'm always comparing myself unfavourably to others; hard core backpackers, war correspondents. I know, weird huh?

The other catchphrase of the Pondicherry spell was in restaurants after eating, 'Well it wasn't brilliant food was it?' A lot of the food was expensive fusion or Indian food with a twist and we didn't enjoy it much. We got excited about a shop almost next door to the guesthouse that sold dried fruit and nuts, soya milk and health food items. I drank almost a whole big carton of soya milk in one go.

Meeting the yoga teacher in Chennai who was so surprised that I did yoga, and the covering up and wearing of ill fitting or unflattering clothes that weren't always my style, triggered yet another minor identity crisis. Yet at the same time, I can feel myself dissolving under these sartorial experiments. Playing with my sense of self, my identity. Being here, that is the work.

We saw Indian women tourists in Pondicherry in short dresses and shorts, albeit near the beach, and I decided to relax my self-imposed modest dress code a little while we were there. Anthony supports me whatever I do but I know he thinks I am overly covered up sometimes. So I went for a walk by myself wearing my lungi dress- above the knee, with side slits, without loose black trousers underneath and without a scarf over my shoulders. I had got so used to walking around with trousers and a scarf that I felt half naked and vulnerable. I walked down the road and to the park, feeling a little self conscious.

I saw no one dressed in as little as me; at the park even though it was daytime, there were people around and there was a policeman at the gate I still felt uncomfortable. I thought a man might have been following me. This could have just been me, I get anxious, you could say I have anxiety except I haven't been diagnosed; anyway I get paranoid at the drop of a hat. I didn't stay long, I came home, put some trousers on and grabbed my scarf.

Pondicherry streets were a mixture. Down one side were pretty coloured buildings with intricate lattice iron work, on the other side grey and dusty concrete with people living in pavement dwellings. Metal grilles like big drain covers were propped at kerbs and pavements outside shops and restaurants to make ramps for mopeds like in Chennai. Chalk rangoli patterns decorated the pavements outside shops like in Kanyakumari. We saw a sign saying, 'Dead body boxes,' at a woodwork place; coffins, we realised.

We went to a big weekly street market. The length of a long main street was lined with stalls selling leather belts, parts for cars and all kinds of everyday household items and products. There was the smell of coffee, citrus fruit, and occasionally toilet smells. Street sellers sold plastic animal facemasks in bunches like balloons. Stalls sold God dresses, and gold gowns like little girls' princess dresses in adult sizes. In the street I saw a woman wearing a floor-length fairy-tale gown made of red and white net with red velvet appliqué flowers.

It was the first time I had seen women's underwear for sale since the UK. First plain white then padded bras in bright colours with polka dots and slinky night dresses. Anthony bought some underpants, they had a pocket in them! The man explained that this pocket, and the top pocket in the short sleeved shirts, was where Indian men kept their money and their phones; as they wear lungis that are essentially a piece of material and so have no pockets. Apparently some Indian women sew a tiny pouch into the tucked in end of their saree and that is where they keep their money. The man on the stall explained how money was safer in the underpants pocket as it could fall out of the shirt top one when you bend over to pray.

We went to the temple at Chidambaram that Yogesh had suggested. Chidambaram is where the God Lord Shiva is represented as Cosmos. The temple was made of several buildings, each one beautifully coloured and incredible to look at. I could have stood and looked at one area for hours and still not have taken it all in; sensory overload, again. We came outside and sat in the shade on the stone floor of the grounds. I went for a little walk across the courtyard by myself. People and cows were asleep under the cool stone walkways. I stood and soaked up the sight of the blue sky above a row of gold minarets and below, a beautiful white cow statue. Those two sights alone filled me to the brim with beauty.

***

The evening before the temple trip an important political figure died in a Chennai hospital, a much loved ex Chief Minister of Tamil Nadu. In India each state has its own political parties and Chief Minister. Yogesh had told us that in Tamil Nadu politicians generally come from the film industry; they are actors or scriptwriters. We had been out for a very late lunch/early tea; we'd eaten light as we'd intended to eat again later. On our way back we saw that the street was almost dark and the metal shutters of shops and restaurants were half closed or closed. We thought at first there was a power cut; in Chennai the power had been scheduled to be off from nine am to five for maintenance. We got back to the guesthouse; several men were gathered in the lobby. The staff explained what had happened and advised us to go out and 'Buy bread,' as there would be nothing open that evening or the next day. We went back out and joined many others in a shopping frenzy. The restaurants were already closed but from street stalls and shops we bought nuts, biscuits, crisps, bananas and water. Within an hour everything had closed.

Overnight there appeared framed photographs on tables with flower garlands and coconut shells, like little shrines. Huge billboard posters of the Minister's face and shoulders, some with huge real flower garlands hung on as if around his neck. It was a level of public adoration UK politicians could only dream of. In the morning we checked out of the guesthouse as planned, intending to go to the temple and then get our bus back to Chennai. We got a message confirming that the temple trip was still going ahead, but in the car on the way to the temple we got another message saying that our bus to Chennai had been cancelled as part of the closures.

We asked the driver if he'd take us to Chennai, he said it was, 'Too dangerous,' and that later would be better. When we got back to Pondicherry we met some Westerners who were also trying to get back to Chennai; they decided to get an auto to a halfway point. They said they had heard that people had thrown stones at taxis in Chennai for being disrespectful by working. We sat on a big concrete step at the side of the road around the corner from the guesthouse with our carrier bags of snacks and our backpacks and wondered what to do. Just then a taxi pulled up on the opposite side of the road. We asked him if he'd take us to Chennai. We told him what we had heard and asked him if it was safe. He asked us which area we were going to, he called someone in that area and then said yes, it was okay to go.

When we got to Chennai diversion signs were up, our driver followed them and ended up at the beach, where buses and cars and scooters and people walking had all descended. There were men waving flags and some of the vehicles had flags on them; we realised it was to do with The Minister. People ahead of us were just parking up and leaving their cars so that it got more and more congested. We had seen police everywhere on the way home but not a single one was here trying to organise the traffic. We were obviously in a taxi, and conspicuous as foreigners. Not only that, there were only a very few women and children amongst a big crowd of men. I was nervous, but the atmosphere of the crowd seemed okay and aside from the usual few glances at me as a Western woman we had no extra attention. We realised the road was a dead end; our driver did an almost impossible u turn and we made our way slowly out of the jammed up area.

While we were in the traffic jam I saw on the beach the signs, 'Live and let live', 'Pigeon feeding station,' 'Donation station.' It warmed my heart to see. I thought about how some people in the UK despise pigeons and even grey squirrels who I loved feeding in the UK. In the morning before work I used to put saucers of nuts and chopped apple on top of our shed. The husband of someone I used to work with used to shoot squirrels in his garden, not even to eat, just piling up the corpses at the bottom of the garden.

Roads were closed and the driver pulled up to ask someone where to go. Everywhere was shuttered and closed, no one was around. I saw a lone flower garland hanging up and realised we were at the crossroads near where we went for dinner; everything looked so different with all the shops shuttered up.

The Broadlands manager hugged me and kissed me on both cheeks like a father. It was about five o'clock in the evening. He told us to go up and have a sleep and that when we woke up at six thirty, seven, everything would be open again. We were in the same room as before but people had been in it since us; there was a folding camp bed put up and glitter on the sheets; I thought probably a family had stayed there. It hadn't been cleaned, probably due to the events of the previous day. 'I'm going to assume they were clean,' I said, but the truth was I didn't really care, I was just so glad to be back.

We woke up later when it was dark and went downstairs. Nothing was open. We saw the yoga teacher, she said that the evening before The Minister's death was announced and then everything had shut within ten minutes. She'd only had biscuits and bananas. One of the staff who worked at the hotel appeared, he apologised for our room not being cleaned and explained that they hadn't been able to get to work. He went out to see if there were any food places open, we and the yoga woman gave him money just in case. He came back once saying that everything in one direction was closed and then he set out again. We thought there would be somewhere; Yogesh had told us you can always get food as there are lots of bachelors in Chennai and they often eat parcel meals (takeaway) from the restaurants.

About forty-five minutes later the man returned with little plastic bags of sambar (curry) with orange sauce and parotta bread. We ate at the little red table in our room. The little plastic bags of sambar were tied with a twist of fine twine that wasn't even knotted, just wound around neatly and expertly. The sambar was hot and the parotta bread was thick and filling. It felt so good to eat hot food after an evening and a day of crisps, biscuits and nuts.

The mosque sounded very loud again the first morning, then on the days after we slept through it or half slept through it like we had before. As usual in India, there was the caw caw of crows. One morning very early the crows were especially loud. I mentioned it to Anthony. He said, 'There was one on the ground below the window making loads of noise, and another sitting right on the shutter not making a sound; I said to it, 'What's the other one's problem?!'' Also as usual, there were barking dogs; a pack of dogs seemed to live on the waste ground below our window. 'Dogs in the UK don't have the freedom just to howl and express themselves like that,' Anthony said. We saw an Indian squirrel climbing on the outside of the window mesh, all four feet clinging on, upside down and doing acrobatics as if it were in the circus.

The mosque car park was a beautifully clean paved area. One day when it was quiet I saw a man and a little boy arrive on a scooter. They fed the pigeons, who arrived and left in great beautiful clouds. When they had finished the man put the boy on the scooter, patted him on head, threw the empty food cup over the wall into the street and left. On Friday the mosque car park was filled with lots and lots of scooters and a handful of cars and on the waste ground beside the mosque, some autos. There were so many people that they couldn't all fit inside and there were people praying in the outside part of the mosque. At night the flats on the other side of the mosque car park had their lights on and the curtains open. The colours of the rooms lit up, one green, one mauve, with the silhouettes of house plants making shadows on the walls. The mosquito mesh on the windows of our room was bent and folded, gently undulating like a sheet of fine wire mesh. When the light caught it, it looked like taffeta, the colour of burnished gold.

The quest for fresh vegetables led us to a Chinese restaurant where we ate vegetables and noodles, big florets of broccoli and chunky carrots in a thick and glutinous msg sauce. We sat beside a fish tank full of big fish swimming sadly back and forth. I brought up some of the things I had been thinking and feeling in Pondicherry. We agreed that being happy can't be the aim; it's pleasure-seeking and a Four Worldly Winds pain-pleasure trap. That kind of bliss cannot be sustained and anyway it would be boring; people need challenges. We agreed that 'the spiritual journey' is a red herring.

Observe yourself and how you are and what you do like a character in a film. E.g. do you react impulsively? Drop down and forget all this for an evening and reflect afterwards, how did I do? That's the work. The trick is to try and maintain the clear awareness even when the key breaks in the lock or the taxi to the airport is late. If not you'd have nothing to do. Most people are locked into feeding the pleasure centres; the 'reward of nothingness' wouldn't appeal to them as worth it for a lifetime of searching. Anyway, most people aren't actually actively looking for enlightenment. But if you are prepared to accept this peaceful serenity, this above-ness from the senses, so that food isn't really so much of a thing anymore; this distance, beyond love, beyond joy… If you are prepared to accept that, then maybe the reward will be to understand everything. That's what makes renouncing worldly pleasures, or rather, drifting away from them and letting them fall away, like when following Buddhism, worthwhile.

***

The Broadlands manager told us that a film crew was coming to film at the guesthouse; apparently the film had a famous film star. It took a whole day to set up with all kinds of props including chicken coops and furniture being brought in. We watched big wardrobes being lowered from the upstairs balcony on ropes. In the UK they would have closed the hotel or at least closed off part of it. Here, we were shown different routes to and from our room via different staircases and courtyards. When they were shooting in the central courtyard below our room, we just had to peek out. 'Shooting,' they'd say, or not. Sometimes we had to walk through their chill out area in between the plastic chairs arranged in a circle for lunch; huge pots of food were carried into the hotel at lunchtime. The pots of food, filled with all different kinds of curries, were laid out on trestle tables. We went down separately to use the internet. The famous actor was sat on the sofa going through his lines. At the end of the filming day they all gathered for a group photograph and there was lots of clapping. I had a cigarette and hung about outside watching them pack up and soaking up the atmosphere.

The yoga teacher next door had complained about the film shoot and told us it would start at six am and go on all night, with flashing lights and loud music. We weren't concerned; after all there was nothing we could do about it and it wasn't as if we had anything to get up for or do and we could always sleep during the day. I sympathised with her for getting woken by building work above her room though; they were doing some pre season alterations and she was woken at six am. She asked for a day's refund but I don't think she had any luck. The film shoot was over in one day, it wasn't noisy and it didn't start early after all.

I can see how one could get really stressed: being woken up, building work, dogs, mosque, crows; plus coping with things being different, food, people, and each other, but we're ok. There are things I could get annoyed about of course, if I had a mind to: many rooms only having one plug socket available so that we have to take turns charging our phones and tablets. The traffic, the pollution, the rubbish. The food all coming at different times. The complicated menus with strict times, this 12-2, this 3-6, this all day, this 12.30-9.30. The occasional restaurant bureaucracy, 'Can I have a cup of tea or coffee?' 'No, only after four pm,' 'Can I have tea or coffee now?' 'No, juice first, then afterwards we'll take your order for coffee or tea.' Not being understood, not understanding things. Some things remaining a complete mystery, others tantalising only half explained. Missing friendships. The poverty. Being sometimes viewed as a walking ATM machine. Even after giving the hotel cleaner so much stuff (he'd asked us to give him anything we were leaving), he still came and asked us for money. How sometimes it seems as if almost every conversation invariably turns to money or trying to sell us something. But the secret is to accept it all and not to judge. If my few days in Norwich Travelodge in the winter taught me anything, it's that the UK isn't perfect. The level of homelessness in affluent Norwich's city centre was shocking. And if things are different to what I'm used to, of course that's to be expected, and that is my issue. And there's so much beauty all around me that my attention is taken up with that.

In the street parallel to Broadlands the houses were painted pretty colours. Just around the corner, at the end of an ordinary street, was an incredibly beautiful temple. There were lots of sweet shops and sweet stalls in Chennai although we managed to resist and just admire them from a distance. We drank chai at a little stall in the backstreets on the corner of Big Street. The first time we sat outside on little stools and smoked cigarettes, the second time we were seated inside amongst the flies and heat. We saw Indian men feeding street dogs in the evening. Even a very humble looking shop had put out puri on the pavement for the crows.

I wished I could show my Grandmother the clothes, or describe them to her. She was a dress maker and interested in clothes until the end of her life. In Chennai I saw flouncy dresses, just below the knee, slightly shorter than I'd seen before, with scalloped hem and lacy lemon or white flowers at the hem and on the bodice; sarees in bold block prints making a 3D optical illusion; others in bold flowers and lots of yellow and orange sarees which matched the colours of the Tamil Nadu autos. In restaurants we saw whole families colour coordinated and wondered if it happens naturally or if the woman picks out the family's clothes? I've maybe seen three outfits ever that I didn't think worked perfectly.

We'd found a little tea shop at the side of the road that did the best coffee, sweet and milky, as well as nice little samosas and melt-in-the-mouth homemade biscuits in jars, it became our favourite place for those last few days in Chennai. We had got our photocopying done and our tickets printed out at a little copy shop, bought reading glasses for Anthony, ticking jobs off the list and feeling pleased with ourselves, and went to the tea shop afterwards. We bought cigarettes and offered them to the staff and a fellow customer; cigarettes can be a good icebreaker when you don't share a language.

We sat and watched the traffic and the people crossing the road. There was the smell of traffic fumes, rubbish and occasionally animal or human waste. We watched two people lifting a big drum onto a scooter. It was common to see scooters loaded with sacks of onions, even sacks of cement or a family of four riding all together. That is the mode of transport that the family has, they don't have a car, so scooters are used for everything.

A girl, a young woman, came skipping down the road. We made eye contact and she came over and said, 'Hi,' skipped off, then came over again, pointed to her cheek and said, 'Kiss.' I couldn't kiss her, I'm British and can't easily kiss total strangers but I offered her my hand and we shook hands. She went skipping off again, almost dancing across the road. She dropped her scarf in the road and picked it up scarily right in front of an auto.

A truck went past laden, absolutely laden with plastic pots, urn shaped but big like garden pots. Instead of being terracotta colour to pretend to be made from clay, or green to blend into the garden like they would be in the UK, these were shocking pink, bright leaf green and bright unsubtle primary colours; as if they were saying, we're plastic and we're proud to be plastic.

When we checked out of Broadlands the manager shook hands with Anthony and hugged me. 'I love Anthony,' he said, 'He has a good heart.' In the taxi on the way to the airport, the driver said, 'Look, look,' said something and pointed. We couldn't understand him, then just at the last moment Anthony realised, 'Parrots!' About fifty small parrots were sat on the electricity wires across the road. 'That is their house,' the driver said. 'One thousand parrots live there. At six pm every day you see them.' It was around four-thirty pm. We were a bit sad that we hadn't known about this before, but happy that we had heard it then and seen some of the parrots.

I kept thinking we were going back there, to Broadlands, to Chennai, and had to remind myself that it was over and we were going to Kolkata when we returned to India. I know we were only there for eight days in total but if it wasn't for the pollution I'd like to live there, at least for part of the year. What would I do? Write, feed cows, put up posters at the bins to tell people to tip food waste onto the floor don't put in plastic bags. Get involved with some kind of rubbish clearing/recycling initiative (Anthony's idea). Learn Tamil, teach English in return. (But Tamil seems so hard! I feel like Hindi would be easier so maybe pick somewhere where the main language is Hindi…) But that's all dreams, I haven't seen hardly any of India yet, I may yet fall in love again many times over during the rest of our travels.

Every moment on earth is a blessing: Thailand

In the courtyard garden of the guesthouse there was a little terrace with a wooden framed roof with plants growing through and around it. Bamboo plants at the sides, tiny pot plants hanging down and a huge aloe vera on top of the roof, its leaves coming in through the gaps. I sat at a metal table and chairs with my water, notebook and cigarettes writing, writing, writing.

This is what I do now. This is me 24/7. There's no distinction between work me and me, I do this all the time, noticing, observing, noting, then typing up most days for a couple of hours. I saw a bird, a lizard and a squirrel, smaller than UK ones with a big fluffy tail and a white belly like a stoat or a weasel.

'I love it here,' I said to Anthony. 'What's not to love?' He said.

A friend from home's message, with money and work concerns. One of Anthony's old work colleagues saying she'd like to travel but she had got work to think about and bills to pay, at only twenty years old. Validation that this is worth it.

'I never want to go back (into the matrix).'

'It's up to us,' Anthony said.

***

The guesthouse had dark brown wooden floors and staircases and walls of bookcases. Our room had a metal four poster bed without the curtains. Mosquito mesh windows looked out onto a garden thick with plants. A bed, any bed, feels so good after travelling. After a little while it rained; we listened to it while we were cosy in bed.

When we woke up we went to a tourist cafe, full of Westerners. It was expensive but so nice; soft flat big noodles that felt sexy in the mouth, creamy hummus and tahini drizzled in olive oil, puffed up pitta bread and pretty coloured pickles which made beautiful swirls on the plate like a work of art.

Later I went out by myself to the 7/11. At the junctions there were birds' nests wires like in India. Crossing the road was much easier than Chennai; zebra crossings work, not the same as the UK but much better than India. The wonders of the 711! It sold everything; vests and t-shirts in black or white packaged like baby grows. All the face cream was whitening and there was even face cream with snail extract.

I'd gone out in a sleeveless black cotton dress, just above the knee, my hair long and loose, bare shouldered and bare legged. I got no stares and felt free and light. I'd become so accustomed to covering up in India that it just seemed normal. People's Instagram pictures of themselves on nights out wearing very short low cut dresses with visible thighs and cleavage had started to look weird.

We went to a Thai place for dinner and ate tofu with broccoli and peanuts; feeling absolutely in love with broccoli which was served fresh and crunchy. I had a beer and afterwards we went for a walk just like we were on holiday. I would recommend anyone travelling to India for a year to take a few weeks out and go to Thailand for the food and vitamins. Anthony said it was like visiting the R&R planet on Star Trek, I am more familiar with the relaxation spaceship of Battlestar Gallactica.

Walking around in the evening we saw a rubbish truck and workers in hi vis with gloves, sacks and raffia baskets sorting through the waste and recycling. The roads were quiet, no beeping. Everything looked so clean and ordered. We walked down the Khaosan Road, once the hippie backpacker area, now barely a hippie in sight. Bars opposite each other played very loud competing music. In an environment like that it's so easy to remember to be in the world but not of the world; no interest in it, no competing, no envy. We walked down a road with a line of trees beautifully lit up with matching gold lights. It was only lit up that one night, Anthony took a photograph of us under the lights.

The rickshaws were completely different, bright pink with fancy metal work and grand looking reclining padded seats, no luggage space behind the seats, not functional like Indian autos.

We had breakfast by the canal, next to a laundry. I arranged my laundry; we greeted each other then the laundry woman got the cafe staff to translate. Everything was so fun and friendly. 'It's like every encounter is a joy.' I said.

A man complimented me on my tattoos. He gave me some fruits, like lychees. He said, 'Say this to your husband,' and told me a Thai phrase. I repeated it back then said it to Anthony and everyone fell about laughing. That's another difference between India and Thailand; in Thailand one can potentially have more of a laugh. Indian people sometimes struggled with the British sense of humour, tending to take things literally, meaning that several of our jokes have fallen very flat. Just before we left Kerala we'd watched a new restaurant being done up on the tourist strip, a sign outside said 'Vegan chocolate cheesecake' which got us very excited. One day we spoke to the chef, he explained that they were just getting the menu ready, and wouldn't be opening until after we had left. 'If you want someone to practice on...' we said as a joke. His face became serious. 'I don't need to practice, I am trained for seven years,' he said.

We met Maeve, Anthony's daughter at the airport. We had dinner and cocktails and then took her to the Khaosan Road. As well as the signs for cocktails and cheap buckets there was one saying 'We don't check ID,' which made us all laugh. The competing music was on again. Little street stalls sold scorpions, roasted to eat. In the middle of all this, *What's going on* by 4 Non Blondes was playing.

The next evening we got the night train south. We met a young British man, he said of Thailand, 'It feels safe. I didn't think I would but I do.' Is this how I felt in India? But then to come to Thailand and realise that maybe I didn't? Or is it just that Thailand provides such an elevated level of comfort? Is this our reward for five and a half months of India?

It's like it's all laid on for tourists. Staff even make the beds up on the train. The seats are soft anyway and then they put a mattress on top and then the sheet. There's a lovely blanket in a bag, white with square raised bits, it holds the warmth of your body and is big enough to wrap yourself up in and cover your feet right up. The sleeping area was very comfortable with plenty of space; there were even three little metal pegs which fold out from the wall to hang your clothes on.

A member of staff, a lovely friendly woman taught us some Thai and took our orders for breakfast. As usual I was too excited to sleep and sat up writing in my cubicle long after Maeve and Anthony had gone to sleep.

The train arrived early the next morning and after a coach, a ferry and a taxi we arrived in Haad Rin, Koh Phangan. Haad Rin was full of Westerners, they were well dressed and looked as if they had money. A lot of the clothes shops were expensive. Having adapted to India, it all seemed like a bit of a culture shock.

'It's probably not that good for my self image being here,' I said.

'It's not that good for me either, Anthony said, 'All the guys are totally ripped and walking around with their shirts off!'

We watched a woman go into a hairdressers wearing her shoes; even after the staff asked her to take them off she still carried on talking and standing inside the shop with her shoes on.

The dogs and cats were big and healthy looking. We saw a woman on a white bicycle with two dogs sitting on her lap, their paws on the handlebars. We saw what looked to us like a giant cat after Indian cats, stretched out, long and fluffy on a table.

Where we were staying we saw cats being carried like babies back to staff's rooms, 'My cat,' one woman said to us as we passed. An orange cat with bright eyes visited us for an hour while we played cards; we fed it left over banana cake from the train, all we had.

Most of the staff where we were staying were from Myanmar. One of the staff sounded like a cockney. 'I copy Danny Dyer, he's my favourite actor,' he said. One of the staff showed me their tattoo, 'It means freedom, I used not to have freedom, but now I do.'

At the party beach, stalls sold little plastic buckets of alcohol and mixers with straws alongside handwritten signs on neon card saying fucking and cunt. One said, 'Jesus loves you but I think you're a cunt.' There were little kids with their parents who were at work, a toddler in a cot behind a cocktail stall near the bar, wearing ear plugs. The trees nearby were covered in lights flowing down. A group of men and boys did fire club displays. People sat in the sand in front of big colourfully decorated screens doing UV body painting. Beach sellers walked around with fake flower garlands, toy monkeys in bright neon colours and even more mysterious, Connect 4.

Feeling tired, but noticing the beauty anyway. At the table next to me, a woman's foot, no nail polish, half buried in the sand. The sand was so soft it felt unreal. My blue Goa ring, blue like the room in Chennai. Thinking, *Every moment on earth is a blessing.* Between the bar and the sea was a row of flags flapping. I looked at one flag, shiny bronze-gold, simultaneously noticing a light out at sea, one of the boats. Lots of lights but I picked just one.

There was a swimming pool where we were staying but it was often busy, with people sitting around the pool on white plastic sunbeds. Some evenings there were pool parties with cheap drinks; signs said, 'Free love for everyone,' and 'Find your lover before you go.'

We found a swimming pool further along the beach, up some steps, part of a restaurant and rooms resort that was practically empty. We ate at the restaurant and asked if we could use the pool, which was usually deserted. The three of us went swimming together, practicing strokes, doing tricks and just enjoying the water totally unselfconsciously, me in my underwear, us having found the pool as a surprise, reacquainting myself with my old love of swimming. Family at its best are people you can just be yourself with.

The swimming pool was surrounded by fake boulders and the complex was done out like a fake temple. There was a sink outside in the open air. The water came out of the tap warm and there were always white blossoms in the sink. There was an outside shower with a faux stone mermaid; I used to think someone was standing there as I swam.

Monsoon clouds and the sea all different colours; green, dark blue and pale blue in patches. The beach full of driftwood; a big piece with lots of branches worn pale, neat criss crossed piles of darker driftwood, old coconuts and huge brown coconut leaves like branches. Plastic bottles and lots of glass, terrifying broken bottles with jagged ends sticking up from the sand.

***

What do you do when everyone else is drinking cocktails, you ordered iced coffee because you have a blog to write? Take a sip. When they can't drink theirs and offer to you, even though you ordered iced coffee? Take a bit more than a sip, even though I don't really want to, but don't finish it. Like the potion Robert from Switzerland told us about! Return to room, start blog, and keep writing until it's the end, after everyone else is asleep.

Me, lying on my back after yoga: 'Why do I feel so bad about everything?' White light above me: 'It's your programming.'

On the beach I thought: 'Enjoying yourself can be its own religion.' I got back to our room, Anthony was listening to this song on YouTube: 'Enjoy yourself, it's later than you think; Enjoy yourself, while you're still in the pink; Enjoy yourself, enjoy yourself, it's later than you think!'

One night I was just outside the bathroom when I saw what I thought was probably a bit of fluff. I honestly thought it was a bit of my scarf which had been shedding fluff but just in case I shouted for Anthony and dived into the bathroom. It turned out it was a big spider, which my brain had very considerately fuzzed out into a bit of fluff to protect me. I crouched cowered on the top of the toilet seat while Anthony dealt with it. One of the many, many reasons I love being married.

Anthony left to take Maeve back. Dark afternoon after they left, reminiscent of when Anthony used to take Maeve and Jude back to London after a weekend with us and I stayed in the suddenly empty and silent house. I beat myself up about not going swimming, 'What have I even done today,' but so tired, hence low mood, maybe PMS? I ask for time alone but it is dangerous. Feeling suicidal, thinking, 'Is all this too tiring and I'll just end up killing myself after all?' With my solitary nature and melancholy disposition am I safer being part of a family rather than left alone?

I pulled myself together and went for dinner. The onsite restaurant had little bells on each table to ring for service. I disliked doing this, but it only made it worse. I'd wait for someone to come, be fearful that no one was coming. Plus I often used the space for writing, which was fine, but meant that they didn't always know if I wanted food or not.

It was a weird place to be alone, a party/couples/young people holiday place. By myself for four days: a bit sad and lonely but safe, with the nice staff and an easy environment, and once I get into it, good for writing, yoga and swimming I told myself.

I spent the first night in a state of anxiety about spiders, having had that big one only a couple of nights before. I stayed out in the evening and kept the light off when I returned so I wouldn't see anything. The second night I heard people coming back at 3am and being sick, and sick again in the morning. Even once my fear about spiders had subsided a bit I still couldn't sleep.

A nice waiter told me about what it's like during the Full Moon Party; more people come every day, the whole restaurant gets full, the kitchen forgets food orders… 'Crying, lost phones, we tell them, don't take out, don't take card, just take enough for how many drinks you want but-' Agghh! I thought. Not looking forward to that at all!

Every day I made lists and stuck to them: do yoga, write, swim, go shopping, collect laundry, make space for J. Stick with the plan, the to do list, then if not happy, at least satisfied.

At the swimming pool, thinking, wouldn't it be nice to be a successful writer and have a swimming pool. But I do spend my days writing and I have a pool all to myself. 'I have everything already.'

The orange cat came by in the evening and was still there after I came back from dinner, as if keeping me company. In bed I tried everything to sleep, all the exercises I know. 'You're trying, that's the problem,' Anthony said when I told him on the phone. The only thing that really helped was thinking about the little orange cat sitting outside on the bench, like a talisman.

As always, WordPress, in synchronicity helped. Bethany Kays posted on her blog on WordPress about how it was much harder to be mindful without her husband present, about how she'd wanted some mindful photography alone time but found that she was afraid without him there and that was distracting. Bethany has real things to be afraid of, alligators, spooked wild horses, and uses a wheelchair. My fears were all in my mind but still, I recognised the timing of this post. I read a post on WordPress about, 'You may have noticed how it's easier to criticise yourself than have other people do it.' That's what 'internalising the negative messages' actually means. After twenty years working in mental health I only just understood that. Dirty Sci-Fi Buddha had been getting very deep and I was struggling to absorb his message. I thought, I wish he would explain his philosophy more simply, and he did: 'Try and be fulfilled; Be nice to people; Enjoy what's in front of you.'

After two nights I realised I could watch Netflix. I mean I *knew* that, but I forget to enjoy myself, I think only of writing and anything that might need to be done, forgetting that in the evening I could watch something. I mean if Anthony is there I'm with him so that's taken care of, we'll spend time together or watch something that he will have downloaded and organised for me. I spent the third and fourth evenings sitting out on the balcony with the cat, my feet propped up on the table watching stuff on my tablet.

'That looks like my kind of evening,' my neighbour said, returning to get ready to go out, looking as if she'd rather stay in.

'I've even got a cat,' I said. And the battery lasted right up until the end, dying seconds after my last episode finished.

I survived the experience and four days in my mood evened out. I got a haircut and blow-dry, the first time I'd had my hair blow dried for months, and bought a pair of earrings and a tinted lip balm. I returned home and ordered a beer- at not quite midday and took it back to the balcony. I listened to music and put on my pink lipbalm and my kohl from India, making mild smoky eyes, happily waiting for Anthony and J to arrive.

***

The first night we went out and drank. Many years ago I used to drink to excess to try and 'get somewhere,' into some alternate reality where everyone was really themselves and we all connected. It took me a long time to realise that alcohol doesn't really raise consciousness; in fact it was a long time before I was even interested in raising my consciousness or knew what it meant. Now, even if I am a bit drunk, there's a bit of me looking down, outside of it all asking, 'What are you doing this for?'

We went to a place in town that did twenty-four hour breakfasts for party goers. It was the night of the Full Moon Party and there were lots of people wearing what looked like a fancy dress uniform of white t-shirts with UV paint splashes. The loo was upstairs, up a flight of steep steps; each step was really high, it was something we noticed a lot in Thailand, how high the individual steps were, like giant's steps.

We ate dinner at a local place. J and I were bothered by them playing a horror movie, even if we didn't look at the screen we could hear the screaming.

'Well we could try to ignore it, or I could ask them to turn it off,' I said. A group of women at the next table were also talking about how they hated horror films.

'Or we could just leave,' Anthony said, so we did. It was a good metaphor for dealing with people or situations that upset your equilibrium, you can work on accepting it or on trying to change them or you can just... leave.

On our last evening in Haad Rin I went for a little walk by myself on the beach. The sea was unbelievably still, exactly like a lake. The colours of the surface- milky opal green, mauve blue looked like oil or glass. Above the sea a sunset, at the shore a little red boat. It was picture perfect paradise but I didn't feel the emotions that I did in India.

We went to the party beach for the last time. J and I had our Tarot cards read. The tarot man looked cool; he had a thin curled moustache and sat cross legged on a blanket on the sand. He turned over the first card. His face broke into a smile and he looked at me full in the face as if seeing me properly for the first time.

'Ahh, sexy lady! Sexy when sleeping, sexy when wake up, sexy walking down the street. Everyone loves you.' He turned over another card. 'Good family, man loves you. You love everyone.' He looked at my hands. 'You are strong!' He exclaimed. 'You look after everyone.' Another card. 'You worry about a young one. Okay, everything okay. You the boss, work, home. You do stuff.' Another card. 'Look after your heart, and your blood. Smoking not good for you. Bad air, sleeping, working, dirty air, not good for you. Potatoes good, cool, warm.' I'd just eaten potatoes and actually commented, 'Very grounding.' Potatoes, in fact any vegetables that grow below ground, are meant to help ground you if you feel your spiritual awakening/frequency rising is going a bit fast. Conversely, if you want to speed up the process the advice is to only eat vegetables that grow above ground.

We moved somewhere quieter with grassy grounds with palm trees, right on the beach with a little bar-restaurant. Away from the day glo hordes, albeit friendly enough, I could begin to be still and catch the quiet moments again. They are so distracted, there's so much to see and do and so many people around. J and Anthony had gone out for a second breakfast. I stayed home and did a full, proper yoga session outside on the veranda, un-distracted and with unlimited time, invigorating for mind and body. I had my period and reminded myself that this is the time when 'the veil is thin.' I did the warrior pose (where your fingertips are outstretched and your gaze follows the path of your fingers). The green-stoned ring on my right hand matched up with a tree. *Strong roots. A base,* I thought. On the index finger of my left hand was my blue ring, I followed it to the exact place it was pointing at: a tree, and part hidden behind the tree, lined up exactly with the blue stone, was the tip of a little red boat pointing out to sea. *Adventure.*

At the bar-restaurant on site Anthony was sorting coins out, saying what's this, what's that, that's such and such, Thai, that's a rupee, Indian. 'I don't know what that one is,' he said, holding one up. 'That's a 10p!' J said laughing, 'I can't believe you don't know your own money!' It really was true, and after only five months away. We walked into town, the curves and diagonal lines of the pavement bricks making shocked parallelograms**.** We heard *What's going on* by 4 Non Blondes playing from one of the bars. At the food market there was a vegan stall, we had huge portions of green lentil curry, it even came with brown rice, a substantial dish like we would make at home.

From the food market there was a weird trek outside and beyond to the toilet, down a muddy deserted track to a kind of run down prefab building where the loos were. On the inside of the loo doors were stickers, photos of pigs. Each individual pig was encased in an oval tunnel made from what looked like green garden wire, totally encased, to the size of the pig, rows and rows of pigs. *'You don't eat, this won't happen,'* said the writing. I felt sick even writing it up, weeks later. J, who eats meat probably didn't even notice them; if she did she didn't mention it whereas I'm still haunted by those images.

***

One day we went to a Tesco, it was the first supermarket resembling the ones in the UK that we'd been to since leaving. There were huge bottles of Pantene shampoo and conditioner and packs of ordinary cotton knickers which I was very excited about, although unfortunately they didn't fit, Thai sizes were much too small for me. The variety of milks in Thailand was incredible, soya milk with green tea or chai seeds; the seeds soaked and swollen so that it was almost like eating tapioca. For snacks we had packets of dried seaweed instead of crisps.

It seemed people had a high tolerance for noise, like in India. A kid on a toy bike which was playing a really loud nursery rhyme, no one seemed to mind. The 7/11 door triggered a tinny automated 'Sawadi-ka' every time anyone came in, it would be enough to drive me insane, again the shop staff seemed able to ignore it. It was nice to see that work and home life seemed mixed up altogether. We often saw kids with their families at massage places and at restaurants and sometimes boys shyly served us or brought the menus. Often the family home was on the same site as the restaurant and to go to the loo you had to go into the family home. At one place when I asked for the loo they got the boy out of bath, covered in soap suds, I protested but it was too late. The bathroom floor was wet, a child sized version of a baby bath full of soap suds and clothes; washing clothes at same time as having a bath made sense. There was a big water butt full, catching drips from a tap; the whole set up just struck me as so totally functional.

But apart from these occasional glimpses, things you had to look really hard to see or be lucky to encounter, the real Thai culture seemed drowned out by the tourism. We went to Ko Samui to extend our visas. On the ferry were almost all Westerners. A group of hungover Brits behind us were talking and swearing loudly. At the immigration office, where signs expressly ask people to dress respectfully and not to wear beach clothes we saw several tourists in tiny shorts and tops. I heard a woman getting annoyed at the counter. Keeping your cool is really important in Thailand, it is confusing and offensive to get angry.

Out for a walk on my own I met a man who used to be a monk. The conversation started with him offering me motorbike hire and tour guide services but we ended up talking about meditation and enlightenment. 'I can't get there,' (enlightenment), he said because, 'I can't do it, one meal a day,' the life of a monk. As far as he was concerned, there was only one route there. I felt sad for him but I didn't want to risk offending his religious beliefs by disagreeing with him. He told me about the local temples and about how important it was to be in nature and how if only we could roll back all the development of the island by twenty years...

Sometimes we'd be woken up by the national anthem or loud pop music; Thai pop music was upbeat, playful and very fast with lots of sounds, almost discordant to our ears.

I felt that I had all the time in the world to do anything. It didn't matter what time I got up or went to bed; as long as I wrote and got some exercise I had no guilt and was happy. I wrote, did some yoga and spent time with J and Anthony. It was the opposite of, 'I don't know where the day went.' I did my writing sat on a bench at a big wooden table facing out to sea; under my feet the sand floor. When I took a break I had a Red Bull and a cigarette with J.

In Thailand, Red Bull comes in little cans or in even smaller glass bottles which look like medicine bottles. It contains B12 and all sorts of other vitamins; different bottles and cans have different combinations, one has Zinc, another has Vitamin C and it tastes much better than the stuff you get in the UK. For lunch I ate rice with tofu and vegetables.

Just metres from our door amongst the trees was a log to sit on. Sometimes late at night before bed I sat there and looked out at the lights out at sea and in the town and the pretty coloured boats on the shore. It was a moment of peace and quiet to close the day with.

Outside our bungalows we heard hard fruits dropping on the ground just like at Osho's. All around were the sound of voices, conversations in German, French and Thai.

In the evenings our neighbour played The Beatles. One night, after we had gone to bed, I heard *Let it be* coming from his bungalow. If this was a film, I thought, we'd all start singing. Us, J next door; the people in the bungalows opposite would join in and before you knew it the whole site would be singing along in imperfect yet beautiful harmony…

Not all those who wander are lost: Tokyo

The closer we got to me going off to Tokyo, the worse we seemed to get on, bickering over the smallest things. Maybe it was the pressure of thinking that our last few days together had to be good. Or maybe we were living up to what we'd been saying mainly as a joke to people we met; we need to build in a break from each other during this trip as we've been together almost 24/7 for six months.

On the ferry to the mainland I sat outside, the wind was quite strong and it felt almost chilly. I got locked in an OCD loop of checking and rechecking my passport and the bus and train tickets. A few rows away, a young woman was being sick into a bag. Her boyfriend's arm stayed around her the whole journey.

On the train to Bangkok I met a couple from Belgium, they said they'd met lots of people in their thirties who had worked hard and then had a realisation, sold everything, left their jobs and gone travelling. 'You go to school and then go and study and then work for years... It seems more and more people are talking about this, questioning the normal pattern,'

'Don't let go of your bag, not ever,' Anthony said when we said goodbye. He was probably concerned, having seen me leave my backpack in an auto and other absent minded behaviour. But it is possibly easier, because it's so essential, to concentrate when alone.

In the check in queue at the airport I met a Japanese couple from Osaka; I expressed my sympathy about the recent typhoon. They smiled, 'Work building gone, home okay.' In the queue as I went through to security I saw a woman wearing a pink t-shirt saying *'Not all who wander are lost.'*

At Tokyo airport I went to the toilets. At the side of the seat were a whole array of buttons including water jets for 'front' and 'back,' each with pressure settings, and a 'privacy button' which apparently played music. But I couldn't find the flush! I had a mild panic before finding it; it was on the opposite wall. There was a queue and only one sink; I quickly brushed my teeth at the sink, unsure about the etiquette of brushing my teeth in public.

The woman at the information centre told me that a taxi all the way there would be a huge amount, over half of the money I'd changed to cover me for two weeks of spending and food money. I thought maybe she'd added an extra nought on by mistake, the figure was so high. The easiest would be the metro, she said but at that point I was terrified of doing that. She told me I could get a coach from just outside to Tokyo train station and then get a taxi from there.

Out of the coach window I saw fuzzy green trees, a dome, a big white bell tent and a bridge that looked like two chairs fighting, and lots of steel and grey. The taxi driver pointed at a little square sign in the midst of lots of other little square signs with the name of the hostel. I got out, feeling a bit vulnerable. Up a lift to the third floor and there it was. Below the desk was a pigeonhole shoe rack to leave outdoor shoes in with slippers to use indoors. The hostel man showed me to the room.

It was a momentary shock, seeing what a capsule pod really looks like. I'd imagined the curtains would be sideways like on the trains or sleeper buses; these were at the end so that you sort of dived into your tunnel cubicle. But it was clean and quiet, and at that moment there was no one else around in the dorm.

The man at the desk gave me a hand drawn food map, he didn't hold out much hope of me getting vegetarian food and said of the restaurants, 'It's expensive, it's Tokyo.' 'I just need to get something to eat,' I said to myself; that's how we always settle into a new place. I walked down the road, I found somewhere that looked okay, the woman understood me saying good evening, after a moment. I'd learned how to say vegetarian: ve-gee-tah-ree-ahn? She shook her head. I tried the next place I came to. The woman looked doubtful at first then said they could make me noodle vegetable soup. I couldn't get coffee, my pronunciation was all wrong, but I got some orange juice and after a puzzled pause I managed to make my 'Thank you for the meal' understood.

My hostel was in the business district near a big crossroads and I explored in all four directions. When my feet began to hurt I thought about stopping and turning around and then I always found something just after that point, something that made the walk worthwhile, so that I could say to myself, 'So that's what I was walking to,' and turnaround from there: An amazing apartment building with Gaudi style mosaic sculpture over the walls and balconies; wrought iron, black metal letter boxes and a hallway tiled in beautiful mismatched vintage tiles, and a cat cafe- the light of the sign went off moments after I'd seen it.

I found a proper coffee shop. It looked like an old fashioned British tea shop. They asked me things I didn't understand, they said things I didn't understand but they brought me coffee in a dear little cup and saucer with cream and chunky lumps of brown sugar. On my left sat a woman in a dove grey kimono. On my right was a woman dressed smartly in black and white using an expensive looking black laptop. Opposite me was a little display shelf of pretty little teacups and saucers of different designs.

I counted out what I thought was the right money, feeling very clever until I realised I had got the coins confused. Anyway, I had got coffee for the first time. 'Now I need a shop to get food for breakfast,' I said to myself. Moments later I came to a shop and bought raisin bread and a banana. I tipped out my money and they counted it out since I obviously didn't know the coins yet.

I kept walking, past a Metro station, I thought, I could just get on a train, go one stop, eat, and return. Or I could do some research and go on a trip. The feeling that I could do anything. There's nothing to be scared of. I kept walking. I saw a 'forest' took my bearings, looking carefully at the buildings around me so that I would know the way back and went up the steps and over the bridge. I passed a bank of vending machines, there were vending machines everywhere selling drinks but this was a row selling pot noodles and even burgers and chips.

I realised a few days later that I had made a faux pas wandering around in my strappy vest top. I had wrongly assumed people wore anything in Japan. Although the shortest skirts and shorts are fine, tops are modest. Some of this is to do with sun protection; girls are taught from a young age to protect themselves from the sun. Necklines are high and sun protector sleeves are worn. There is a fashion sub culture that does seriously tan, but it is definitely not the norm.

It was often raining and surprisingly cold when it did. Most people had the same almost identical see through plastic umbrellas with white or black handles. I learned to carefully put mine in a certain place in the umbrella racks, to remember it but even so I lost one and had to buy another. I realised I'd left it and went back but it had gone; there were others the same but I didn't want to take someone else's. I discovered afterwards that these umbrellas are all kind of shared by necessity.

One sunny morning I had a nice encounter on a bench; mine was the only dry one and an older Japanese man was looking for somewhere to sit. I moved my bag and gestured, then said good morning in Japanese. Unfortunately I'd left my language notes and couldn't remember hardly anything else. We used sign language and his little bit of English. We couldn't really make ourselves understood but it was such a nice encounter, he and I so keen to chat with each other.

Usually I got coffee from the mini mart, it was cheaper and I could sit outside or take it back to the hostel. On a good day by rehearsing in the lift on the way down I'd be able to say in Japanese, Hello, Good Morning, Coffee, Please, Just as it is/no bag and Thank you. You couldn't say it was a conversation, but it was a decent attempt at a polite interaction.

One day at the bench near my hostel where I often ate breakfast there were four or six baby sparrows with mum and dad nearby. I checked the prohibition sign with its pictures: No wine, no fireworks, no camping, no fires, no cars or bicycles, no litter, no dog fouling, no loud music. Another sign warned people that there were mosquitoes. Nothing about not feeding the birds. I let a few yellow cake crumbs fall, the baby sparrows looked, I made more by rubbing the wrapper of my cake so that tiny bits came off. I moved benches so they wouldn't be afraid and they came and ate it all before disappearing back into the hedge.

In many ways Tokyo was the opposite of India. It was so quiet and peaceful. The buildings were grey or neutral, the clothes too; neutral, black and white, grey, taupe, pistachio, and everything ordered and conventional. Because of the lack of obvious colour, when I did see it I really noticed it: clothes of moss green, plum, a subdued sea blue, a purple top barely discernible in a dim alleyway. In the street a burgundy dress really stood out- like the woman in red in *The Matrix*- and immediately after I saw a pair of shiny burgundy shoes. I saw lots of fire engines leave the fire station, they looked brand new; so shiny and such a bright red that the scene looked almost unreal.

I experienced pockets of absolute quiet, the traffic still, no one talking. Most people walked alone on their way home from work so I really noticed when there were people talking in the street.

Near my hostel I saw women and men on bicycles with kids in child seats, presumably dropping off and picking up at day care. It was a contrast to Thailand, where kids seemed to be with their parents and work and family more intertwined.

There were poodles and little fluffy dogs all on leads. No stray dogs. There were no bins but no litter either. Even the cars seemed quiet; sometimes I would be walking down a little side street and a car would surprise me, making just a little purring noise, barely audible. The taxis were boxy looking, in black or colours, orange or green. There were lots of bicycles, vintage style with baskets or bags; I saw one painted bright pillar-box red, another with a dog in the basket. Mostly they were left unlocked, including a child's one, new looking, rose pink with wicker basket, left for days in the business district of central Tokyo untouched.

It felt safe to walk about anytime, and no male attention whatsoever. A Japanese woman approached me one evening as I was walking and we chatted, she had been to eighty countries. 'I am so proud of my safe country, I hope it stays this way,' she said.

Nearby my hostel were some road works with a temporary walkway made by coning off part of the road. The cones were lit up from the inside by lights and some had flashing lights on top as well. Pedestrians were guided onto the temporary path by a model of a waving man with a lit up wand. Two actual men, one at each end of the path waved wands like truncheon sized light sabres, directing the pedestrians. All of the many road workers were wearing hi vis with lights built into the waistcoats. And in Japan *everyone* waits for the green man, even at the tiniest side road with nothing coming.

***

I went to Tokyo to see B, a fellow writer and blogger I met on WordPress. We met out of town for our first meeting; she sent me detailed instructions about the trains. 'It might seem a bit daunting, and Tokyo station is very large but there are signs everywhere in English;' when I was unsure of my way in Tokyo station, which is huge, and with lines that seem to be then divided into sub lines, I asked at the office which has an English speaking tourist counter. Trains run on time and standing at the station waiting for trains was peaceful with just the sounds of approaching and departing trains, the announcer and the sound of fake cheeping to discourage birds.

'I probably look terrified,' I thought, 'But I'm actually not.' On the first train, a crowded commuter train, I was surprised when I felt people press into me. I first thought, 'Well that wasn't as polite as I'd expected people to be.' But later Anthony said, 'People in London aren't polite enough to squash into each other to let people on, we like our personal space too much. Whereas in Tokyo people know the trains are busy and that everyone needs to get to work so they squash up so that other people can get on.'

It is frowned upon to eat on the metro; the only people I saw doing this were tourists. Talking on your mobile phone or having loud conversations is also not done. In Tokyo, where people work hard and there are lots of people, the idea is to make the commute and travel as peaceful as possible.

B told me that at the weekends people bring their musical instruments to the park to practice, even full size harps, as Tokyo apartments don't have the space or sound proofing for home practice. She said she saw someone bring a pram full of cats to the park. In the restaurant in the park where we went for a late dinner I did see a dog in a pram. Not a dolls pram or an old cast off child's one, this was a super smart new looking pram with a medium sized pug faced dog lying quietly in it. Two other women arrived and sat at a nearby table, one of them had a dog who squeezed itself out of a long tight bag as if emerging from a chrysalis. The dog in the pram sat up to look at the new dog. No one (other than me) batted an eyelid. B told me it is common to see young couples walking happily together in a park with a pram with a dog in it.

I found out from reading that tattoos are not really socially acceptable in Japan despite my previous impression of Japan as a great place for tattoos. Lots of bath houses do not let people with tattoos in but others are 'ink friendly.' B told me that outsiders' ideas about Japan and technology are also a bit off; she said that at her work they use fax machines and very old photocopiers. She pointed out how many people on the train were reading paper books and how few were using electronic readers. I remembered that wandering into a bookshop at the weekend it had been very busy.

The reputation of Tokyo's working hours culture though was accurate. Employees such as teachers are expected to stay until the most senior person goes home, which could be ten pm at night. People go jogging at midnight because that is their only time. And then there is after work drinking, particularly on a Friday night, where people say and do anything and it isn't mentioned afterwards. I had read in an etiquette guide that the last train on a Friday is when all the rules go out the window. I saw for myself people drunk in the street on Friday nights, groups of men and groups of women smoking in the street and I once saw a man in a suit on his hands and knees being sick on the pavement.

B said that women in Japan are very shy about people hearing them urinate, 'It's not okay to just let out a stream of wee;' they rattle the loo roll holder or door handle, hence the privacy buttons on the toilet panel, the sound of flushing or music, not just for poos!

B told me that brushing teeth in public is absolutely fine, everyone brushes their teeth after lunch and she sees colleagues walking around with toothbrushes in their mouths which is strange to her as a South African like it would be to me. In the UK I was unusual in and self conscious about brushing my teeth after lunch at work. Later in my stay I saw women brushing their teeth in public bathrooms in Shinjuku Square after lunch.

B said that, like in Thailand people don't say 'no' in Japan either, 'You hear a lot of 'maybe,' which can confuse foreigners as it actually means no.'

Under pressure I can't remember anything but this is the most I've got into a language since trying to learn Hindi in the UK before we left. Me saying a formal thank you for the meal in basic places and good evening to dogs may be over polite or wrong but even so

***

Even in my first couple of days I never thought the black and white and grey was cold, it was just very different to India and after almost two weeks I began to see it for what it was, beautiful. The difference between the clothes and buildings of India and Japan was like the difference between butterflies and moths. The longer I was there the more colour I began to notice and the more beauty I began to see in the buildings. I saw a lot of circles, big circular brick designs and windows in the walls of buildings, curved balconies set on top of each other like cut out cylinders and black metal spiral fire escapes.

B told me about the buildings not clashing with nature; at first I didn't get it, why aren't they painted blue or green to blend with nature but it's not about blending, it's about harmonising and not competing, hence the neutral colours. Clothes follow the season's colours, umber, maroon. Nature is revered, planted or allowed to be. I saw planted walls at the Metro station and trailing bindweed with pink flowers making fine curtains over the side of a building in the park.

'Everything's beautiful,' B said.

The clothes were subtle and stylish. Smocked blouses with puff sleeves; long artists smocks in taupe or black; modest print dresses in brown or blue and long dresses with circle prints and asymmetrical hems. Sticky out skirts with net underneath worn with cute blouses; a woman dressed up like a doll in a big bright pink lacy dress with a laced up bodice. A man dressed Andy Warhol style in a tight black sweater tucked into high waisted black trousers. During the week lots of office wear; men in suits with white shirts, women in black or navy pencil skirts and white, cream or pale coloured tops. On Sunday clothes were a bit different; lots of wide leg slightly cropped trousers in black, navy or taupe and smart clinging wool skirts, like soft office wear.

When I was out with B we bought snacks from the mini marts, B showed me what I could eat: rice triangles wrapped in seaweed, little pots of sticky soya beans, tofu rolls filled with rice and wasabi, miso and tofu salad and pouches of cooked chunks of soft pumpkin.

In the evenings I mostly ate at the same place. Customers had to choose and pay at machines at the front and hand the order ticket to the kitchen staff. I usually ordered a soup of noodles, seaweed, Japanese leeks and thick triangular slabs of tofu. I managed to eat with chopsticks, even cold tofu, like a kind of thick blancmange. The cold tofu was part of a slightly strange meal made up of side dishes, along with kimchi, mashed potato and salad.

One evening after dinner I went for a walk past the amazing office buildings; my favourite was a huge glossy white sided building that rose up from the pavement like the side of a ship and was a landmark for me. After the big office buildings, into the restaurants area I saw a multi floored pink building. A pink building! I stopped and stared: I saw a sign, it was a music school. At the end of one of the side streets near the hostel was a tiny pale pink faded apartment at the top of a neutral coloured building. A metal fire escape ran from the top down to the bottom. I changed my mind from the Gaudi mosaic apartment building, I'd live there instead.

I walked to meet B in Shinjuku East Side Square, this involved many little twists and turns which meant I had to hold my tablet and follow the blue dot all the way there. It was a sunny day and the sky was blue above the grey and pale fawn buildings. I saw apartment buildings from a different view, from side roads and little alleys and from down flights of steps; above me so many apartments packed neatly in. I concentrated on remembering landmarks; a blue bridge, an animal hospital. Further on were smarter buildings, a huge one like a big city office block but it was actually apartments. It looked like the side of a spaceship, all these little apartments, so many rows, so many columns, so many deep; I tried to count them but it made my head spin.

At the crossing I got confused, a Japanese man asked me if I needed help. 'Cross over, turn left, look up and you'll see it, big building,' he said. B had sent me a photo of Shinjuku East Side square. One of the buildings was white and made of sleek shiny white bricks which interlocked, and was instantly recognisable.

Down a quiet little street I saw a row of three open umbrellas hung up on the outside wall of a house. Each was a different shade of light pink; it looked like an art installation. The umbrellas and a few bits of laundry hung up on balconies were the only colour. A little further on down another alleyway, amongst buildings which seemed to all be different shades of cream I saw some brightly coloured delivery crates outside the back of a shop; red, green and yellow, the only colour in that scene.

Shinjuku Square, with its big modern buildings outside and shops and cafes inside was beautifully designed in circles, ovals and spirals. In the centre was a teardrop shaped pond. B told me that things are inspired by nature and designed with meaning, so that the pool might be the shape of a raindrop, for example, as well as also having a specific spiritual meaning.

***

I decompressed at the hostel. I laid in my cubicle and thought of myself as being 'back in the tank,' reconnecting with myself. It didn't feel weird or claustrophobic and it was kind of comforting to have people around me. Near the reception desk was a small communal area with a low table and chairs with no legs. Sitting there I met people from all over the world.

I met an Italian man. He'd been travelling alone for five months and been to so many places I couldn't remember them all, several places in the United States, as well as Peru, Brazil, Argentina, Bolivia... He'd left his job to go travelling and said he'd met many Europeans, especially Northern Europeans who had done the same. I explained that Anthony was in Cambodia and we were doing some solo travelling for the experience and whereas some people said, 'That's interesting,' or needed a long explanation, he got it straight away, 'Yes, because when you're on your own, if things go wrong it's just you.'

A woman asked if I could read English then asked me to help connect her new Bluetooth headphones; I had no idea what to do but she thought I'd helped and was really grateful. She didn't speak any English and one day when I was indoors writing for most of the day she used a translation app to ask me, 'Why don't you go out to play?'

I met a woman from Thailand. I asked her if Thai people get fed up with all the tourists. She worked as a tour guide and said, 'Some tourists, they do what they want, even if you tell them, they say 'I'm here travelling, I'll do what I want.'' She said sometimes it wasn't the tourist's fault, the rickshaw drivers take them to a temple, are only interested in the fare money and don't tell them anything about how to respect the culture.

She went on to talk about how no one talks about sex, or about condoms, how girls don't speak up if when they start having sex a boy does not use a condom; no one tells her she can speak up, so there are many teenage pregnancies, although people don't talk about it. 'We need to get more open, its 2018!' she said.

I asked her why restaurants in Thailand gave out chopsticks. 'It's because of the Chinese, when a Thai person and a Chinese person go into business together Thai people take on some of the culture.'

'But they aren't very practical for Thai noodles though, they are so sticky?'

'Oh I just use one (chopstick) and twirl the noodles around it, like spaghetti,' she said. I thought of me, trying to learn the rules of chopstick use from YouTube, getting really stressed out because I couldn't do it 'properly.' 'Do you get the food into your mouth?' Anthony had said, exasperated, 'That's all that matters.'

Thinking about travelling on an evening walk, the realisation, we all eat, we all wear clothes, we all communicate, we all go to the toilet. It's like, let's see, how are we going to manage that here? In Japan eat with chopsticks, in India eat using the fingers of the right hand. Different clothes but still clothes. Different languages, but 'We all want the same things,' as David in Chennai had said about using sign language to ask for food, a universal communication across languages and cultures.

***

I had met fellow writers on creative writing courses. I'd met fellow seekers on Buddhism and meditation courses. And I had good friends. But in meeting B, which as she said was, 'Magical, that in this vast world of billions of people we connected on the internet, which you use sparingly compared to most,' and then that we met face to face in Tokyo, and connected. Here was a peer: a woman, similar age, seeking but also largely self realised. Who has wandered away from her family, who like me has some family guilt, tensions and mysteries to either process or simply accept. And who is a writer. Who is really writing, is writing a book, who has total dedication to writing. 'I don't like wasting time. There's no chance it won't get finished. It's the most important thing.'

Meeting B gave me validation, permission, to put in the time, to be driven, to spend time on this, to take it seriously. *To stay in while others go out to play.* We spoke about the struggle women sometimes seem to have to commit to art especially if they have a family.

'What would you rather, to have given up on your art but still have friends and family around you or to have become a successful writer but end up alone?' 'Which would you rather have and would it be worth it?'

'What if when you're old and you have no family,' for B if she has no kids, or both of us, if we'd lost everything, 'What if you were disabled, ill, couldn't look after yourself?'

'Well,' I paused. 'There's no guarantee that if you have kids they will look after you anyway. The state... depending on which country you were in, maybe...' 'Money, that's what you'd need!' I said. I suddenly realised that's the solution, for her, but for me and Anthony too. Or just to not worry about any of it.

Valuing our time together.

'I don't want to waste it talking about the weather.' B said. B asked the big questions that swirled around my mind like koans. 'If you think it's all an illusion, why do you recycle, why not eat animals?' 'What do you believe right now?' 'Have you done healing on yourself for psychological issues?' At the same time we explored doubts. Should we be doing more, demonstrating, getting involved? B has friends that are political or environmental activists. My family are active environmental activists.

B said she had always struggled with the idea of infinity; she had found it overwhelming as a child and still does. We are told that our minds aren't capable of understanding it, but what if that's just to keep us down? What if we can't comprehend it because it's not true? I've often felt that the night sky was just scenery, like in *The Truman Show*. And it's not even necessarily that I think there's a 'They' keeping us down, it could just as easily be ourselves, the forgetting we did as part of this human experience, necessary obstacles as part of the journey of discovering or remembering who we are.

Mountains are meant to be quiet: Kolkata, India

It still felt warm, even at one am. I saw Anthony suddenly, a surprise; he had walked to meet me and was nearer than I thought he'd be. We had a big hug, it felt slightly surreal; one day I'm in Japan and he's in Cambodia and the next we're back in India together. It's such a miracle, travelling.

My first impression of Kolkata was lots of bright lights. A blazing strip of blue lights on the road and big smart brightly lit buildings including one which in my sleep-deprived state I thought said 'Government Enlightenment Institute,' (it actually said Engineering.) And I'd forgotten about the 'only in India' signs: 'Give blood but not on the road.' Then we came to run down buildings; I saw a thin cow eating out of garbage, cycle rickshaws and lots of people sleeping outside on the top of taxis and out in the open on the pavement.

The guesthouse was a beautiful old building with marble stairs and wrought iron bannisters. One of the staff, an old man who didn't speak any English had stayed up to let us in. Our room was clean enough although it smelled a bit musty. I saw tendrils of mould growing under the beds, from the floor up the wall a good few inches, like thick embossed wallpaper in the shape of knobbly little trees.

There was a shared bathroom with a padlock and a key, 'No one much else about though,' Anthony said. The bathroom had blue dolphin tiles on the wall and an orange bucket. It reminded me of the bathroom in the house before last which also had blue dolphin tiles and orange walls the same colour as the bucket.

We had a shower together and then we had sex on the bed. Husband-and-wife-back-together sex, yet with such a force it was almost like strangers having sex for the first time. That first trip to the bathroom was all about sex but even after I kept saying, 'Come with me,' every time I went to the bathroom; I just wanted to be with him.

At Tokyo airport I'd had a short video call with Anthony in Kolkata, him with no top on, sweating under a familiar Indian fan. It was the first time we'd spoken in two weeks; we'd wanted to have our own experiences to share in full face to face, and to deal with things alone.

The room was very hot and the wet from the shower was quickly replaced by the wet of sweat in minutes. We spent most of the time covered in a layer of sweat; it made the back of my knees itchy.

When we went out for the first time Anthony told me to look out for the bumps in the road, like invisible sleeping policemen that would otherwise trip you up. There were walking and bicycle rickshaws on the corner near our guesthouse. We got a bicycle rickshaw to Sudder Street, which is meant to be the backpacker area. Watching a man's sweat and muscles take us along was a challenge to my sensitivities but a bicycle rickshaw was a great way to experience the narrow streets. The view was super sensory overload, so busy with loads of tiny shops, birds' nests wires again, and meat.

'Don't look right, look straight ahead,' Anthony said a couple of times. He said I looked like a rabbit in the headlights. Tokyo to Kolkata was a shock to the system.

'Maybe something easier would have been better for my first day,' I said.

'I don't think there *is* anything easier,' he said.

There was a traffic jam and a row ensued involving our man. They looked like they could have stood arguing all day. Anthony got out and helped our driver reverse. We paid the asking price plus fifty percent tip, obviously still a pittance but isn't it worse to not use at all? I had read that bicycle rickshaws, at the bottom of the pecking order are especially disadvantaged, having areas they aren't allowed to work in and that their offered prices are correct whereas autos can be vastly inflated for tourists.

At Sudder Street there was a long street market with stalls selling cotton dresses and brightly coloured trousers and scarves. There were lots of families shopping. We got caught up in a huge queue, which we found out was going into a new shopping centre with an opening day sale. We wanted to say, 'No, no, no, don't do it!' but that's not how it works. As Anthony says, everyone's got to experience it for themselves, it's no good us who have had it all, telling people who haven't not to bother with capitalism, consumerism and stuff.

When Anthony arrived he'd eaten at one of the hole in the wall places with huge cooking pots as he couldn't see anywhere else. He said he'd watched a man stack a pile of dirty plates and then when a customer came in the man took a plate from the bottom of the pile, wiped it with a dirty rag and put the food on it. This was why Anthony always said, 'Whatever you do, never look in the kitchens.'

We found somewhere else for dinner, smarter than we'd normally go to; there didn't seem to be anything in between. Men were building towers for a festival with wooden canes bound with fabric ribbons. There were lots of coloured lights, falling down in strings. A man said, 'Hello,' and 'Welcome.' I noticed two white rabbits in the form of litter bins. There was a market selling plastic lunch boxes and drinks bottles, kitchenware, headphones and gold jewellery. Small stalls were packed with metal and plastic bangles in all colours. I saw an underwear advert on a post. The model was voluptuous by Western standards, soft and with a tummy. Seeing underwear pictures and pretty underwear on open display made it feel easy to buy. I hadn't seen knickers for sale very often. The stalls had both men and women serving. I pointed to my hips. I bought two pairs of cotton knickers which fitted perfectly.

We passed pavement dwellers with little houses on the pavements, a community of homes with cooking set ups outside and people washing at standpipes in the street. On the corner near to our guesthouse was a group of young men, I felt nervous walking past them. I'd returned to India a bit freaked out after reading news stories about rape and murder in India. But despite what I read in the papers, people in India had shown us nothing but kindness.

We went out to get my thyroid medication. The fourth pharmacist was able to help and I bought a three month supply to last the rest of the trip. The pharmacist asked what we did for a living back home, 'We're in the same business,' he said.

Walking down the main road it was busy with lots of people asking us for money, children following and tugging on our sleeves, young women and girls saying hi. If we stopped still for a moment we got approached. Once, we reached a big junction, decided the idea of crossing it was too crazy and turned back. Near the junction there were pavement dwellers sleeping out in the open right on the main road, a boy on the pavement right next to all the traffic and exhaust fumes. I saw the inside of one of the pavement dwellings, a single room with a fan and a lot of people inside all sat very close together.

Anthony and I were in different places; me vulnerable and loved up after all the back-together-but-felt-like-new-sex. It was like how I used to feel the day after being drunk; feeling hungover and emotionally vulnerable and not wanting to be left alone. He was adjusting to us being together again, having been alone and ill for most of his two weeks in Cambodia. I got upset when I thought he snapped at me. Kolkata was not the best place for getting upset, crying in the street. I was afraid it would go back to how it was in Thailand, us bickering and not appreciating each other.

We found a soda place to sit and have a drink. In the street were chickens, cats and thin dogs. A tiny shop was packed with hair products, costume jewellery and sparkly earrings. There was a mosque, and beside it was a pile of rubble and beyond that a derelict street. Grey houses were made colourful with washing. Two very well dressed Indian tourists with new-looking suitcases stood looking like they had just arrived in the wrong part of town. The buildings epitomised the descriptive phrase 'faded grandeur.' A house with newly painted shiny maroon shutters stood out. The details were still there; the coving, the arches. Now black and white or sepia but when new they must have been so beautiful.

Before we left I looked again at the mould tendrils under the bed. It wasn't mould raised like embossed wallpaper, it had been cleaned and just the marks were left.

We got a taxi to the train station for our overnight train to Varanasi, which gave us a view of Kolkata while being insulated inside our ac car; shops full of pipes and sheets of steel, the odd newly painted or well-maintained building stood out amongst the grey. Pavement stalls sold basic provisions; I saw a stallholder sitting on the floor measuring out handfuls of rice or flour into newspaper packets. We drove past a big metal bridge and huge grand colonial buildings, one big and red; apparently most of them are banks now.

Kolkata train station was busy outside and in, a huge board displayed all the trains. There were a few dogs lying down, sleeping right in the middle where people walked and lots of people on blankets waiting for trains. The colours of Kolkata station seemed to be navy blue; a woman in a navy blue kurta and blue leggings, another woman dressed all in navy blue with a white scarf, a Sikh man wearing a navy blue velvet turban. We went into a busy food place, it felt a bit daunting but upstairs it had a quieter seating area. The manager came up to us and shook Anthony's hand.

'See, there's always someone,' Anthony said. Always in India there seemed to be someone who offered to help or came to befriend or talk to us.

On the platform itself it was dirty and dusty. A man hung around and stared at us a lot, in the end Anthony shouted at him to go. I felt uncomfortable but it seemed like he was after money rather than being a threat. There was a man standing near us and I felt as if he would have helped had we needed. Another man asked Anthony about the train; although we were at the correct platform, platforms can change at anytime which meant no one was certain. It meant we made a connection with someone on the platform.

On the train a grandmother with a baby came to see us, 'Say hi,' she said to the baby. She gave me the baby to hold, nonchalantly. The baby's parents came to chat. They explained that they were a party of eight on a thirty-six hour journey to visit a Hindu pilgrimage site. A family with a tiny baby on a thirty six hour train journey, that's how important their religion is. We showed the family pictures of where we had stayed in Kolkata; the Grandmother's face was a picture, they didn't share our enchantment with the old buildings. The grandmother tried to encourage the baby to take Anthony's glasses when he wasn't looking. She called us Grandfather and Grandmother to the baby.

'Not Auntie and Uncle?' I asked.

'No no, Grandfather, Grandmother,' she said firmly.

The baby's mother pointed at my Om pendant and asked me if I knew what it meant. I gave a solid explanation and she nodded and seemed satisfied.

'Why are you going to Varanasi?' she asked. Indian people can be very direct. Anthony answered that one. 'India is one of the holiest countries in the world and Varanasi is one of the holiest places in India and the feeling you get from being in such a place is something we really appreciate even though we aren't Hindus.'

I brushed my teeth and got into bed. There was a clean white cotton sheet and a thick heavy charcoal woollen blanket. I felt the train, lots of shaking and movement, and relaxed. I felt myself come back into India, and India come back into me. Moving, clanking, like gears, like a chiropractor, my body adjusting and assimilating into India again. I felt safe, and I slept.

At four am another family nearby started chatting and woke us up. At five am they got off and more people got on, people just talking normally with no concession to people sleeping. 'This is India,' we had to tell ourselves. At six am I gave up trying to go back to sleep up and got up. I stood looking out of the door- at least one of the doors is usually wide open on the trains. Outside there was miles and miles of green. There were derelict buildings, some being used as dwellings. In the middle of the expanse of green there was a little gold temple. I wasn't afraid anymore, and all the love was back.

Two young women on a station platform were standing perfectly coordinated in mint green dresses next to a green hoarding. As we got closer to Varanasi we saw red brick buildings, it seemed strange to see red brick again. Each individual brick had a pattern carved into it. Some of the buildings were square shaped with turret shaped walls like unfinished castles. Two had mosaics of glittering mirrors. As we got closer to Varanasi station, two yellow butterflies landed on the outside of the window.

The guesthouse had said they would send an auto to meet us. We wondered for a moment how they would find us before realising we were the only Westerners at the station. The auto ride was very unpleasant; the streets of the main town were choked with cars and bikes and full of dust. I saw a little exchange take place at a corner, a near miss between a scooter and a bicycle. The cyclist had gone out in front of the scooter causing the scooter to stop sharp. The rider of the scooter looked about fourteen, with a boy of maybe nine or ten standing up at the front of the scooter, the stop made a mild jolt and jerked the younger boy forwards. Both riders stopped, made eye contact, there was a pause; the moped rider gave a head wobble that seemed to serve both as chastisement and to acknowledge acceptance of the cyclist's apology and off they all went with no words exchanged.

Our driver went as far as he could then parked up and led us on foot through the narrow alleyways; we had to walk fast to follow him through all the twists and turns with him only occasionally turning around to check we were still there. I was excited to see monkeys again in the alleyways, up high, jumping from side to side but there was no time to stop and look.

The guesthouse was painted shiny mustard yellow. The manager said people move to Varanasi, swelling its population; hence all the pollution, because it is believed that if you are living within its boundary when you die you go straight to Nirvana, guaranteed.

He said, 'The weather is changing all around, because humans have interfered with nature.'

'Too many cars,' I said.

'Yes, and too much chopping down of trees, and interfering with mountains.' 'Mountains are meant to be quiet,' he said, 'They are not for picnics.' He asked what I liked about India, I said as always, the colour. He said 'Yes, I watch the news reports for Europe, there is no colour, there are no shining faces. Even the poor have shining faces in India. Even people living on the street smile.'

Anthony had his answer, 'Because in India you feel free.'

'Yes,' the manager said, 'Even the animals in India are free.' He and I bemoaned the problem of cows eating plastic. 'People are lazy,' he said. 'When I was a boy, every house had a cow that would come, and you would give it the food waste. Now people put it in plastic bags. The animals have suffered since plastic came to India. You see,' he said, 'They don't have hands.'

At the top of the guesthouse was a roof terrace covered by a metal cage to keep monkeys out. I sat up there with a Sprite and a cigarette just watching. So many buildings, all different heights, some brick, many grey with age and dust, some painted with the colours faded; white, cream, pale blue, pink, red, yellow and blue-green, and the colour from the washing hung out on the rooftops. Boys and young men on rooftops flying maroon and purple coloured kites made out of wood and paper. Circular windows reflected the light and looked like mirrors. There were lots of mosques, mainly white. Out to one side was The Ganga, huge and beautiful, with colourful wooden boats carrying pilgrims and tourists. And so many monkeys, effortlessly jumping from building to building, thirty to forty altogether, tiny babies, medium babies, some hanging under their mum's tummy or sitting on her back. The highest building in the near vicinity was painted pale and dark pink with a wrought iron decorative balustrade. At the top of the building there was an adult monkey sitting on a wall, looking on top of the world.

At the reception we met a couple from the UK, a man and a woman; he was originally from Norwich, my home town. They were in their thirties, had left good jobs in London and were on a one year trip. They planned to go and work wherever they could earn the most money e.g. Dubai or Singapore in order to stay on road, keep travelling and not get stuck.

'More and more people are doing this, rather than follow the school then work then buy house and work until you retire,' the man said. 'If I went back to London, I'd get promoted, I'd get stuck,' the woman said, 'It's a trap.'

We were staying in the old town where narrow alleyways criss crossed and went down to the Ghats, the steps at the side of The Ganga. Hole in the wall shops sold tobacco, cigarettes, water, toiletries, crisps and biscuits. Stalls sold hippy clothes, scarves, thin trousers, silk, jewellery and ornaments for the tourists. Varanasi is on the backpacker route and everything was suddenly easy in terms of availability of clothing, toiletries and food. The stallholders offered as we went past but were not really pushy. We bought loose cotton trousers and tops, feeling more relaxed already.

There seemed to be butterflies everywhere in Varanasi; even the clock in the cafe had butterflies on. The menu was in Chinese and English. It was a family business; there was a little boy bored with no toys, opening and closing the sliding glass doors of the cupboards, moving chairs, and getting told off by the two women sitting at the counter.

The people looked like they were doing well. The cows were the best we'd seen; cows in holy areas seem to be well fed and big. The dogs were not as good; many looked mangy. The narrow alleyways were full of bikes, noisy and polluting and meant you always had to be moving out of their way. People born here seemed happy like the people born in Hampi. When we asked the man from the clothes shop how he was he answered, 'Everything is perfect.'

We met a sadhu and went to his house for an astrological reading. 'It is one hundred years old, some of it is broken,' he said as he showed us inside. We sat on the stone floor near an altar or shrine. He looked at our faces and hands, we did some meditation together, he gave us a blessing, some information and advice and we gave him some money. We entered into the spirit of it and of course embraced the bits we liked or that rang true.

He told me I was a very spiritual person, that I have good intuition but that I overthink things; he said that I get close, almost to my mission, to enlightenment and then fall back. He told me not to have wine or marijuana or smoke cigarettes. He told me my past life was in India, that I died in Howrah near Rishikesh and that one day I will do something like open an ashram or a yoga centre, an NGO or a school for poor people, 'Something like that. You've thought about that?' He asked, well yes, I had thought about it.

'Rachel only your body name,' he said, 'Meditate on your soul name.'

He told me to, 'Pick a guru.' He gave us a blessing as a couple and told us to stay together until death. 'If he get angry, you be quiet, if she angry, you quiet,' he said. 'Past is bullshit, Future is bullshit, Mind is bullshit!' he said.

We walked around the ghats. Bells clanged at temple time. Incredible looking sadhus, some naked and covered in ash sat on high stone platforms beside the river. A man offered to sell us opium. 'Why not, it's Sunday?' he said when we said no thank you.

In the evening we watched the ceremony on the steps of the Ganga. There were lots of families, small children and babies, and women in beautiful coloured sarees. Someone had told us, 'It makes no sense to non Hindus, but get stoned then it will.' Performers in orange robes played music, there was fire and lots of candles and at the end the little candles were put into The Ganga. Afterwards a plate was passed up the steps for donations.

At a stall selling bananas, a cow stood there looking as if they were about to help themselves to the bananas. I bought some bananas for the cow. 'Good feeling, good karma,' one of the men at the stall said.

I said optimistically, 'Let's go out for dessert.' We found a little place down an alley and were shown to a room upstairs. We had tea and fruit salad with nuts and dried fruit. The man was very friendly and put a pile of books about Hinduism in front of me. I looked up about the red mark on the forehead which I saw a lot. It is called

Tilak and symbolises the quest to open The Third Eye. Opening The Third Eye, the book said is the unification of the conscious and the unconscious; the point at which all elements of duality merge into one universal entity.

There were was lots of Lassi- Indian milkshake shops. Shops sold big round blocks of what looked like solid cheese, and curd in little clay pots with newspaper lids wrapped over them. We found a good food place; aloo gobi and spinach potato, the spinach pureed into a dark bright green sauce for the chunks of potato, a different vegetable curry each day and chilli chips which were wet with red sauce.

In the restaurant we met a woman from Spain travelling alone, so brave. I don't even like eating alone, she has to do it every meal. She'd done volunteering with a family, an ayevedic treatment course in Kerala and was soon off to Dharmshallah to volunteer in a Nunnery. She said, 'Sometimes it gets tiring, there's no one to watch your bag, you're all alone.'

We bumped into the man from the banana stall every day. He wore the same red t-shirt every day. *One day at a time,* it said. He told us he used to be a Brahmin, but because when he was younger he was addicted to heroin he has spoiled that and is no longer a Brahmin, despite having been clean for many years. At the chai stall a man chatted to us and showed us pictures of his two girlfriends, one in Nepal.

'Do they know about each other?' I asked.

'Are you crazy! If you had a boyfriend would you tell Anthony about him?' he said.

One evening we bought a selection of homemade Indian sweets from a little shop between our guesthouse and The Ganga. We sat on the steps at the ghats and looked at The Ganga and the boats. We watched a dog going from little rowing boat to little rowing boat, three tied up parallel to the shore, looking under all the seats then back to the bank, looking for food. A smartly dressed man with a plastic carrier bag came down the steps. He took a big framed picture out of the carrier bag and threw it into The Ganga. In front of us was a red boat, it matched the red scarf Anthony was wearing. 'We're a long way from Harleston,' he said. Yet at the same time, we're only a visa and a plane ticket away, the same amount of money some people will spend on a sofa or new carpets.

Another man came down with a red bucket and tipped out food for the dogs. He tipped one pile, the dogs all fought over it, he moved along and tipped out another pile, all the dogs went to that one, he made another pile and the same thing happened again before one dog eventually went back to the first pile where there were no other dogs. In spite of the initial squabbling, six dogs all got fed.

'Hello, Namaste,' the man called to us.

'You are a good man,' I said.

'I try to be a good man,' he answered. On the floor of the stone steps were red, orange and yellow smudges of powder from the ceremonies. I fed the rest of the sweets to a dog with puppies; I thought I was being kind but behind us we heard lots of angry barking as if I had caused a family argument.

***

The Ganga was high and so we had to walk the long way through the busy part of town, rather than walk along the river to the Burning Ghats where cremations take place. It was a really awful walk, with the heat and the pollution. We stopped at a stall and bought scarves to put over our faces. The walk was hard but I saw faded red stairs inside a house with pale pink walls, and above the open door a tiny lemon on a string with green beans threaded horizontally above and below making a decoration, or a talisman. As we got near, people called out, 'Dead body burning?' and told us which way to go. It seemed so inappropriate to treat this as a tourist attraction, even though that was what we and other people were doing. We do it, but we don't want to be open about it. But people in India are direct and things in India are out in the open, especially death.

A man came up to us and took us around. He took us into the burning room where the bodies of Brahmins are cremated. In metal frames raised off the ground were piles of fires which were almost out. We were very close, it felt very weird. The burning takes several hours and the family stays for the duration. We saw a family; it felt intrusive although our guide appeared relaxed about it. The room was up high; from one side we looked down and saw piles of firewood, from the other he showed us where everyone else was burned on the ground level. Amongst the ash were gold pieces that looked like foil decorations. The man showed us a small fire smouldering, 'The Shiva fire,' which never goes out.

He told us that he was a social worker at the hospice in the building next door, doing massage and caring for the dying. At the end of the tour he asked for donations for poor people's cremations. He told us how many kilos of wood it takes to burn a body and how much the wood cost per kilo. 'How many kilos are you going to buy?' he asked. 'Is that all?' We both left feeling guilt tripped about our contribution being too little.

On the way back we saw a body being carried through the streets on a simple stretcher of fabric and sticks with a blanket over; the person's body was so thin, so flat. It was an overwhelming walk back again with the heat and pollution.

It was so good to be back in our alleyways; the old town is not so polluted. We stopped at the nearest of our regular cafes and ordered fizzy drinks. I went to the sink and washed my hands. With a bottle of Sprite in hand I immediately felt better before even drinking it; just by being back there, in the land of the living.

I still felt a bit strange from the emotional impact of it all. 'Tea and cake,' or an approximation of it, was required. I bought biscuits from a little shop and we went to a little coffee shop with wooden benches and tables. Sitting near us were an Indian man and a Western woman. There was a long wait for coffee, and they struck up a friendly conversation with us.

He was from another state, travelling, trying to find something different to do, she was from Europe. She said it was her second time in India but her first time in Varanasi. She said she couldn't do Varanasi the first time, it was too intense. We spoke about being tired and about the heat. He said, 'Do stuff before ten am or after ten pm,' the implication being, in between do nothing. They ordered more chai. They said, 'How many chai have we had now? Four or five? We've had one every half an hour since ten thirty this morning.' They bought us tea. The coffee shop encounter and chat, the biscuits, provided me with the comfort I needed. Anthony said, 'There's always something, for every bad experience, there's a good one.'

We got back and told our guesthouse manager where we had been. He said, 'People say they are social worker,'

'Yes,' we said, 'They do massage, care for the people and need money for wood.'

'No,' he said, 'There's no hospice there. That building is a place for families to stay. The family pays for wood and if they are a poor person the community supplies the wood.' I told him how many kilos for each body, how much per kilo. He shook his head. 'How many kilos did you buy?' His face was a picture. 'You should have asked me first,' he said.

I felt much better though, finding out we'd been scammed was better than feeling guilty about not giving enough money for wood for a poor person's cremation. We'd paid for the man's time and we probably wouldn't have had so much access without a guide.

The English couple were worried about their train bookings, one had been cancelled and the guesthouse manager was sorting it out for them. 'You worry too much, he said. 'If God is angry, things won't go well, if God is happy, things will go well.' I loved his attitude, and the fact that he was so accepting of us even though we were so different to him. 'For Indians even t-shirts have to be ironed so we couldn't travel with back packs like you,' he said to me.

On our last morning we woke up early and went up to the rooftop. People were already up, sweeping, doing exercises and prayers. Women were making breakfast in caged off rooftop rooms and hanging up laundry outside on the open rooftops with sticks to protect them from the monkeys. People had put chapattis out on the roof terraces and squirrels were eating them. There were monkeys all around including lots of babies; there was even a baby monkey sliding down a pole like a fire station pole. We watched a monkey pick up a lost kite and just destroy it piece by piece; picking it up, looking at it as if interested, eating a bit then tearing it to bits. Some birds that looked like swallows were making a huge noise. A black and white dog chained up watched the monkeys and barked when they went past. A fluffy orange dog was loose and chased the monkeys; once there was a near miss. The sun was just risen, an orange ball above the Ganga.

***

We got an overnight train to Delhi. People were in our seats, lying down; they had used all the pillows and a lot of the sheets and blankets. We had to ask them to move for us to sit down, which they did grudgingly, the woman still half laying down so that Anthony and I were squashed up on half a seat, all of them seemingly thoroughly put out that we were there. Soon after they announced they all wanted to go to sleep. We were in three tier ac again and when the middle bunk gets folded down no one can sit on the lower bunk anymore. Anthony had the lower bunk. I lay on the top bunk, meditated, and tried to sleep. Then someone put the big light on. I woke up at 2.15 am and then at 4.30 am for good.

It's always a bit noisy; people's alarms go off and people get off at stops along the way. From early morning there are men selling chai coming through the carriage saying loudly, 'Chai chai coffee chai.' *Well I didn't want any, because I was asleep, but now you've woken me up I actually do!* But this journey was particularly bad, with loud snoring and farting in the night and in the morning one of the party sat doing really loud burps. Of course the fact that we felt annoyed with the people we shared a space with and they didn't seem nice made it all the worse. But when we arrived into Delhi station the adult son came up to Anthony and shook his hand, ending any (or at least most of) the hard feelings.

We arrived in Delhi very tired. 'I'm never doing three tier again,' Anthony said. We went out for breakfast at a rooftop cafe overlooking Main Bazaar, Anthony found us a hotel, we treated ourselves to ac because of the pollution.

Anthony got ill with an upset stomach almost immediately, from the first meal he ate, at funnily enough the same restaurant as when he got sick last time. It didn't necessarily mean he had got sick from there but he certainly didn't feel like eating there again. While he was ill I went out on my own to eat in Main Bazaar. A man said the usual, 'Hi where are you from,' and 'I'm not trying to sell you anything,' which was almost certainly not true, 'No talk? He said, acting all offended. When he caught me again on the way back I said, 'I must get home, my husband is ill,' which worked a treat, and the man backed off. I went out to eat several times by myself and it was okay, I met people from Korea, China, Japan, all super friendly and chatty. One of the staff remembered me from back in March, he said, 'If you need help with anything,' heart hold, 'You are a very nice person.'

Just as when we arrived in March, our room had a balcony which looked out over Main Bazaar. I saw four adults and two kids on a scooter. Outside the restaurant opposite, a black and white dog was leaping up, wagging its tail in front of a man, the man acting cool, the dog jumped up on the man and then finally he gave in and fussed the dog, it was nice to watch. I had a masala dosa at that restaurant and chatted to the owner who was from Kashmir. Later on I saw the kitchen, which was a couple of floors up, from our balcony. The table and walls were black with dirt and grease and a man was wiping the table with a very dirty looking cloth. I got sick just after Anthony. Again, I got sick after eating a meal at the same restaurant as I did last time.

'I feel defeated by India,' Anthony said. Our frequencies were really low, thinking about the UK, everything, the realisation that, 'We took the red pill, there's no going back,' and what taking the red pill really means. Planning how we will go forward into our new life, the UK life, beginning to turn twenty-five percent of our attention to the UK and what happens next, practically. 'We don't want to have a life changing experience and return to the same life;' was our mantra, while still being present in India and me still completing the book.

The bed had a really cosy duvet that we appreciated in our sorry states. We watched a lot of old X Factor clips on YouTube, it's not what I usually do but I enjoyed it. 'In my job I see a lot of pain... a lot of joy and happiness, but a lot of pain...' a priest said, before singing *Everybody hurts* by REM. I tried meditating, focussing on my out breath, feeling a sense of peace, enjoying the big duvet cosiness. Feeling almost chilly but knowing that my new comfy soft sweatpants from Tokyo were available was comforting.

I'd been trying to meditate again since Varanasi, I thought it had possibly helped me deal with vomiting. I said, 'Oh God,' a few times but felt calmer during vomiting. I really hate being sick and get a bit scared sometimes. In the bathroom was a little plastic seat, opaque white with worn out mauve and silver sparkly flowers, it was my favourite object in that place. I had a dream about a silver palace. Waking up, the first thing I saw was the gold and silver leaf design of the curtains which were lit up by the sun.

I sent my son, who's doing really well, a message, 'Well done, we're both so proud of you.' At same time, cutting the cord. You can cut the cord and still be loving. In fact doing that, rather than being distant actually sets you (both) free. Same with my mum- little messages with a few photos, and no angst from me. This sets me miles and miles away. I thought being distant does that, but it doesn't. Pain and conflict can keep you enmeshed just like being all cosy cosy can. This isn't enmeshed. It's kind, it's nice, it's fairly non emotional- as in, it's happy but not riddled with guilt, or upset like before; or feeling trapped. My son's doing better set free from me. I'm doing better set free from my mum.

It's so simple put like that. Is this the magic secret, all there is to it, the how to transition from child to adult relationships that I never previously understood? Parenting a troubled teenager and twenty-something had been an emotionally devastating experience. At the same time I'd remained overly enmeshed with my own mother throughout my thirties. Was this how to transition into my own life at last?

Delhi is known for being polluted and while we were there the air quality was particularly bad. Bryan Adams did a show and tweeted a photograph of himself barely visible beyond the smog. We wondered whether it was better to have the ac on or to leave it off and keep the windows closed. We researched it and discovered that ac only gives a false sense of security and doesn't get all the dangerous particulates out. We came across adverts for companies selling bottled air in Delhi. My heart went out to the people who live there all the time.

We were going to Rajasthan next, we had booked trains ages ago and had planned for a month; a week in each city. But when we researched, one of those cities was as polluted as Delhi. We'd just experienced a lot of pollution in Varanasi and after Rajasthan we'd got flights booked to go to Kathmandu, also known for poor air quality. In addition there was an outbreak of Zika virus in Jaipur which was meant to be our first stop in Rajasthan. Although very dangerous only for pregnant women, neither of us wanted to risk getting ill with something else.

We procrastinated for ages, the two of us. It was a balance between what we wanted and felt up to doing now versus would we regret not going to these places once the trip is over. In the end we ripped up the plan, cancelled all the trains and decided to just go to Pushkar, the smallest and least polluted place on our Rajasthan itinerary. All the trains to Pushkar were sold out- which was why we'd booked them so far in advance- and we could only get there by bus. As there are no loos on buses we had to wait until we were well. We felt trapped in Delhi; we felt like the food and the pollution made us ill, or at least didn't help but we couldn't leave until we were well.

We stayed six nights in that room in Delhi. On our last morning we ate porridge with banana sitting out on the rooftop. It was so nice being outdoors together, it felt like an outing. The past few days had been mainly spent indoors, one of us only going out for food or drink or to the pharmacy over the road. Once or twice we went to the cafe downstairs, which was a bit sad and greasy and with doors that opened into the pollution of the street. From the rooftop we watched a Westerner, he lived right at the top above the dirty kitchen, completing Hindu rituals, or possibly just washing with a water bottle, we weren't sure. We watched him doing his laundry on the roof. What a life. What was his story? Divorced? Pension? Hindu convert? Disappeared?

That night we got an auto from the hotel to catch the night bus to Pushkar. I tried to soak up the sights of Main Bazaar/Paharganj; the neon lights, the mopeds, the cows including a cow and calf with big floppy ears, knowing it might be our last time. I lost concentration for a few moments and then it was gone. We were into a different area, we saw veg restaurants, pure veg places; I thought, why didn't we go here? Oh, yes, because we were sick and ill and indoors the whole time!

    And then, utter craziness, worse than Kolkata. We saw the Delhi smog close up. Thin cows trying to eat non- existent grass in the middle of road or central reservation, licking a stone in the middle of the barrier. A group of calves eating from a trough. Everything grey, dusty and dark. Buildings that looked like they had been derelict for decades or would be for demolition by UK standards. Birds nest wiring amongst them and then a few inflatable toys, bright pink balloons and big brightly coloured teddies wrapped up in cellophane.

It looked like a market had finished and was packing up. There was every type of transport; lorries, cars, rickshaws, oxen and cart, men with carts and men with sacks on their heads. Men pulling, some with another man pushing but some alone with huge loads. A man was carrying a huge load on his shoulders, wrapped in plastic, two leg ends and castors poked out, a chair or a table; he carried it up to the top of a ladder to a vehicle alone then men at the top took it. A sign said: 'Men at work.' Oh God yes. If ever that sign was valid, it was here.

Dust, dark and traffic jams. Everything within a thick smog. It's unbelievable how anyone survives and does this every day. How there's any old people in Delhi. A cycle rickshaw got caught on our auto. Everyone around just shouted instead of helping. Usually touching of vehicles, even a scrape, does not result in shouting, not like in the UK. Maybe this was because it held up the traffic, and maybe it was a status thing, with bicycle rickshaws considered lower in the pecking order than autos.

On previous night bus journeys I worried about needing a pee, this time it was worry about diarrhoea, which was much more of a worry, eclipsing the pee. Then oh great, blood: period. The bus depot was dusty with rows of numbered stalls, travel agents each with a desk and a tiny office with seats. The toilets were down a path, there were lots of men hanging around and big dogs. By the toilets there was a big room with men sleeping on the floor. There was a sink for hands outside but nothing in the loo and it was not very clean. Even if I took a bottle of water for the moon cup like I had on the train, I'd not be confident enough about hand hygiene to use it, so cloth sanitary pads and lungis would have to suffice. On the bus we saw a dreadlocked young woman, the first thing she did was spread out a white lungi on the bus seat, it's good to do for hygiene. I did my (purple) one double layered just in case but my cloth sanitary pad didn't let me down, as they say in the ads.
    These buses apparently doubled as goods transport too; before we got on men loaded sacks into the luggage hold and all down the aisle inside the bus. When we got on there were people lying in the aisle, using the white sacks as makeshift beds. Although it was a bit

crowded the atmosphere was very friendly and people moved to let us in and out which made it feel kind of fun.

We had a double compartment with a sliding door, like a big hutch. It felt nice and cosy with the door shut and there was plenty of space for us and our bags. We'd heard single people say they'd booked a single and ended up sharing a double with a large stranger! Above us was a family with loads of kids but after a short while they went quiet, for the entire journey, no complaining, no toilet.

There were quite a few women travelling alone; the dreadlocked woman with the white lungi, and near her a Western woman dressed in white. The bus man came to see her, and came back again; there was obviously some kind of problem. She said to us, 'They want me to leave the bus, they say I am on the wrong bus, that mine is a cheaper one.' I instantly thought, towards the man, Just leave her be. Or, that she could just share with us; there was quite a bit of room, we could switch sides so Anthony was on the far side, although I didn't mention it as I wasn't sure if Anthony would mind or not. We were both worried about her being dropped in the night; Anthony looked for her as she was talking to the man, ready to intervene if they started arguing, but all of a sudden she was gone. I said that I wished we'd intervened or checked she was okay. Anthony said, 'I was going to say she could have shared with us but I wasn't sure whether to suggest it.'

At the first loo stop we saw her, all the buses often stopped together, she was completely fine and on another bus. She said she'd refused to get off our bus unless the man walked her to her new bus. We were relieved to see her and find that she was okay, but far from being vulnerable, she was more experienced than either of us; this was her fifth time in India. She said she couldn't believe how many Westerners were on the bus as usually when travelling on buses she was the only foreigner; she said she'd always been fine.

The bus stopped again in the middle of the night. The brick wall in the wash area at the loos was painted shiny mauve which seemed to shine, vroom vroom, luminous in the dark in my tired state. At around seven am we had to get out and change buses, we all got on a cheaper looking bus and met the woman again. As we got closer to Pushkar a woman said, 'If I don't pee soon I'm going to die.' We shared an auto with the woman we'd met, our bags balanced on a shelf at the back, us needing coffee, breakfast, toilet and sleep.

Outside was Rajasthan: desert, a green mountain, green bushes and trees, birds with baby birds, peacocks on a wall, and walls with cut out patterns like rainbows.

Sab Kuch Milega: Pushkar, India

At the guesthouse entrance we met a Russian woman, 'I love India, there's everything... If you get into the water, then there's everything.' She told us about the Jain temple at Ajmer. 'You must go, it is an ancient temple and yet they portray rockets in the sky. Their knowledge of civilisation and the fact there's so few Jain temples left points to them having been built by an alien race,' she said.

Ganesh was there all the time running things at the guesthouse. In the garden were three tortoises. Ganesh said he used to get stoned and go out into the desert on his scooter and bring animals back with him. He said, 'I bring them, it's up to them if they stay.' Ganesh said he had also brought a porcupine home but, 'They didn't stay, they went off into the market.' I thought about a porcupine wandering into the market and what that would be like; and gave thanks yet again for being in a place where such an event could occur. Ganesh told us he had brought the three tortoises back seven, nine and fifteen years ago; he said they come and nibble his finger when they are hungry. 'They are good, then they go, they come back ten minutes later and I have their lunch ready for them.'

A cat often sat on a wall near the entrance to the guesthouse. On my instigation, Anthony tried to stroke it and got scratched- not for the first time on the trip. When I told Ganesh about this, he looked sorrowfully at us and explained,

'I have tried so hard to make that cat love me. As you know there is no meat in Pushkar;' Pushkar being a holy place there was no meat, fish or eggs or alcohol, at least officially. 'I went on my scooter to the town several kilometres away and bought fish and chicken for the cat. I fed the cat the chicken and the fish, I put my hand out and it scratched me! Then I showed the cat YouTube videos of cats on my phone for twenty minutes. The cat sat and watched the videos, then still it scratched me. Three times that cat scratched me that day. I don't love that cat anymore.'

Wait, what, you showed a cat YouTube videos of cats? For twenty minutes? Not only did the cat watch for twenty minutes, but that you sat there for twenty minutes and did that. I love Ganesh, what a wonderful person.

Ganesh said that in his village they still grind their own oil from seed, using a bull. They grow the seed themselves and they give the residue of the oil to the bull. People all give seed to pigeons; Ganesh described how each day a hundred pigeons go to his house to eat, then to the next house, then the next. In his village, if you get God's gifts; extra grain or seed you give big percentage to birds, pigeons and cows.

He told us that in his village, if someone makes a mistake or commits a crime, the police are not involved, instead everyone talks, they talk with both families and decide which family is in the wrong. The family in the wrong make restitution, offering so many kilos of grass for cows, so much seed for the pigeons. The pigeon as well as the cow are holy- hence the pigeon feeding station on Chennai beach, I realised.

'Pigeons are loved in India. Not cats. But I know tourists like the cats, especially the British, love cats, love animals,' Ganesh said. 'Pigeon not very clever, if cat comes, they shut their eyes and think the cat has gone away!' Later someone on WordPress told me that cats are actually liked in some places in India and in the Northeast and parts of Eastern India they are adored. Ganesh also told me that the camel owners and sheep owners have dogs and if one of their dogs dies they come to Pushkar to give food to the street dogs in their memory.

Monkeys came right up to the guesthouse, over the flat roof and into the tree by the courtyard near our room. The first time I saw one close up the cook was there, he smiled and went and fetched some puri to feed it. He fed it out of his hand and gave us some; I was more cautious and put it on the ground. The staff were so kind, they knew it was special for us even if monkeys were no big deal for them. One day a monkey was sitting on the door of the kitchen as if waiting for dinner; the cook gave it some left over chapatti.

There were two types of monkey in Pushkar, the black faced ones which are big with really long tails and the stockier, shorter tailed red faced ones. The black faced monkeys were welcome at the guesthouse and do not cause any trouble. 'They are family friends.' Ganesh told us. The red faced monkeys were disliked by the staff, who chased them with sticks. These monkeys can be aggressive to humans, 'Make trouble' for the black faced monkeys and fight badly amongst themselves, even killing each other sometimes, Ganesh said.

At the guesthouse the arrival of monkeys was announced by the sound of them jumping heavily across corrugated metal roofs, a sound like firecrackers. Both types of monkeys sometimes went up and down the stairs to the rooftop and garden like guests but the red faced monkeys were braver and bounded unafraid into the area right outside the rooms. Once when I was sitting outside typing, Ganesh came to stand beside me with a stick.

'I come to protect you.' 'Be careful of them, they come, you move.'

Ganesh knew I was writing a book and often told me interesting things and encouraged me to go and see interesting people or sights. I couldn't explain to him that just walking up the guesthouse steps was happiness; that his stories were so rich I could hardly capture them and that just being in Pushkar was enough, almost more than I could write down.

Pushkar is built around a holy lake. Ghats- wide sets of stone steps- lead down to the lake. Shoes are not allowed on the ghats or the walkways by the lake. There were cows by the lake and on the steps there was cow dung and pieces of broken pottery to avoid. The lake itself was grey-blue and still like glass.

Unlike at the Kanyakumari black temple experience when we had been bamboozled into buying flowers, paying for a guide and been rushed around the temple on a very fast tour, in Pushkar we were totally aware. We knew not to take a flower if someone offered it. Anthony had been here twenty years earlier; as he'd arrived a man had caught him and given him a flower, Anthony thought it was just something you did in Pushkar. Before he knew it he was having a blessing at the lake and was then asked for quite a bit of money, all before he'd had a chance to think.

Most days we went for a walk around the lake. We saw a cow walking down the ghats wearing a colourful collar and a bell then watched the cow nuzzle at the offerings on a shrine; casually picking up and discarding pieces of paper before eating the yellow flower garlands. We watched a monkey just take a garland from a shrine and eat it. A succession of monkeys ran along the ghats, each one leaping up to slam against a half-open metal door apparently just for fun; the door banged loudly shut then sprung open again ready for the next monkey to do the same. White herons, smaller than UK ones, stood at the side of the lake quite near people, apparently unafraid and feeling safe. Indian people don't seem to hassle animals, instead allowing them to be free. A group of women in pink and orange sarees, there for the day with handbags and big tote bags, a brown and white cow standing beside them looking like part of the family, until the cow looked inside a tote bag and one of the women shooed it out.

Little stalls sold plates of what looked like unpopped pop corn, different types of grain, and little 'cakes' for people to give to the cows. People put the food on big old metal tables; on a busy day the tables resembled an informal buffet, thickly covered with the different kinds of snacks for the cows. There was always corn on the ground, which was sometimes painful on our bare feet. Corrugated metal roofs of buildings near the lake were thick with corn and pigeons. A man fed slices of bread to the fish in the lake. A monkey sat on a wall eating a piece of fruit just like a human.

Near the bridge there was the smell of greens; women sold armfuls of green stuff to feed the cows. You pay then they put more and more bundles into your arms, encouraging you to feed the cows who are only too happy to eat whatever they can before you realise that each bundle is charged separately; very quickly all your change is spent. You had to take off your shoes to walk over the bridge; I liked walking barefoot there even though it was bit dirty and there was lots of cow dung.

At the other end of the bridge was a small courtyard garden area. Two nearby trees were full of monkeys. A man warned us not to stand underneath the trees, 'They may go to the toilet,' he said, 'This is India, everything is out in the open.' He was from Pushkar but lived in France and ran an Indian restaurant. There was a small shrine in the courtyard garden; the man said he does pooja, leaving offerings to honour his late father but the monkeys destroy it. 'I don't mind,' he said, 'This used to all be jungle, they were here first.'

At a restaurant where we ate masala dosas, sweet little birds with yellow beaks came right in and ate out of the partly open packets behind the counter. Staff shooed them out, they put food down for them outside. The restaurant staff told us they gave the first chapattis and dosas of the day to the cows.

There was good healthy food available in Pushkar. Juice bars sold muesli with fruit salad and soya milk and delicious soya milk smoothies with dates; you could even add cacao or spirulina. The portions of muesli and fruit salad for breakfast were almost too big to eat (almost.) The small seating area had a great view onto the main street full of shops selling Rajasthani goods, brightly coloured cushion covers, clothes and blankets. Rajasthani women walked past in beautiful clothes; thin scarves in red, pink or green decorated with tiny round mirrors, draped across with midriffs showing. Shop keepers getting ready for the day; sweeping the road outside the shop, beating the clothes hanging up outside the shop, sprinkling water on the ground to damp down the dust and then doing a morning ritual with incense and a flower garland. A man arrived on a scooter laden with boxes and boxes and huge bags of fruit and vegetables. A woman delivered on foot, a big bowl of white-stalked vegetables on her head, carrying plastic bags of what looked like cauliflowers; she was dressed in a deep blue saree with a silver nose stud and bindi, under her arm a purple handbag. Just like in Varanasi, there were a lot of motorbikes and scooters. The motorbikes made dust clouds from the desert roads, drove too fast through the streets and parked outside the juice bar, spewing fumes and blocking the entrance. But at least there were no cars; cars are banned from the main streets. Motorbikes and scooters used to be banned too but gradually everyone stopped obeying the rules.

After breakfast we usually walked around Pushkar looking at the sights. A cow looking inside a restaurant as if waiting for a table. An enormous cow standing in the middle of the road, bikes going around it and tourists stopping to take photographs. Three cows sitting in a row on the road, their legs neatly folded, the ends of their bent knees like velvety paws, the skin wrinkled like old tights. The cows of Pushkar were very big with humps, huge curly horns, long tails with a tassel at the end and floppy ears. The calves had thick ruffled grey fur and with their big ears looked almost like donkeys. Shops and stalls sold jewellery, bangles, bags, drums, masks and huge gold swords. We saw children in heavy theatrical makeup and ornate dresses, like living dolls. Women sat on the pavement in the blazing heat making and selling beaded jewellery. Some had small children with them and tiny babies in cradles made from cloth with wooden frames. In the quieter back streets were small shops with big cooking pots, vegetable shops and small jewellery wholesalers. The peacefulness of the back streets made it easier to notice the little details; a building in breathtaking blue, a periwinkle wall beside a mauve corrugated steel building like a shed, a tiny shop with very little stock.

In the centre of the main street were two falafel stalls who dragged passersby in with smiles and handshakes, free chai and promises extracted to come back later. At the falafels we bumped into the woman we'd met on the train, Heather. Her name suited her, I remembered it by thinking of purple flowers. She had beautiful eyes, grey-blue like the lake. She was English, aged thirty-one, she'd been away from the UK for seven years, teaching English in Spain for a few years but otherwise travelling using Workaway and Couchsurfers, next stop Australia. Heather said, 'I trust myself to keep myself safe, I listen to my instincts.' We spoke about women's safety and inevitably the incident referred to as 'the Delhi bus rape,' Heather said she raises it with all Indians she gets to know, 'I say to them, do you realise the effect this had; a grandmother in Devon will know this about India.' This is true, although someone else rightly said that the US has awful crimes but people don't tend to judge the whole country on it, perhaps because we are more familiar with the US from television and films.

Heather introduced us to Jack, twenty-five, from Scotland, he had been away from home for four years, again using Workaway interspersed with spells in a 'proper job' earning money for the next stage; his CV included doing the online marketing for a trekking company in Nepal, building clay ovens and teaching English.

Meeting people that lived like this, even if they were younger than us, was eye opening and showed us that 'Sab kuch milega/Everything is possible,' as they say in Pushkar.

Heather asked me about my eyeliner- how I did it, where I got it from- an attempt at messy smoky eyes or just got out of bed having slept in makeup, also a look I covet having been a punk, made with a kohl stick from a Himalaya shop. It felt good to be complimented about my appearance. Arriving in Pushkar, my Varanasi loom pants in mustard and burgundy suddenly felt all wrong, when they'd felt fine there, being modest and the colour mustard or saffron feeling religious. Pushkar was more laid back and more touristy, it was interesting how the vibe changed from place to place. I'd been shopping in Pushkar and bought two strappy t-shirt dresses, one blue-grey stone, one maroon, plus thin black trousers to wear underneath and a black scarf to drape around my shoulders; I felt elegant and quite pleased with my look.

The four of us went up in the cable car to see the sunset, a rare tourist activity for us. 'I don't do anything either,' Heather said. After the cable car trip we all went to a cafe and had lemon sodas. The cafe had the main kitchen inside but outside they served street food with the ingredients all out in the open. The mosquito fogging scooter came- a scooter with a kind of leaf blower on the back blasting out grey clouds of insecticide. We all covered our mouths and noses and rushed inside until the worst had cleared. We looked out at the uncovered street food; some other tourists said, 'I'm not going to eat that.' I felt really sorry for the cafes and street food sellers. We saw mosquito fogging again later; they came right along our road and the smell carried up to the guesthouse. We saw kids chasing along behind it, right in the grey cloud. The guesthouse staff told us that the kids take selfies in it.

Heather, Anthony and I went out for dinner at an Italian restaurant: mushroom pasta, pizza and ginger beer. Heather had a little rum in a bottle that someone had tacked onto their alcohol order, delivered from a neighbouring town. After dinner we went back to her hostel; she was staying in a dorm but outside there was a big green space and a tea stall. We carried on chatting for ages over mint tea. Heather and I had drunk some real coffee earlier which probably helped but it was an effortless evening, no awkward silences, just feeling totally understood; it felt like we were on the same frequency. Eventually we said goodnight and goodbye as Heather was leaving the next day.

We walked back through the town to our guesthouse, it was around one am. We walked right through one pack of barking dogs and then another and past one big dog on its own, whining and howling. We reminded ourselves, 'They are not interested in us, just each other.' We felt calm enough but even so it was weird to walk through so many dogs barking and growling. The dogs did that every night; although muffled we could hear it from our room.

We had got used to bumping into Heather most days at the falafels and we missed her after she had gone.

***

The guesthouse had a rooftop like in Varanasi with amazing views. In Pushkar the rooftop was a restaurant and decorated beautifully. Indian parasols and quirky lightshades hung down from the ceiling and the walls were draped with printed bedspreads and padded fabric rings in bright colours with gold thread. They looked like chunky bracelets but were actually, I found out much later, to put between the head and the basket when carrying things. There were wicker tables and chairs and day beds which doubled as beds for the kitchen staff. During the day heavy blinds were lowered to keep the sun out; it came in through gaps at the edges and was still too hot to hang around for long in the middle of the day. We'd go up and eat or have a drink at least once most days; Sprite in glass bottles, aloo jeera- delicious curried potatoes, dal and rice, mushroom, olive and tomato toasted sandwiches, homemade finger chips and banana pancakes. As in Varanasi, Bhang Lassis- a kind of weed milkshake were legal and available everywhere and it was fun being around stoned people lounging on the day beds and eating banana and Nutella pancakes one after the other.

Ganesh's joints were very strong, weed only no tobacco, he referred to them as AK47s. Once, referring to the owner who didn't smoke, Ganesh said, 'If he smokes one of these, he will see aliens.' The owner wasn't there all the time but most days he'd come up to the rooftop restaurant and talk to us for a bit. We had an open and surprisingly easy conversation about periods; him talking about cooking and explaining how in his house he cooks, as for five days the women don't do any cooking.

'You know, on period,' he said, in case I hadn't understood.

'Good idea,' I said, 'We should do that.' He said to me and Anthony, 'Yes you should do in UK in your home!'

One evening the owner cooked for all the guests, huge pots of food and round balls of bread called bati cooked outside in tin foil in a cow dung fire; all of us sitting on the floor in an open outdoor area just beyond the restaurant, eating with our fingers.

'My first time,' one of the young Western man guests said, his face glowing, 'I just did my best.'

The staff were not supposed to smoke marijuana openly at work. One day the owner appeared as he often did, quiet, like cat. I tried to distract him by asking what he'd got in his bag. He'd arrived carrying a bag of what looked like baby lemons. I described what I'd seen in Varanasi: a tiny lemon and what looked like green beans threaded on a string and hung from a doorway of a house, and asked him what it was for.

'How to explain...,' he said, 'Say someone jealous of you and Anthony's relationship...' 'Like evil eye,' I said, 'Yes!' he said, high-fiving me. In Kerala we had seen black masks with scary faces for sale in shops and hung outside properties. We had asked the man we bought lungis and bananas from what they were for. He paused for a second then said matter of factly, 'Someone break in, they break leg.'

The owner pointed out across the rooftops to a small peachy orange and white temple. He told us that his late father had built that temple. At the time his wife and children were not happy, especially his wife as it cost a lot of money. But the father went ahead and did it anyway. On his deathbed he called his son to him and said, 'You wanted to know why I built that temple, I shall tell you. When I die and you have the guesthouse, you are going to make a lot of money. You may be tempted to spend it on women, gambling... If you get tempted, you look out there and see the temple that your father built.'

The owner told us how to reach it and we went one evening. Along the way we passed several camels pulling carts full of tourists. I felt so sorry for the camels that I didn't want to look and turned away.
'Don't turn your back on them,' Anthony said, 'They need your support. You can give them some love; show them that you acknowledge their pain.' Sometimes I cut myself off from my feelings, other times they seem to rise to the surface; and maybe since getting into (almost) veganism and being in a meat free, almost vegan place, where it was so religious and so beautiful, all had the effect of making me feel more tender.

Up close the temple was much bigger than we'd expected, with arches and alcoves containing small shrines with Gods. The paint was slightly faded which had turned the colours to delicate pastels. It was almost completely dark by the time we got there and the crescent moon was beautifully framed by the outer arches.

The owner was in the process of having another area made, on one of the flat roofs outside. He explained that it would be just 'For relaxing,' he wanted somewhere other than the restaurant so that guests could sit without feeling that they had to order food. He was going to have books to read and was also working on clearing the grounds below to make nice view. Creating a relaxing space and relaxing itself was considered a decent aim. I'd often thought that I'd come to India at least partly to learn to relax. I knew how to work hard but I didn't know how to completely relax. The owner told us about a politician who he said had 'Done lots of good' including the creation of a big garden by the temple which was opening soon for all, Indians and Western tourists, 'For relaxing.'

Like in Chennai, we met ordinary people doing extraordinary things. A British man, fifty-two, who had spent fifteen years living and working in Japan, first as a DJ in a gentleman's club then teaching English to kindergarten kids and then working at a bar in Thailand with free meals and accommodation. When that ended he returned to the UK, initially working most of the year and travelling to Southeast Asia for a few months during the winter. Via careful budgeting he had now got it to six months in the UK working, six months travel. 'When I'm in the UK, I don't go out, I'm a hermit,' he said. This was the fifth UK winter that he had missed.

A mother and ten year old son from France travelling for a year; they had been to Malaysia, Indonesia and French Polynesia. After India they were going to Myanmar, Thailand and then either Cambodia, Laos or The Philippines.

'A year is so short!' the boy said. He said they'd met a family with kids aged four, seven and ten who were travelling around the world on a boat for six years. 'So much time!' he said. He did his studies happily on a tablet in the restaurant and proudly showed us his worksheets.

Pia, a thirty-four year old woman from Costa Rica had come to India to do a yoga and meditation course and was now sharing what she had learned, creating educational and inspirational videos on YouTube; she didn't know anything about making videos before. Up until recently Pia was married with a house, a business, two cars and all the trappings of what is thought of as a successful life but she wasn't happy. She separated from her husband, disbanded her business, sold the house and cars and went off to California to trim marijuana plants. 'But you have a doctorate!' her parents said,' 'Yes,' she said. 'But you may never get a visa again!' 'Yes,' she said and went anyway.

Pia met a man in California but continued with her plan to travel for a year and to travel around India alone; she wanted 'To know I can do anything' and 'To toughen up.' She said she could hear her biological clock ticking; she may go back to the marijuana farm and the man in California and have a baby with him and build an alternative life together. She had felt inspired by the many families in Pushkar, including babies and small children, some with parents who looked like they had been on the road a long time.

Me always 'on,' things to do with writing the book: noticing, writing things down, ideas pop in, memories; and 'spiritual journey' always 'on' too. It was tiring, the answer: Eat potatoes. Pia agreed. 'I'm obsessed with potatoes!' she said, ordering them at every meal. We discussed an image I'd seen on the internet: 'What people think a spiritual awakening is like:' a serene looking woman sitting cross legged in a meadow versus 'What it's actually like:' a woman in bed at night, sweating, saying to herself, 'I'm not crazy, I'm not crazy.'

Angela, thirty-three years old and from Portugal, she was dancing to mantras in the rooftop restaurant when we met her. An organic farmer, she showed us beautiful photographs of avocados, glossy purple aubergines and figs, of which she grows thirty varieties. Together with other environmentally minded people she successfully persuaded the local authority to vote to protect her local environment, not working along political lines, just to 'Protect nature.' It was her fifth time in India. Angela travelled alone; she made sure to arrive at good times i.e. not the middle of the night or the early hours. She comes to India for the spiritual and healing aspects and comes as often as she can when her business is quiet. 'When the trees are asleep, I run back,' she said. Angela couldn't leave us to get her bus; she kept showing us photographs and talking about all the different varieties of figs.

Nora had been brought up in an artist's commune and produces Human Postcards, sixty second snapshots of people with interesting stories. She had done a TED talk and encouraged me to promote myself. 'I prefer to stay in the background, typing,' I said. 'But one day the time will come when you will have to step forward,' her partner said.

It was great to meet all these people living a life outside of the ordinary. It soothed our anxieties; suddenly what we'd done didn't seem that strange after all.

We met lots of solo women travellers, and despite the horror stories, no one had said they had a bad experience. Morag, a young woman from New Zealand said, 'In my experience Indian people only want to check I'm okay.'

Ganesh told us he was going to Brazil to be a Baba for the summer, courtesy of some previous guests. 'I will tell them I do this (work at the guesthouse), that I am not a full time Baba.' One of the women said, 'Ooh, Brazil, you'll see women wearing just thongs and bras!' Ganesh said calmly, 'It's okay, I've been to Goa; I've seen Western women having a bad trip, running around and taking all their clothes off.'

We met Greg from Poland, fifty something, travelling by motorbike with his partner. We talked about poverty, guilt, people begging.
'I had this moment where I felt like, if I accepted this, I was in danger of totally understanding India.' He described watching a man with no legs or arms rolling down the street. People gave him money and treated him okay, seemingly not phased, whereas Westerners would be squeamish.

Anthony had noticed this time that there were fewer people with disabilities and fewer people begging generally in Main Bazaar. I looked up why. Apparently, to clean the city up for tourists, begging had been made an offence and people doing it were moved out of the city centre to beggars' homes where they were forced to live in unsanitary conditions with filthy water. So Westerners with bleeding hearts agonising about poverty had actually had a negative effect.

Westerners are targeted for money and assumed to be rich. Greg said he did not like to be overcharged and bargained hard, which was usually expected but sometimes he got it wrong and felt badly about it. He said once he bargained hard for a pair of trainers and walked away; the man came running after him and agreed to his price. Initially Greg felt pleased that he had 'won.' Later he realised that the man had been absolutely desperate, that's why he had agreed to the price.

He told another story about how one day having got totally fed up with being targeted to buy stuff, he had gone off walking into a forest. In the middle of the forest was nothing but a cottage and a woman standing by the garden gate. She was selling chocolate and asked if he wanted to buy some. Automatically he said no and carried on walking, irritated about being asked to buy something even out there in the woods. Later, that night he regretted it. 'Her face came back to me. It was desperate. Why did I say no? She was just selling chocolate!' he said.

At the juice bar we met an Austrian man in India for the winter with his partner and children aged two and four. He said they've been good with the food- although they can spot French fries and Fanta on the menus- and their guesthouse has a big outdoor space where they can play. Next they were going to Goa for the rest of the winter where they have friends; he said there is even a kindergarten for the Western kids.

'It's great because here I have time for them, at home I'd be at work, but here, there's nothing to do,' he said.

'I know,' I said, 'The only thing to think about is, 'Do I need to do my laundry or do I need some more shampoo?'' I said.

'Yes, go to the Himalaya shop, that's it,' he said and we both laughed.

Drinking ginger lemon tea one evening at the tea stall we met a man from Spain, forty-four, who had spent the past year cycling from Spain to India on a tall bike- the height of two bicycles put on top of each other. To stop or get off he has to have space around him to tilt the bike and let it fall over to one side; he described cycling through Delhi, coming up to traffic lights, having clear space and then an auto coming up at the side. It sounded terrifying; I asked him why he did it. 'To make people smile,' he said. People everywhere take photos and ask for selfies.

He camps, which he tries to do after dark as he attracts so much attention and interest from the locals- albeit all positive. Arriving tired and wanting to wash and rest he often has curious visitors descend on him, he tells them to go away and come back in forty five minutes, while he showers, eats and rests after cycling all day. They don't go, they just wait. One lot come, they tell their friends, another lot come, then another. He showed us a photograph of a big group of local people who had come to his camp to meet him, to see how he cooks and to ask questions about his bike and his trip. They say they'll come back at seven am, he says to them that's too early, come back at eight am; they don't, they come at seven am on their scooters and wake him up. But on opening the tent to see lots of little faces peering at him he said it was impossible to be annoyed.

I wondered at the time if he realised how lucky he was being able to do this. Being a man, that a woman would not have been able to do this, or not as safely. Or was I wrong? Would they have been just fine?

We got close to Jonathan from Israel, an artist.

'Sometimes I think, what am I doing, staying inside in a studio making art, should I be out there, contributing instead?' Within days of arriving Jonathan had made many friends and connections and become known for his art, with many people requesting him to do portraits of them. We'd ask what he was up to, he'd say, so and so has asked if I can do a picture, and someone else. 'If I can fit it all in, I'm supposed to be leaving soon,' he said. He could have stayed there full time and done portraits. One day he went off to buy a man a goat, a poor person he had met who sold homemade instruments in the street. 'A goat would change his life,' Jonathan said.

We spoke a bit about family, and relationships. 'There's something strange about adults getting involved in other fully grown adults' lives,' he said. He was single, 'I came to believe that to find The One, I would need to travel.'

Jonathan got invited to an evening of music and chanting at a small Shiva temple near one of the main ghats. He took us along, outside we met up with the friend who had invited him. We were typical Westerners, 'Doesn't it start at nine?' 'Shouldn't we go in?' 'Smoke first,' the friend said, 'Then go in.'

Outside at the bottom of the steps were all the shoes, then up a few steps and into a small room with heavy Indian blankets on the floor. There were young and middle aged men smartly dressed who looked like businessmen, an older, poorer looking man in traditional dress, a Baba who was quite old and several other Westerners both men and women. We found a space and sat on the floor. I was squashed up by a backpack and people's knees. Just as I had settled in and accepted my slightly cramped position, a man rolled out another carpet, people shifted and the older man beckoned me to go and sit in a new, bigger space where I could get comfortable.

Behind the musicians was a small alcove with a shrine. The God's clothes sparkled in the candle light. There was the smell of incense. The music was like meditation; music and mantra chanting, chanting Shiva's name over and over. Another musician arrived and simply sat down and seamlessly joined in. The old Baba began preparing a small clay chillum on a tray, he was sitting just in front of me to my left; his slow careful preparations were mesmerising. The chillum was passed around and then small paper pots of chai. We left in the break but the musicians carried on all through the night until four am. They did this once every two weeks.

On the day of Diwali we went to see Aloo Baba (Potato Baba) with Jonathan. Aloo Baba had eaten only potatoes for the past thirty five years. 'Aloo Baba is okay but he smokes too much marijuana,' Ganesh said. 'Well if *you* say that,' we said to ourselves. 'He is a tourist Baba.' Ganesh said some Babas are tourist Babas, some are for Indian people. Ganesh arranged an auto and advised us to take him the makings for chai: packets of milk and spices and sent one of the staff out to shop for us. 'Everybody takes him potatoes and marijuana,' Ganesh said. Although we couldn't resist taking potatoes as well! It was a very bumpy journey along the desert roads in an auto. We passed women and children on the road herding goats and breaking twiggy branches, collecting firewood and carrying it on their heads.

Aloo Baba was sitting outside, near a white ashram. He was very friendly and welcoming with good English; people from all over the world came to see him. He had left Varanasi a long time ago and travelled for years before coming to Pushkar, where he said all religion started. He said he had been there for many years, from when there was nothing there and had built the ashram and planted a lot of trees. Unlike Ganesh and the staff at the guesthouse, Aloo Baba preferred the red faced monkeys as he said the black faced monkeys jumped around in the trees too much and broke the branches.

A younger man made chai. There was also an older man there, Aloo Baba said he was from the village and comes to the ashram during the day for peace.

'He is old, he has big family. Too much talk. Talk talk, problems. He comes here morning, go home evening.'

Aloo Baba was in his seventies and looked fit and well; he said he still walks up the nearby mountain to keep fit. 'The body needs work,' he told us, 'Hard work is good for it. Not this (miming hunched up over) computers.' He spoke about control. 'Control eating.' Hence only eating potatoes, which he cooks with salt and a little chilli. 'Control words. Control looking. Every woman my mother, my sister.'

'No good no bad,' he said. 'No one person all good, no one person all bad.' He told us he had a sister somewhere but he hadn't see her for a long time. 'No family,' he said. 'Only God. Family life or God life, can't have both.'

Aloo Baba sat peacefully outside. He feeds the birds. He looks after the trees he has planted. He meditates. 'Every day Diwali,' he said, when we wished him Happy Diwali.

On the way home we passed a group of young men and scooters on both sides of the road, wearing bandanas and with axes or machetes in their hands. We were in the middle of nowhere, just us three and our auto driver. Is this how it ends, I wondered. It seemed totally surreal. No one else seemed at all concerned though and we drove past and through them no problem; they were only cutting firewood or something.

It was an honour to experience Diwali in India and especially in Pushkar. We had bought sweets for the staff at the guesthouse, admiring the layers upon layers of sweets like terraces in the shops, so that the men in the shop had to climb around to get to them. We went out for dinner with Jonathan and heard the fireworks going off all around. Kids threw bangers down onto the street that made our ears ring.

The poojas go on indoors, in homes and businesses so there aren't things outdoors to join in with but the restaurant owner who was explaining all this said that the priest was coming soon and we could join their blessing for the business. We joined two Western women, the father, the son who ran the restaurant and a younger boy who was trying in vain to control a tied up Dalmatian dog who wanted to say hello to everyone. Prayers were said into the fire and then the priest tied thread around our wrists making a bracelet, as he did so he said, 'Good life, good business, good health, good marriage.'

We went back to the guesthouse, hastily past the boys with their bangers. The street near the guesthouse was covered in the litter of fireworks and there was smoke everywhere. We went up to the rooftop and listened to the fireworks. Everyone smoked marijuana and I had some beers; although Pushkar is a holy city and officially has no alcohol, unofficially it was possible to get. Later lying in bed, the fireworks nearby actually shook the room a little.

Ganesh did not like fireworks, or kites because the strings injured birds. He would go and clear up the discarded string he was able to reach but not all was possible to get. He never had fireworks as a child as his family were too poor so he used to help if the firework had not gone off and once a big one hit him in the head. Also the fireworks scared the pigeons; several lived down the alley near the guesthouse, and the monkeys. Ganesh said all the monkeys went off into the mountains during Diwali.

On doorsteps all around the town were little people made out of cow dung. In the days after Diwali some got messed up by dogs, cows and scooters and some remained intact. Ganesh told us that after the camel fair the children take them out into the desert and make little houses for them out of grass and put a candle inside, 'To say thank you for the festival, and see you next year.'

The morning after Diwali, the streets were all cleaned up. That such a big party could happen and then be tidied up so fast was yet another thing I admired about India. We sat outside a cafe and watched people all greeting each other and giving money in the street. When we'd finished our breakfast and the man was adding up our bill, he had to break off from his task to shoo a cow away, another wonderful 'Only in India' moment. At the guesthouse the party atmosphere continued, Ganesh and the staff had a bottle of whiskey open, they gave me some, 'Because, Rachel, you don't smoke joint, you don't drink Bhang Lassis.'

The waiters at the guesthouse tried to teach us Hindi, 'Everyday you learn a new word,' they said. They would test us when they saw us on the stairs or back at the restaurant. Hi, how are you, okay, fine. The owner, a Brahmin, the highest caste, corrected our responses; what we were saying was not correct for us, too casual, we should say xxx instead. Obviously we'd learned the casual version with waiters, which we were fine with. It felt like he undermined them by saying that in front of them. 'We don't observe the caste system,' was something I used to say in private to Anthony. Meaning, I don't observe the caste system myself. We just talked to whoever talked to us.

As soon as you trust yourself you'll know how to live: Pushkar, India

I wrote at the table and chairs on the outdoor courtyard near our room. There was a low wall next to me, beyond which was a view of the street and some of the rooftops. The brick wall had a design of square gaps in it, making an ordinary thing pretty. I began writing the Tokyo chapter: *Not all those who wander are lost.* Later the same day the man in the cafe where we ate lunch was wearing a blue t-shirt with *Not all who wander are lost* printed on it. It wasn't as if this was a common t-shirt either; I never saw a t-shirt with that on again in India.

One of the few times I felt really stuck was in Pushkar, on Tokyo, the words dancing around, I couldn't make head or tail of what to do. 'I can't do it,' I said, childishly. But I just needed a break. I needed to sharpen my axe. If I'm okay, I can write. But writing is part of what makes me okay. It is to be respected and managed, a balance of feelings and instinct and head and discipline, like food.

One of the psychologists at my old work, Rebecca, told me this lovely story: When she was in the middle of doing her PhD she had got herself exhausted and super stressed and was taking it out on the house, frantically cleaning and about to set about vacuuming. Her boyfriend, concerned, tried to get her to stop and have a rest. At first she refused, but then he wrapped his arms around her, walked her to the sofa, got her to sit down, put a blanket over her and said, 'I'm going to tell you a story:

Once upon a time there were two woodcutters. One chopped wood all day without a break, and even though he began to tire and his axe got blunt and he was hungry and thirsty, he did not stop chopping wood until night fell. The other wood cutter chopped until it was lunchtime and then stopped to eat a lunch of bread and cheese and took time to sharpen his axe and to rest his tired muscles. After his lunch he returned to his work until night fell. Which woodcutter do you think ended up chopping the biggest pile of wood? Rebecca,' her boyfriend said, 'You need to sharpen your axe.'

Thinking about writing and spelling and what gets repeated and what is important and what gets noticed. Thinking, Slow down, stop, just write, slowly and deliberately rather than this scramble-to-catch-everything. Realising about rooves and roofs 'Pronounced like rooves but it's antiquated to write it like that.' Wow, since when?! I just thought everyone else was doing it wrong! Like déjà vu or the Mandela effect or like when they change the pronunciation of Boadicea or of Diplodocus. I mean the dinosaurs weren't actually called those names anyway let alone had a correct pronunciation.

At the 'Not all who wander are lost' t-shirt cafe we ate puri sabji; a local curry, a rich red colour made with peas and other vegetables and served with puri- puffy fried bread which was deliciously chewy. The cafe also served real Italian strong black coffee and homemade brown bread toast with peanut butter. A portion was four slices, we accidentally ordered a set each and couldn't eat it all. I wrapped some up to take home for later but on the way home I gave it to the cows at the rubbish dump near the guesthouse. The rubbish dump was cleared every few days, in the meantime cows and even a pig and piglets ate from it. I often saw cows in Pushkar chewing and eating cardboard. One day I saw a cow eat an entire plastic bag; I was too afraid to intervene as it had very big horns.

Pushkar was so good for shopping, with a huge variety of beautiful things to buy and lots of courier services; it was buzzing with people buying stuff to send home for themselves, as presents or to sell. We met a Dutch woman buying to sell for the first time.

'Money is energy,' she said. We saw her again later, with more stuff to send, 'I can't stop buying stuff!' she said. We got to know Shiva who we bought a lot of things from and who sent them home for us. We often sat and drank chai and chatted with him. He said,

'Westerners going about like Indians, with their dress, meditation and yoga, and Indians dressing in jeans and forgetting about yoga and meditation.' It was like Osho said, what was needed was a merge of East and West. Shiva did meditation each morning, 'Up at 5.30am, and sit.' On business he said, 'Business always good; feel good, business good, money come, money go.'

After breakfast one day Anthony went to see Shiva about shopping, I went home to write. On the way I passed a man, disabled and on crutches, I put some money in the bucket he was holding out and went to go off sheepishly as usual. He took my hand and shook it so firmly, while looking me straight in the eye. His eyes, his face... It was embarrassing to be thanked so thoroughly for so little, enough for a cup of tea; British awkwardness. My hand still felt his hand when I opened the door at home.

I didn't go out alone that much. When I did, I enjoyed it, but I didn't often really feel like it. Pros: I could sit and stare and really take it all in whereas Anthony would get restless, also I orientated myself better when I was alone and having to concentrate on where I was and directions. Cons: hassle, me on my own got the most hassle, me with Anthony less, him alone, least; the assumption being that women like shopping, also I always felt safe and unselfconscious when I was with him.

So I took alone moments when I could, in the small outside area beyond the back of the restaurant, not in shade, where I could look out across the rooftops in peace and quiet. I watched a man on another rooftop; he came out from under a white stone structure like a pagoda onto the flat roof and filled bowls of water for the monkeys that went across the rooftops. Likewise from the other way, towards the entrance, you could sit on a low wall and watch the sun go down.

**

Babas lived out in the open by the lake with bedrolls, blankets, fire pits and cooking pots. One had lots of plastic pink Ganeshes all around the base of a Banyan tree. The Babas often called out as we walked past, 'Chai,' 'Coffee,' inviting us to sit with them.

We drank coffee with one Baba who lived near the tree where the monkeys hung out. He was wiry with a twisted posture, his head to one side, with long clumpy black dreadlocked hair, his face and body covered in ash. He sat on a concrete plinth with a few blankets, some framed pictures decorating the wall behind. He heated water on his fire and gave me coffee in a glass cup.

He was very friendly but he couldn't speak English and we couldn't speak his language. A man who happened to be there acted as an interpreter. He said he was called Naga Baba, he went to live with a Baba when he was a child. The man explained that sometimes families give their child to a Baba in thanks for help they have received.

Naga Baba can lift great weights with his penis.

'All real Babas have a talent,' the man said. 'They have to have a special talent or they are not a real Baba or if they are drinking, they are not real.' He said of the Naga Baba lifting great weights with the penis, 'If you meditate for fifteen years, you become very strong.' Naga Baba showed Anthony a video, whether of him or another Baba doing this I wasn't sure but I looked away and focussed hard on drinking my coffee.

The friend told us that his big brother has a factory business but that he himself was a stoner guy and they argue if he stays in Pushkar; so he goes to Goa to sell stuff for his brother. He said he was addicted to smoking marijuana and to chai. He reminded me of people from home who have a similar lifestyle, no work and wander around on the streets or in the pub or smoking indoors, only he had somewhere really exotic to spend his day.

The other Baba who invited us to sit with him was called Ram Dass. We spent more time with him as he spoke very good English. He had lived beside the lake for ten years. He was based under a Banyan tree which was decorated with colourful material with framed pictures set up underneath. His home was his temple. There was a place to take off and leave your shoes, shelves with cooking pots on and blankets on the ground to sit on.

Ram Dass made us chai, he even had a stack of little disposable paper chai cups. The pots and pans were kept very clean, as cooking on the fire is considered a spiritual practice. He explained that it was a holy fire which never goes out. He said that the fire 'Cleans the air. Too much bikes, fireworks, trains, cars, planes. Sky getting dirty.' Ram Dass told us that the fire contains the whole universe. He meditates every morning from three to six am, meditating on 'All the world and all the people. That is my work,' he said.

As a child Ram Dass was taken in by a temple when his parents died. 'No family,' he said. Ram Dass explained that real Babas have been with Babas since they were a child. Although he spoke good English, Ram Dass had never been to school and could not read or write. That is how to tell a real Baba, he told us.

There was another Baba with him, we saw him carrying firewood and fetching water, sometimes he made the chai. 'Not a real Baba,' Ram Dass said. He told us that sometimes men go a bit crazy when their wives die and they go to live with a Baba. They look like Babas but they have been to school and can read and write; they have had a previous life. The assistant Baba couldn't speak any English though not like Ram Dass.

Babas travel everywhere free, 'Train free, bus free, food free.' Some Babas travel all over India continually, although they don't have passports so they can't travel outside of India. Ram Dass received donations of money, or food, ghee or milk, or blankets. He told us that a French couple had been coming every year for fifteen years, they bought the pots and pans. Ram Dass teaches meditation and yoga, one man who was very grateful for yoga bought him plane tickets.

One day when we visited Ram Dass he was just back from getting his laundry done; he explained this was not allowed to be done in the lake. He was wearing a new looking hoodie on top of his orange Baba robes. It was kind of heart warming to know he did some of the ordinary things that we did. A couple of times we saw him in the market carrying a bag of groceries; standing up he was tiny, much smaller than me, even.

Passers-by, tourists both Indian and Western sometimes took photographs without asking or tried to do it sneakily when Ram Dass said no. Ram Dass pulled the skin under one of his eyes down and looked at them as if to say, 'I see you.'

'I can't read, but I know people,' he said. We were annoyed; people didn't ask, didn't offer money and were disrespectful, treating him and his home like a tourist attraction but he let it go.

Ram Dass built a second fire pit while we were there, out of clay; a square built onto the stone of the ghats with smooth rounded walls, perfectly and beautifully made. I saw it when it was freshly done, still wet and drying out. He was preparing to move into a small tunnel under the bridge, like a cave where he would spend the nights during the winter. In the hottest months of the summer he goes to stay with other Babas in the Himalayas, as Pushkar got, 'Too hot, dangerous,' he said. We swapped phone numbers. Ram Dass had his numbers carefully written out on paper and a simple old scratched phone, 'No music, no crazy,' he said about his phone.

We talked to Ganesh about Babas. He told me about a Baba who works with Indian people to get djinns out of them. This Baba starts work very early in the morning and people queue up and wait to see him. Ganesh told us that he, 'Works really hard,' that he meditates for eight hours a day, 'To get the new information to deal with new things.' Ganesh explained that Naga Babas was the name for the type of Babas who lift weights with the penis; I had thought it was that Baba's name. Standing Babas, I'd read about them in Shantaram, they never ever sit down, their legs becoming swollen and distorted. Also Ganesh told us about Bone-Eating Babas who eat the marrow out of the bones that are left after the fires. 'I've seen them, in Varanasi,' Ganesh said. Ganesh told me that during the Kumba Mela festival in Varanasi there are women Babas, including Westerners. 'As white as you,' he said. I was amazed. 'Are they accepted?' I asked. 'Do they sleep outside?' 'Are they safe?' 'Yes,' 'Yes,' 'Yes,' he said.

As our month in Pushkar came near to ending, many more Babas and other people began arriving, some setting up homes under a Banyan tree, some sleeping all together out in the open in a small square opposite Naga Baba. Ram Dass told us there was a five day festival starting soon, where all the Gods come down to bathe in the lake and people come to Pushkar to bathe in it too. I did see a female Baba in Pushkar, one of the 'new' Babas we had seen arriving for the festival.

Anthony and I spoke a lot about the Babas. They have opted out and let go of fear. Fear about money, fear about health, old age, and death. Money is a way of control, if it is made the most important thing, it can control people. Those in power can control the economy to punish or scare people or just to create distraction; the hooks of news stories about 'the economy,' fear about jobs. Money works to control and distract via the desire for goods (which can never be satisfied), the desire for security (which is fake anyway), and via fear of not having money and/or not having security. Is it possible to refuse to believe in it, refuse to participate, and to place ones faith in something else?

Babas let go of attachment to good/bad, happy/sad, well/ill. What if I'm old or ill with no one to look after me? Answer- someone will look after you, or you die. People will bring food, or they won't and I will die. Health problem? Benefactors will help, or they won't and I will die. But we all die. The craving for security, the fear of ill health, the fear of old age, all comes down to fear of death. Get rid of that, get rid of all fear. We will all die so why be scared of death or of anything else? Get rid of fear= total freedom.

Returning to the guesthouse after Aloo Baba and before our Diwali evening out, Jonathan went to his room to read, Anthony went into our room to relax. I, from immediately we got back until it was time to go out again went out to the table to write. I worked hard and I finished Tokyo *Not all those who wander are lost,* and I paused and acknowledged my achievement.

A day or two before, after sex I had this insight looking in the mirror, not at myself, just at the mirror on the wall opposite the bed. The mirror was brown, a funny shape, a kind of oval or curved oblong. A few items on its shelf, a few clothes reflected in the mirror. Nothing interesting about it, even for me.

Wondering, Will I know? If this is a simulation? What this is? Then thinking: You don't get given the meaning until you detach yourself from everything here: looks, ego, news, self, possessions, family and friends, even.

I remembered having that insight before from being stoned, but I always forgot it. *You have to let go, detach from everything and everyone, first. Then you find out.*

So this feeling distant, going through the motions with family, that is correct. Sex, food.... and then the next day or the day after, we go to see Aloo Baba: *'God life or family life, you can't have both.'* Can you do it, can you do it fully and live in the world? I had already thought of letting go of appearance- I'm older, let go of it, not my time.

Interestingly, this came to me after a day of being quite sociable with Anthony and Jonathan, not much quiet time. My quiet time e.g. in Tokyo doesn't always benefit me that much.

I've always liked this line from the book *Wetlands* by Charlotte Roche: *'To stay with someone even though you no longer love them.'* It's in the context of a young woman upset by her parent's divorce when she was a child. *'Falling out of love is not a good enough reason to divorce, when you have children,'* she says. *'If you really want to promise something worthwhile, try this: I will stand by you even if I no longer love you. Now that's a promise. That really means forever.'*

Why had I remembered this for so long? I was worried; I took it at face value. I knew I loved my husband, and I also knew I'm not the kind of person to stay without love; I can barely put up with a few hours of friction and discord, so it wasn't a literal message for me. As a writer I take words much too literally sometimes and miss the metaphors, which I so easily see in the rest of life.

But it's this, it's can I be in the world, while being absolutely detached? Stay in the world and fake it, pass as here? Go through the motions with presents, socialising, while knowing you are far away? Our conditioning is so strong that you can't explain it, hence my guilt re detaching/'not loving' family. The film '*The Matrix*,' where people are plugged in and machines harvest their energy, is a metaphor. To 'unplug' is to let go of attachments. Attachments to people, ideas, things and pets. Attachments take your energy.

That's why we have divisive leaders, all the news stories. People even stop speaking to friends and family, 'the friends and family we no longer speak to,' on WordPress re two years of xxx, about what, a political view on the internet/news? What if they didn't watch the news?

The more I extricate myself, no newspapers, no Google feed, the better. There's the occasional temptation; the more I extricate myself the more tempting the news stories are. Like an extinction burst, as psychologists call it. Not getting involved or telling people what to do. Just live as light as possible and vegan as possible, live on the boat, simplify, maybe set an example and influence like that. Someone I used to work with feeling more able to give herself permission to extricate herself from a stressful job, status, money and career because I'd done it.

Anthony would go on his phone and read out news stories in the morning while I was getting ready and doing yoga. He'd often been awake for hours already; I sleep like a cat, so he'd already had his quiet time and was waiting to talk. I was coming to, wanting to do yoga in peace and wanting to observe a news blackout.

We have to share space and he hasn't got anyone else. He needs to talk when he needs to talk; it doesn't work to save it for over coffee after breakfast, my preferred time. He gets restless; I like peace and quiet. Many women complain their husbands don't talk to them. Still, it bothered me. Saying something caused conflict/bad mood, as it would the other way around; yet he never says anything to me, I can talk whenever about whatever for as long as I want.

'Waking up' or 'unplugging' doesn't mean going somewhere else. Even Neo in the film at the end is still there, he's just seeing the world in a different way/for what it is. That's enlightenment. Maybe it's not that it actually is a simulation; it's that the way you interact in it is simulated, not real, or programmed. So maybe it's the change in how you interact with it that's the key rather than the thing itself changing.

I had a dream I was shouting in the street 'It's a matrix, it's an illusion!' and wondering, Will I be arrested/put in a mental hospital, but also, when I shouted at it, it froze. Then thinking, Just think it- no need to shout out loud, but feel it in yourself as strongly as if you were shouting. It freezes/falls away.

Let go/unplug from everything, then all that's left to do is enjoy eating, sex, until exit... But that's a form of attachment, or at least entanglement, and it's back to the beginning again...

Like the time I thought I was dead but carrying on in a simulated universe with everything and everyone seeming the same, while in the real one you are dead. You go through the motions, but these people are not actually the real ones, they are just kind of there as a comfort to you. On accidentally purchased fake MDMA we went out for a drive, later I thought we'd died in a car crash, I remembered a moment of seeing some lights, I wondered if it was then. I imagined being above our mangled bodies with a choice: come back and face pain and a long journey of rehabilitation or let myself drift easily away. My son was about to start Art School, I imagined everyone wrapping their collective arms around him, my friends supporting him, his peers and the university supporting him, him having an interesting back story he could use. We are dead, we don't need to eat but we do because it and all the associated things that go with that- cooking, cleaning up, doing the dishes, going to the toilet, going to the supermarket, getting the money to buy the food via working, getting the work, all the associated things around that, years of schooling, dress codes, policies, attitude, alarm clocks; all that, gives you something to do. It's something to do, we do it to pass the time.

It's something to do and it enables, risks, allows for you to be plugged in but as Pema Chodron says all those things also allow for you to use them to wake yourself up. It's not about running away e.g. Anthony reading the morning news and me doing yoga and getting annoyed or trying to ignore it. Or ignoring family, or distancing myself from the whole world or only breathing no eating. Aloo Baba controlling eating by only eating potatoes is a good example of using something every day to wake yourself up.

Meditating helped me be calm, and I thought, We do it to help us with the day to day; to help us to be calm, to help us to be aware, and to help us to be in control, like Aloo Baba said.

***

In the masala dosa restaurant, Anthony saw two older hardcore hippies looking disdainfully at two younger hippy-ish travellers, apparently judging them. Sometimes we are underestimated because we don't dress up alternative or people don't realise what we're into. We talked about our dear friend DW, one of the coolest people we know but who outwardly looks perfectly ordinary. But if you underestimate him, more fool you. He doesn't care. He is not interested in so-called cool people identifying him.

'Style is saying who you are without words.' It's a tempting idea, but it doesn't work for me. As Anthony said, 'Saying who you are without words,' usually means just emphasising the cool aspects. So I'd emphasise the writing, go about all in black with a sleek laptop and a cool black Moleskine notebook? Or, on a sexy pretty day, do my hair and put on makeup and something nice? Or emphasise the yoga, the meditation and the spirituality? Why not emphasise my anxiety or my OCD? Show it all. Or none of it. Be plain, and more fool people if they write you off based on that.

Thinking about the boat, the future and reminding myself to live in the now and that we aren't trying to get anywhere. Everything is as it should be. We are us, we are realised, whether we are in Pushkar or Northamptonshire. Whatever we are doing, writing, washing up, trips, it's all the same, no difference to the core of us. Nothing wrong with where we are, what we are doing or who we are now, so don't imply it by looking forward to an imaginary future. After all, what could be better than now?

Towards the end there were so many in tune times; when I looked at clock and it said 04:04, that kind of thing. We went to somewhere different, a rooftop restaurant hang out decorated in Rastafarian colours with murals and quotes handwritten on the walls. Opposite where we were sitting there was a Goethe quote: *'As soon as you trust yourself, you'll know how to live.'*

Ganesh said that on the television news everything awful is reported, all the hideous crimes from all over India. He said that he watches it all, to know that there is bad. 'I know there is everything,' he said.

I read a blog post by Adie about therapy, about 'The places;' the place where everything is bad and nothing is good. The place where everything is good, 'Unicorns farting rainbows;' people who get into spirituality can get stuck there. The functional place is the 'And And place,' not All Good, not All Bad.

We watched Big Mouth, a sad episode about the effect of separation on children. We had a discussion about commitment to children versus adult selfishness. Although Anthony was talking about people more generally or about him, it got me thinking about how I could have just stayed, but I didn't think that way then. My mood plummeted. Thinking about how my son had an unhappy life- or partly- without a dad. His dad has three more children now and has lost touch. Round and round and round to: Face the reality. Forgive yourself.

In Tokyo I had sent healing out, having not done it for a while, a friend had asked me to send some, so did B. I sent some to my son, a blaze of gold; the next day he messaged me to say he was getting his teeth done. For ten years he has had teeth problems and refused to get help, and we have all watched as they got worse and worse and worse. Although of course our sadness is of nothing compared to his experience of having such serious problems and yet being afraid to go to the dentist. But it often felt like a kind of slow torture, there were times I felt suicidal; part self punishment for my failings, part because I couldn't bear to keep on watching, and of course you can't avoid someone's teeth when you see them.

After several false starts and cancellations, the treatment was done in one go one day while we were in Pushkar. He sent a video message from the recovery ward that evening. I sent one back saying to let us know when you are ready for a call, thinking it would be in a day or two. He messaged straight back, 'Now is fine.'

We went out onto the open air bit just beyond the restaurant, past where we had all eaten dinner sitting the floor, to the place I went sometimes for a quiet moment, where I'd watched the man under the white arch put water down for the monkeys. My son seemed fine although seeing him in the hospital wasn't nice. Out of view of the video call I clutched Anthony's hand as he told us the extent of what had been done.

It was a weird anticlimax; everything I'd been dreading all these years, everything I'd been hoping for, and afterwards just a kind of stillness. We stayed up until two in the morning with me talking, trying to explain how I felt and to process it. On one hand and really, the only thing that matters, is that he got the treatment, it is all done and completed and now he is healthy. But on the other hand I wished none of it had ever happened or had to happen. I wished that we could go back in time and do whatever it was that could have been done, to go back to a place before the damage was so bad. I was sad for a past that couldn't be returned to or altered. Round and round, to, *The past is the past. It's all okay. Forgive yourself.*

***

Suddenly it got cold in the evenings sitting up in the rooftop restaurant. Our bathroom was like an oven so we left the bathroom door open while we went up for dinner to heat the room up. We went shopping and bumped into lots of other travellers also suddenly buying warm clothes, all of us laughing about being caught unawares.

For a couple of nights our neighbours were a young Indian couple, they played music loud at night.

'They do that thing that young people do, not playing a whole song,' Anthony said, which makes it more annoying. Ganesh told them to be quieter, he said to us, 'I told them, the British, they like to go to sleep at 9.30!'

At the same time Des on WordPress wrote a post about how his twenty-five year old daughter had phoned up to tell him that she listened to a whole Beatles album- *Abbey Road* all the way through; that she understood the context and its location in time from listening to the whole album rather than single songs. Des wrote that it was unusual for a young person to listen to a whole album, and that individual songs apparently have only a 48% chance of being listened to all the way through!

The evening after reading Des's blog we went to a nice restaurant for what felt like a date night; we sat in a very green garden which was decorated with lights. Unusually they had alcohol and eggs openly on the menu. I had mojitos and a whole pizza all to myself. They played REM- *Automatic for the people,* the whole album all the way through. It has the track *Everybody Hurts,* which was a real-life call-back to our week sick and tired in Delhi before coming to Pushkar. Then they played The Beatles *Help* all the way through too.

On our last day we bought sweets and took group photographs with all the staff. We were so well cared for there, the staff were so warm and kind; the delicious food, the monkey feeding, the Hindi lessons. While we waited in the garden for our taxi the cooks and waiters swapped Facebook contacts with Anthony.

We left early so we could go and see the Jain temple at Ajmer, a huge model, made up of many smaller models, multiple scenes and many worlds which filled a huge room. Everything in the room was gold and overwhelmingly richly detailed; people and houses and chariots on the ground and in the air, worlds and other worlds built upon circles and according to the explanations on the wall, our own universe was just a small part of the whole scene.

So many ways to dance upon this earth: Nepal

Having got sick both times we'd stayed in Main Bazaar, we booked a hotel near the airport for the one night and one day between Pushkar and Nepal. Our plan was to eat room service and spend most of the time in the hotel room. This time the Delhi air quality was 'unhealthy' rather than 'hazardous' as it had been last time.

Two young men gave us advice about a better Delhi station to get off at which was closer to our stop and even looked for us to check that we were okay.

'You are guests in our country,' they said. Our taxi driver dropped us at the wrong hotel, but seeing us with our bags, people came to give us help and directions, people actually ran after us to offer help.

We were on the fourth floor, I used the stairs for a bit of exercise. There were unusual wall designs in brown tiles and shiny brown wallpaper, on one side a mosaic design, on the other side giant pebbles, elsewhere there were even giant buttons. There was a round window in the wall, I looked through to outside. The wall of the building opposite had a hole in, like where a fitting had been removed, making a messy circle. Inside the hole were a pair of pigeons huddled up together. On the roof of another building a bird was drinking from a terracotta saucer of water that someone had put out.

I went out for a little walk. I was nervous about getting lost, but on my own I really looked: an OYO sign, a hotel sign at the end of our road. A tiny shop, a crossroads, side streets, barbers, two juice stalls, more tiny shops and street stalls. The road was broken and bits of it were flooded a little. A man went past wearing a t-shirt I only caught half the words of.

At the crossroads there was a momo stall, 15 rupees for half, 30 rupees for full. There was a room behind the street stall where people lived. Above the shop and across the road was a perfect bird's nest of wires. A sign saying Health and Hygiene Institute. A block of faded flats. A little girl stood on a balcony holding a red balloon.

On my way out I'd made a point of saying Namaste and Good Morning (even though it was the afternoon) to the man at the hotel door. I got back to the hotel but then decided not to go straight in but to go on past it a little way. There came a man and a dog which I thought was on a lead, but then I felt its wet nose in my palm. It was quite a big dog, with a collar but not on a lead and not with the man. The dog started being super friendly and started to hump my leg; I tried to shoo it but didn't want to be too forceful in case I made it angry. I was on my period; the dog's attention was embarrassing. I quickly walked back to the hotel and asked the doorman for help, he opened the door and shooed the dog away.

'Friend,' he said.

'Too friendly,' I said. It was like I should have gone in straight away, quit while I was ahead, but it turned out okay.

The area was made up of faded buildings interspersed with hotels. 'Our least India view,' Anthony said, it could have been any city. I fed the previous day's samosas we had bought at Ajmer train station to sweet little birds on the windowsill, poking the pieces through the bars.

I wanted, needed, to see the strange giant button design again. Sometimes I look at something but I don't stop long enough to feel I've soaked it in or made the most of it and then afterwards I regret it. Am I a pleasure denier, even for things as simple as that? But then I realised that the same wall covering design was actually right there, in a corner of our bathroom.

I told Anthony about the t-shirt I saw when I went out for a walk, then later I spent a while sitting on the floor, going through all my papers and notebooks, chucking out and decluttering in order to get the weight of my bag down, and what did I see? The very same phrase that I'd half seen on the t-shirt on my walk, 'Fortune favours the brave,' which I'd noted down from a billboard during a taxi ride from Kerala airport months ago. Can it be like this in future, just picking up the things of beauty as I go without on purpose seeking any more?

***

To people newly arrived from Germany and France, Kathmandu felt warm and they wandered around in t-shirts, bemused at the

Nepali people bundled up in their hats, fleeces and North Face quilted jackets. To us, newly arrived from India it felt very chilly. Our room had two single beds and thick heavy synthetic blankets. We settled in fast. 'It's good how we get used to a new room so quickly,' we said. The trip and travel there seemed so easy, like we were used to it more. There had even been a tiny Body Shop concession stand at Delhi airport just before the gates with handbag sized tubes of my favourite hand cream!

We went to get tea and a sandwich on the rooftop with the woman who owned the place. There was washing hung out, a child's play tent, a little boy, a little girl, a small baby and a cat! I think I'd even mentioned when imagining what it would be like that maybe there would be a cat there! In the evening the woman's husband cooked dinner in their kitchen and talked to us about politics. The food was good: veg curry and a dhal soup which was poured over the rice.

The room had its own loo and sink, the tap sprayed out a bit from the basin and the water was so cold it made our teeth ache. There was no loo seat so we had to sit on the cold porcelain toilet, and the bum gun water was very cold. No towels so we used our cotton lungis; the sensation of being cold and wet with the cotton lungis sticking to us was unpleasant.

Our room had a big plate glass window, the sun shone in during the middle of the day but it got cold as soon as the sun went down, and there was no heating. From the window we could see the roof top opposite and enviously watched women hanging out their washing in big fleeces and woolly hats. We didn't have enough warm clothes; fortunately warm clothes were cheap and plentiful.

Stores with tables out on the street piled high with plain fleeces, cheerful furry fleeces in bright colours, warm sweat pants, woolly hats and socks, thick fleecy trousers for babies and toddlers and the thick heavy synthetic blankets like we had at the guesthouse. I loved the fact that warm, practical clothes were everywhere and affordable. A Nepali man said to us, 'Cheap, yes, you can get a good jacket for £10.'

Outfits were a juxtaposition of styles and colours with an emphasis on keeping warm. Many of the women were dressed in sarees or Indian dresses and trousers with shawls, knitted cardigans, shiny padded anoraks or blankets on top, and sometimes they had thick fleece bottoms on too.

People wore snoods and scarves both in the street and inside restaurants and shops. Babies with their mums in shops were dressed in knitted hats with ears flaps. Toddlers wore cuddly fleece trousers, bright pink with bows, with Hello Kitty type designs. Small children were dressed in hoodies and ankle length wellies.

As well as the ubiquitous North Face padded jackets, men also wore suits or suit jackets. I saw an older man wearing a smart traditional hat, a dark grey pinstripe suit jacket, navy blue shiny tracksuit bottoms with piping, and trainers.

In a shop window I saw a Nero style jacket, silvery grey with red embroidery with tight leg trousers and a Nepalese hat. On mannequins in the windows of women's wear shops were velveteen hoodies and leggings, knitted trousers and thick leggings; a bright yellow long hoodie like a dress, long cardigans and jumper dresses, the shops full of winter coats and jumpers.

Young women wore smart jumpers and jeans. Young men wore trousers and smart jumpers, jeans and leather jackets or smart hoodies. A few women were dressed glamorously with makeup and red lipstick, but most people seemed focussed on just being warm.

I saw more women working and had more conversations with women than in India. I had a sign language conversation with a lovely woman who gave me pieces of orange, I admired her nose stud and we showed each other how many ear and nose piercings we had. She picked bits of fluff off my fleecy and told me in sign language how many children she had, nine. Nine! I said on my fingers, she stuck out her tongue cheekily. Our guesthouse was like a homestay, the woman who ran it hugged me, I loved the easy physical familiarity so un-British and which felt so warm.

It also seemed easier to socialise with Nepalese men who are famously respectful of women. I went out on my own to get a takeaway for us, while I was waiting I had a beer and chatted with a group of men who gave me cigarettes. We saw two women and two men playing a board game on the side of the street; we didn't see a mixed group playing outside like that in India.

Everywhere was cold. The front of the cafe where we had breakfast was open, plus the pollution came in from the road, we sat farthest in away from the door but it didn't make much difference. A young woman served us wearing a bright pink warm fleecy coat. In a lean-to extension outside a chef cooked the thinnest nan bread, light and crispy which we ate with sabji, a vegetable curry.

At another restaurant we ordered tea and a Nepali food plate, the food was all cold: black eyed beans, dry beaten rice like rice flakes, potato cubes with chilli, a slimy fermented dish with olive oil, onion and garlic, and vegetable spring rolls, the only hot dish. On the table they had reusable plastic water bottles, the expectation was that you pour it into your mouth without touching it with your lips, which we couldn't do. The door was open, there was no heating and the other customers, all Nepalese people, were wearing coats indoors. Through the open back door we could see the blue sky and, very excitingly for us, several eagles flying about.

There were lots of jewellery shops, lots of gold, and one shop had a man in a smart navy uniform outside with a knife in a holster. There were lots of little stalls selling oranges and peanuts and people roasting peanuts to sell at the side of the road. Women carried goods on their back in raffia cones with padded head straps. Mini shops made from bicycles: a big metal basket full of oranges on the back, under the cross bar a round raffia basket and sometimes on the handlebars a pair of scales. The houses and buildings were a mix of colourful and not, some looking in need of repair, standing a little off centre, some modern, some shaped like pagodas. Dogs were sturdy and thick-coated, honey coloured, black and white or black and golden brown. One had a tail like a husky. There were lots of tiny little tea shops; we went in one for a break on a long, polluted walk. The woman was wearing a multi-coloured crocheted poncho, grey jumper and green print loose trousers. Everywhere sold loose single cigarettes and we ended up having one in spite of the pollution.

We went to find a samosa place that someone at the guesthouse had recommended. We had two each, they were the baked kind, not greasy, with thick pastry, and chai. Across the road a parent put a baby in a green knitted hat down on a flat cart laden with satsumas. Like babies everywhere the baby picked up satsumas and threw them on the ground, everyone was laughing. Catching sight of a row of scarves hung up in the samosa cafe, one made of devore: (also called burnout) velvet with burned patterns in it. I know that because I did a fashion and textiles course at college. I thought about all the different things I'd done. Again, I thought, *You made it difficult but you made it interesting.*

I bought a new notepad; it had an eagle on it.

'Wow, how many times do you come across an eagle,' I said, excited having just seen the ones at the restaurant.

'Well maybe quite a lot if you're in Nepal,' Anthony said.

In our room, thinking about my old idea for reminder bracelets for my personal mantras, *Awake, Aware, Calm* and *Centred* and regretting that I never followed through on getting them. And then the very next day we went to a temple and saw people sitting at little stalls all along the temple path, loads of people, making up letter bracelets to order!

Pollution was a problem. I wore a fabric mask that I bought in Delhi and we operated a one day out one day in kind of routine. After being out for a long time it felt almost nauseating and the taste in my mouth was like the day after smoking a lot of cigarettes. The homestay was one of the best places for meeting people so it wasn't much of a hardship to hang about indoors a lot.

Matt, who had told us about the samosa place had worked for his dad since leaving school then at the age of forty had given everything up and gone travelling, he had been on the road for four years. He was very handy and used Workaway but then as time went on rather than booking in advance he'd just turn up and something would come up. He'd helped a woman put in new windows, done decorating and worked at a Buddhist monastery. Friends from home would say things like, 'But what about security, what about when you get old?' But the longer it worked out, the more confident he became. In between he'd climb mountains, which he described without a trace of ego. Fascinated, I asked him a lot of questions.

'Of course it is physical, but it's as much mental as physical. If you feel the fear beginning to rise, you have to push it back down again,' he said.

Harrison, twenty one, from Australia; the four of us spent a lot of time in the kitchen talking and smoking weed (Anthony and Harrison) or drinking beer (me.) Opposite the kitchen was a dorm room where people seemed to spend most of their time sitting in bed under the blankets. We even got told off for making too much noise one night. Us, the oldest ones in the place! Harrison said, 'This is nothing, last time I was here it was really crazy, we were cooking up crystal meth in the kitchen!'

Traveller's diarrhoea is a well known side effect/price of travelling. So much so that when meeting fellow travellers, talk invariably turns to the state of everyone's bowels.

'Yep, it's not all about having the trip of a lifetime, it's also about having permanent dysentery,' Matt said.

'If I had guts like this at home I'd be in hospital,' said Harrison.

Maybe as a result of the stopper tablets for the ongoing diarrhoea, maybe as a result of a change in diet, I'd actually got constipated in Pushkar and it got worse during Nepal. I eventually went to a pharmacy but it didn't help much.

**

Since arriving in Nepal Anthony and I had been meditating every morning, taking it in turns to lead and both feeding back afterwards. It made such a difference and I was very happy that we were back on the path together. I always want the quest for self realisation or increasing awareness to be a central part of my life. We're always on the path of course but it's easy to talk the talk and not walk the walk. Those ten minutes each morning honours our commitment and permeates the entire day, and it's only ten minutes!

One day music came through from the balcony of the dorm next door, Nick Cave 'Into my arms' and The Righteous Brothers 'Unchained Melody' and then during the meditation, Portishead then Morcheeba. The music belonged to Harrison, the twenty-one year old Australian, but it could have been ours. In meditation I thought/felt: No time, no place, no past, no future. The timeless nature of travelling. The impermanence of travelling, transient friendships. Now India, now Kathmandu. No one else from home or past around.

The journey is to accept the moment, accept yourself, be where you are; to really be where you are. That is the work, the journey and the destination. Every time you find yourself planning, dreaming, projecting re the future, wanting something, worrying about something, thinking you want to change your life, thinking you're on some kind of journey. Remember that 'the journey' 'the place to get to' is not a place but an attitude. An acceptance that here is where you are, where it is, where everything is.

**

We decided to go for an overnight trip to Nagarkot to go and see the Himalayas with C; we'd spent a couple of evenings together and got on well. She introduced us to a guru, Guru Sadhguru 'There's no higher power or cosmic being. It's you!'

It felt good to get out of Kathmandu and to see countryside. From the car window I saw rice terraces making green steps in the landscape and straw stacked in peaks like little round straw huts. A pile of straw fanned out against a wall and onto the ground in perfect symmetry and in the centre of it all slept a sandy coloured dog, perfectly coordinated. To one side of the unmade road was farmland and alarming drops as we ascended. On the other side was a wall of roughly hewn sandy coloured rock with big fallen chunks of rock on the ground below; the sandy rocks sparkled in the sunlight. As we went up into the mountains we felt our ears popping like on a plane; it was the first time Anthony and I had been somewhere as high.

The place we were staying was called The Hotel at The End of The Universe. We were staying in wooden chalet style accommodation. Later we found out that Robert from Switzerland had stayed there in 1990! It was reached via going up some wooden steps. To one side was a rock wall with delicate looking plants growing out, beautiful like a natural rockery. Close up I could see that the rock sparkled.

The place was owned by the beautifully named Oasis. He told us that his dad was a hippy and had bought the land in the 1960s as a place to hang out with friends and smoke weed. In the evening Oasis played cards in the restaurant with the three of us and two other tourists. When someone said they wouldn't be able to play because they were stoned, Oasis said, 'You're still the same, it makes no difference.' There was much laughter that evening with people forgetting it was their turn and getting confused learning a new game. Oasis just sat laughing and smiling like a Buddha. When we said goodnight we asked what tomorrow would be like and wished him a good day. 'Every day beautiful, Every day shit,' Oasis said.

In the car on the way there I made the mistake of allowing myself to be provoked during a conversation about vegetarianism and veganism. As every vegan-baiter and vegan knows only too well, the fastest way to annoy a vegan or vegetarian is to bring up the suffering of plants, refer to cavemen and lions, question the vegetarian/vegan about the origins of their essential prescribed medication and then regale them with tales of family hunting expeditions. Still, I shouldn't have lost my cool; even though to do so gave me a temporary rush of energy- I almost never get really annoyed. The subsequent come down, alongside going over and over the whole thing in my mind, seeing where I had acted ineffectively and regretting my part, had caused my mood to spiral downwards, all the way through feeling fat and ugly, down to social awkwardness, paralysis, right the way down to self harm and suicide fantasies.

The wooden chalet was freezing cold. There were lots of old heavy duvets, it was like sleeping under carpet. Eventually we warmed up enough to sleep. We set the alarm and got up at six to walk a short way to a half-finished hotel that had become a sunrise viewing tower. We did a kind of half hearted meditation, focussing on our breath while looking; half hearted as it was cold, our feet ached and there were two other people about. We'd skipped the previous day due to having to get up early to leave. It was the first time we'd missed it since starting our regular morning meditation and a bit of me wondered whether that had contributed to the previous day's drama.

In front were pine trees, some fuzzy to look at, as if my eyes were blurred, reminding me of the trees I saw leaving the airport in Tokyo. I saw an animal in a tree, I thought at first it was a monkey, then I realised it was long and slim, more like a big black stoat. One of the staff back at the hotel said it was probably a mongoose. As the sun rose it lit up little pieces of one peak, then another, then more and more, first tinged pink then lit white and silver.

'I don't feel anything,' I said to Anthony as we stood in the midst of a perfect Instagram/Facebook photo opportunity, standing at the top of a viewing platform with the sun rising over the Himalayas. I refused to be in the sunrise selfie, still in a 'feeling fat and ugly' mood from the previous day's argument. The mountains did their work on me though, even if I didn't realise it immediately.

We got back and had breakfast, black coffee and fruit salad. I still had bad constipation and spent a lot of time in the loo. The walls and the floor of the loo were black with little flecks in the stone that looked like stars.

Afterwards I stood at the edge of the guesthouse's sunny terrace, looking out at the view which was so beautiful it was unreal, talking with Anthony and crying about the previous day's incident. As an observer of myself, it was interesting to watch and reinforced what I already knew: that confrontation and argument is not beneficial to my wellbeing. However, I learned a lot: use such encounters, and everything, to develop or wake myself up, not to try and develop or wake the other person up. And it forced me to let myself off. 'We're not Buddhas,' Anthony said. My husband remains my best teacher.

I stood outside on the terrace in the sun and then sat, near the others but alone, near the big German Shepherd that lived there. I had to keep moving my chair to stay in a sunny patch. I could feel the warm sun, and the sight of The Himalayas, the trees all around and the clean mountain air provided me with restorative relaxation.

The others were talking with Oasis, I listened for a while before moving my chair to join them. Oasis seemed to have an easy relationship with death. He was a Buddhist and maybe it was also because of the earthquakes and the mountains. He spoke about taking risks in the mountains.

'So I die,' he said, shrugging.

'What about the people left behind?' Anthony asked.

'Two, three days, then they, 'Okay, okay, he die,'' Oasis said.

We all talked about the journey towards self realisation. I expressed that maybe once you find it there's nothing left to do but die, so maybe it's best not to get there until death. 'You can just enjoy yourself.' Oasis said. 'Smoke, don't smoke. Drink, don't drink, it's all the same. So many ways to dance upon this Earth. Live in the moment don't be concerned with death.' Oasis said of his grandfather that he 'Never saw him not happy,' and that he just died in the night aged ninety-six years old.

Oasis said, 'Head life ok if you just have a head. Otherwise; music, juggling, making juggling balls... And people, I love people. Tourists, all different, being with them, understanding them, that's my meditation.'

Meeting someone new, talking about our spiritual awakenings and telling our personal stories felt nourishing. I heard Anthony say to Oasis, 'I'd marry her again tomorrow.'

During the discussion C asked, 'What if you regret it (our process of decluttering?)' 'Well, hopefully it (the year) will have made it a price worth paying,' we said. Later, I thought to myself, Well I would write about it, and grow from it. I could write a blog post called 'A eulogy for missed things,' and go on from there. Chances are it wouldn't kill me.

During our discussions that morning Oasis remained so totally centred, even in the midst of C's disagreements and comments which I perceived as almost rude, although as I reminded myself later, maybe it's only rude if you allow yourself to get offended.

'Focus on yourself, not what others are doing,' was something Oasis said to C by way of advice. 'You have to manage your thoughts, because when you get to a certain level, what you think about, comes.' I told him that I was at ease with that now, because I feel good and see how it all works but that in the past I'd been anxious about that concept, getting into a panicky loop of worrying about fearing and manifesting spiders. That's why it's so important to maintain a feeling of wellbeing, I thought. Even a tractor, certainly a dog, and us, operate best when they are 'well,' i.e. well maintained and happy.

I felt emotion on occasion but I took some quiet moments, breathed and reminded myself that people who seem difficult are struggling. Anthony offered me some of his second breakfast, a fantastically delicious fruit salad with curd. It grounded me and filled me with pleasure. It felt like a reward for coping better today, as if today was a do-over, a chance to have another go.

I experienced C as challenging but really she was just asking me the questions she was really asking herself: Re meat eating, is it really wrong if we've been doing it for years and my own family hunted and killed? What about if you declutter and regret it, is it all worth it? What is this spiritual journey thing all about exactly?

We walked down to the bus stop and caught the first of the return buses. Astroturf flowed over the dashboard gear box and front seat area, delightful.

Moments of fear on the journey: the drop, the unmade road in a bumpy bus. Just breathe, accept, and be. Moments of luminosity: a woman walking quickly towards the bus. She was wearing plastic slip on sandals with thick socks, a cotton saree, a cardigan and a crocheted pink hat. My heart pinged open, again. Just breathe, accept, and be.

Between buses we stopped for food, I got black coffee, a plate of chopped fruit and a cool glass of water. Luckily there was an Indian style toilet right there because suddenly the medication worked. We sat inside looking out onto a lake. It reminded me of Pushkar.

I bought two cigarettes and they brought them on a white saucer with an ashtray and a box of the thin matches that I often find so difficult to light. I remembered on a day trip to Kolam in Kerala, we stopped to look at a fish market and I bought a cigarette from a little stall. Under pressure, worried about using a poor person's last few matches, I couldn't light them and Anthony helped me. Here there were plenty and I didn't worry, and I lit it first go.

In front of us was a big tree, beneath it were women selling vegetables and fruit from blankets spread out on the ground. In the water I could see the reflection of the big dark green trees on the other side of the lake. At the far end of the lake was a group of women in different beautifully coloured sarees, all reflected in the water below. The water was so still. I thought about how water needs to be still in order to reflect the world and about how this is a metaphor.

My mind is full of stories, my eyes are full of pictures: Varkala, India

Our room got the sun and became blazing hot in the afternoons, it eventually cooled a bit then strangely got really hot again during the night. As before there was the sound of crows and barking dogs- an awful howling outside the window and the noise of the sea was closer and louder than before.

We saw the pretty woman who was heavily pregnant last time, on her stall with the new baby. She always looked just perfectly lovely, wearing a bright yellow or sky blue saree.

On the beach we saw five dogs lying in the sand, they all looked the same. Maybe they were the litter of puppies we'd seen on the beach in August, all grown up. I saw the brown and white beach dog that would have been 'my' dog had I not nipped any emotional attachment firmly in the bud. Walking back to our guesthouse along the cliff I saw 'the dog with the funny teeth,' and 'the Disney dog-' a white dog with markings that looked like it was wearing eye makeup.

Maybe I shouldn't have been so pleased and surprised to see the same dogs, after all it had only been three and a half months. The sea had turned a deep holiday-maker blue but still turned greenish in the late afternoon. The beach itself was smooth, no extra channels, no walls of cake-like sand and so much wider now that the monsoon season was over and the sea had receded.

I arrived in Kerala still in a lot of pain from toilet problems and the first week was mainly spent lying down on the bed. Views and objects loomed large. There were two switches on my side of the bed, one was set in the middle between on and off, I didn't know what it did. The other turned the fan off. The only time we turned the fan off, other than when going out was one morning when it actually felt cool.

In bed in the evenings we watched Netflix and ate small handfuls of chocolate éclairs just to experience something sweet. Pain and illness was so exhausting, just getting through each day trying not to push it away, trying to keep ones mood up or at least level.

Sitting then lying down on the floor and accidentally finding a position that was comfortable. Me squeezing my own arm. Anthony asked me what I was doing. 'I'm just trying to feel a different sensation, not self harm, more like deep pressure.' Not wanting to be touched. Not wanting to be in the body. In the midst of the worst, standing on one leg in yoga tree pose or brushing my hair and looking in the big full length wardrobe mirror, trying to have some other experience or view of this body I was in.

One day unable to feel better in the room I went for a walk along the cliff top. I bought an ice cream, remembering something I'd seen: 'Be in the moment, unless the moment sucks in which case eat a cookie.' The big white-headed eagles and the sea still looked nice. I stepped down over the rocks onto the beach and had a paddle then stood and looked at the sea. The crushed shells from last time were still there although this time they were in tiny fragments.

Anthony had got a nasty bout of food poisoning with lots of pain and diarrhoea every hour night and day. We probably both thought about going home but that would have meant returning to a freezing cold UK and to getting jobs, so no, not yet.

In Kerala I went to the doctor twice and then finally went to the hospital. At the hospital I got examined and diagnosed properly with a small fistula caused by the earlier constipation. I got proper treatment at last; salt water baths, pain relieving and treatment creams, laxatives and pain killers. Anthony got a check up at the hospital at the same time as me and they ruled out actual dysentery and said it was traveller's diarrhoea and would resolve itself.

We stayed in Varkala longer than we had initially planned, near the hospital, people we knew and good safe food. We lived out of what was always our favourite restaurant and which was luckily a stone's throw from our guesthouse, Cafe Del Mar: parcel (take away) clear vegetable soup and vegetable rice, soya milk and banana smoothies.

When we arrived I'd said to the woman in the little salon downstairs that I'd get my hair hennaed. I settled into the waiting chair, a slightly reclined, very padded cane armchair with a foot stool. I fell in love with that chair. It was the first time I'd felt comfortable sitting for ages. As I got better I noticed my usual aching shoulder and took that as a good sign, normal aches and pains returning; I hadn't been able to feel anything else for weeks.

We went to Aranmula to buy a mirror for Maeve. These mirrors are special: called Aranmula Kannadi, Kannadi is the Malayalam word for mirror and made not from glass but from a secret alloy of metals by a secret method known only to these particular families of master craftsmen. They lack the imperfections of traditional glass mirrors and hence famously they show you how you really are. A few days after we had left Kerala in August to go to Thailand, the monsoon rains had caused the worst flooding in Kerala in almost one hundred years. Hundreds of people lost their lives. Aranmula was badly affected by the floods of August; the mirror sellers showed us how high up the temple wall the water had been. Their house had been under water. Our taxi driver translated.

'Where did you go?' I asked.

'To the top of the temple. We had no food for two days, then the helicopters dropped food.' Even though this area had been so badly affected just back in August, the shops and workshops were all up and running and open for business.

As I got better my mood lifted. I noticed when I noticed things: a big black and white cat on a corrugated iron roof. Looking out into the velvety night and appreciating the nearby palm tree, luminous in the dark. My sense of pleasure returning.

'I thought about having sex,' Anthony said. 'I mean, I don't want to actually have it yet, but I thought the fact that I thought about it was a good sign!'

One evening we weren't going to go out for dinner, I was going to skip eating altogether or just get a parcel soup but I didn't really want to go on my own. Anthony said, 'I don't mind going out,' so we went and ate dinner together; soup and salad, fruit salad and smoothies.

We spoke about pain.

'I grip my arm, I find a speck on the bathroom wall to hold onto.' In Nepal there'd been the little sparkles in the black wall and floor of the bathroom which looked like stars. Here, it was the bucket with black pants in, following the bubbles from the surface of the water down to the black at the bottom; the black pants were both a reflective surface and reflected in the water. 'And I sing sometimes,' I said. 'What do you do?' I asked Anthony.

'We're completely different like that,' he said, 'If it's really bad I'm just with the pain, I'm not trying to go anywhere else. It's like how you keep the light off when you go to the bathroom in the night so that if there's a spider you won't see it. I put all the lights on and look.'

I suggested we make a plan of something to do when we both felt better, to look forward to and to celebrate our recovery. We'd seen a vegan fry up advertised at a coffee place, or vegan chocolate cheese cake at the cafe which had opened since we'd been away. Something I'd read ages ago, a rich and famous person in an interview saying, 'You need three things to be happy: something to do, someone to love and something to look forward to.'

Anthony said, 'I don't agree with any of those. Mine would be, you don't need anyone, you don't need to do anything and just live in the moment. We summarised Anthony's 'beliefs:' I don't believe in anything, but I have many suspicions- Robert Anton Wilson. Do what thou wilt- Aleister Crowley. Do nothing- Krishnamurti. I brought up the conversations about nihilism we'd had on Kovalam beach when we were last in Kerala. 'Oh yeah, I forgot I was a nihilist, have I been being one?' Anthony asked. It was the first time we'd really laughed in ages.

We had been meditating almost every day since Nepal. Sometimes this meant nothing more than lying on the bed and trying to follow the breath for ten minutes. Sometimes it had meant doing something we'd do anyway like walking, but intentionally and mindfully.

Anthony led a meditation on being unattached to beliefs and possessions, and being all alone. We began with the pillar of energy spin, visualising things which had stuck to us flying off including ideas and beliefs, then cutting the cords or etheric connections between ourselves, people and places and then the main meditation.

We cling to possessions, people, places, our environment because we come in as babies. We cling on to anything and everything around us because we're scared. But if we knew like Krishnamurti that it's just about us and knowing ourselves and turning attention inwards, would having that as our mission mean we weren't afraid? By turning inwards not outwards for security, we'd be stronger and not need to cling.

We often saw Lyn and Renate at Cafe del Mar, sitting for a bit over coffee or food. One day after seeing them I led a meditation, to walk along the cliff path while being aware of the soles of our feet and our breath. At first all I could do was look at the cobbles underfoot, to get a rhythm with being able to follow breath and feet, not trip up and keep near and in step with Anthony.

What about the beautiful sea from my previous walk, I thought. It's okay, it'll still be there another time, it's okay to just focus on the cobbles. Of course then everything relaxed. I looked up and saw the trees and the sea. I coped with my gaze going all the way to the far side of the bay, the sea so big! And still I was in contact with my breath, my feet, even as my gaze and my mind wandered away in space. 'The mind is as big as space,' was something I always remembered from a meditation retreat years earlier. After having just seen Lyn and Renate, chatting, listening to their stories, my heart felt so open, so full of love. When I looked at the sea it was like when I first started meditating and only needed to follow my breath to go into bliss.

Another meditation from Anthony: Imagine you are in space all alone. Then think about the people you are connected to. During the meditation I thought, 'So in space the connections would exist only in your mind.' *That's the same as it is now.* Discussion afterwards, Anthony saying, all the connections we've made, even the transient ones, what do they show us? They are all a mirror, of an aspect of ourselves, or of the effect of an aspect of ourselves on that person. Even our dress. Most people are younger, does that show that we are young in places, or that age is irrelevant? Remember that everyone you meet is a mirror. Does this make all your interactions more poignant? And mindfulness even more essential?

Although Renate said that she was never bored: 'My mind is full of stories, my eyes are full of pictures,' she did love meeting new and interesting people to talk to. She called it 'Cosmic Recognition:' meeting people you connected and wanted to talk about ideas, life, everything, with. I read a lovely blog on WordPress from The High-Heeled Papergirl:

> *'I came to the realization that when you are unconditionally honest, people bond with you, and most of the time they accept you for who you are.'*

So if the reason for doing all this is the pursuit of enlightenment and the definition of enlightenment is to see things as they really are... Can you have light in some areas and not in others, just as some bits of life can be going 'well' and others 'not so well'?

It's been a source of some anxiety and a fair amount of guilt that my family relationships aren't as close as, as what? As some other people's family relationships look from the outside? As my idea of what these relationships should look like? Except that I have no idea... As what they were? No, that had to change.

In the midst of my painful illness I had a moment of clarity: I realised suddenly: *Maybe they are happy with it being this way.* When I went to live and work in New Zealand for a year I had a similar experience of interpersonal conflict to the vegan argument in Nepal. I emailed my mum; she emailed me back a long pep talk and was probably quite concerned. Even when things were going well I used to phone her from New Zealand a lot. I was thirty-five years old.

My son seems to do better the more independent he is from me, who worries about him. Having someone anxious who seems to think there's something wrong, because they focus on what's wrong, can make someone question, should I be living differently or maybe I'm not in charge of my life; well I wouldn't like that.

With my son, just relax. Yes, it's hard to lose the habit of concern. The teeth, which had been the source of such distress, just days after, even hours after, he seemed okay and a month later it was as if nothing had happened at all. It doesn't escape my notice that he was able to finally take charge of himself and his health while I was away.

Property, security and female independence were pillars for my mum. As a child, teen and young woman I was conditioned to be anti men, anti marriage, anti creating a world with another. And yet that's what I've done with my husband and it's amazing. Right now, reading Krishnamurthy, discussing ideas, being on a joint quest.

I thought about what I could have done differently on my part. The thing would have been to keep separate, not share boyfriend details, not spend each holiday there, not run every decision by her, not do everything she said. Yet at the same time it was hard as I was nineteen with a baby, twenty and a single mum of a toddler.

So maybe like with my son's teeth there's nothing that could have been done differently. And of course now there's definitely nothing that can be done. There's no time machine. It, things, all things can only be fixed in the present.

So exchanges of emails with my mum, photos, a few lines, video calls with my son and me living my life, in India, writing a book, discussing philosophy, deepening my relationship with my husband, creating an exclusive world. Things are as they are.

I've been a big fan of the idea of illuminating the darkness and taking responsibility for everything that's 'wrong' in one's life, for any sadness. But I've realised that it's also about accepting responsibility for my own happiness.

Returning to Kerala where we'd spent so much time before, being holed up ill in our room and the fact that we were eight and a half months into our twelve month trip prompted a kind of reflection or review. What about our decisions? The charge of, will we regret it? Could we live with having gone crazy and regretting it and own it, the good and the bad? We discussed the worst case scenarios and solutions but still I maintained that it's better than dying without having lived.

I imagined thinking in life that I couldn't have done any of the exciting things. Then imagining that on death all the possibilities go flitting through your mind and you realise, Oh my God, I could have done. I could have gone out and done X, X and X and X! There wasn't anything to worry about.

'Your life is your life,' Bukowski, the best message for all.

We had lunch at the coffee place and talked about keeping hold of this attitude to life once we return to the UK. How? Manage fear. Don't take life too seriously. Remember the people we met travelling and how it works for them; Heather in Pushkar, Matt in Nepal. We've cemented voluntary simplicity and minimalism and reduced consumerism by having bought a boat to live on. There's no space to accumulate, there's a physical check on it! The moorings are in a completely new area of the country. There won't be any old influences. We've given ourselves the best chance we could.

***

When Anthony was ill I went out on my own to go to the doctors in an auto. On the way I chatted to a woman. She pointed out a Western woman dancing by herself on the beach, 'She's having breakdown,' the woman said. She shared with me the latest horror story from the newspaper. But I still felt okay going out alone.

One evening on the cliff a group of young Indian men, they didn't seem like locals, maybe tourists or day trippers walked past us making comments and looking me up and down.

'You don't have to be so obvious about it,' Anthony said, annoyed. On the way back one of the men bumped into me, I suspected it was on purpose.

At the coffee place we spoke to the owner's friend, he helped us with menu queries and we admired the music, Leonard Cohen. We could easily have spoken to the owner. Later I mentioned going there to Renate, she obviously didn't like it. We asked her why, she said the owner was a convicted UK child sex offender and that everyone knew about it. Renate said, 'I've been here too long, I can't be somewhere where this is.'

Contrast with Michelle newly arrived from Germany for the first time, enchanted with the overloaded autos and vans- she'd sent a photo to her boyfriend who was a delivery driver. But it's all true. Like the therapy exercise I remembered from twenty years ago: the pebbles held in the hand of the children bereaved by suicide, the jagged pebble representing the nature of the death itself, the beautiful smooth one representing the happy times, the heart one representing love, all three held together in the palm of one hand.

So many things to love: Hampi, India

I still had to bathe in salt three times a day,
'It should be easy to get salt when we get there,' I said, tempting
fate. The staff at the restaurant in Bangalore where we ate dinner
seemed very friendly so I wasn't expecting any issues when I asked
for salt, offering to pay for it.

'No,' he said. I thought he must have misunderstood me. I asked
again. 'No. It is getting dark. People will talk. Come back tomorrow.
Tomorrow morning, no problem.'

I felt frustrated but I knew it was pointless to argue. If I'd realised
I'd have sneaked a little into a napkin but by this time we were stood
up ready to leave and they would have seen. I asked the man at the
desk at the hotel and told him what had happened. He sent a young
boy off to the kitchen. Two minutes later there was a knock at the
door and there was the boy with a small bowl of salt. I resigned
myself to this being yet another thing I didn't understand, and felt
very grateful to the hotel.

We went to Lalbagh, Bangalore's Botanical Gardens and walked
back to the hotel. We talked about the future, about fear versus
bravery. We talked about what to do with the money we had left,
whether to keep and spend it slowly as we needed things or be brave
and try and do something with it. Buy somewhere cheap in Europe
and maybe try and make money or at least do something creative; a
retreat or just a gathering of people we met, and have people from
Workaway to help to do it up.

I sat downstairs in the lobby, the only place where the Wi-Fi
worked. After I had finished writing we went out again. Stepping
outside it had cooled down a lot and I felt the familiar feeling of
being sorry that I'd missed the best part of the day, when it's still hot
but not too hot. We went back to the same restaurant and ordered
two mild curries and rice to share.

Over the road by the little shops there was a chai stall open, they
had paper cups which were more hygienic. In Varanasi at the chai
stall we went to I'd seen them washing up the glasses in dirty
looking water and resolved to use only paper cups from then on.

When Anthony was here twenty years ago chai was served in little clay pots that afterwards were thrown on the ground and broke and went back into the earth; it was a shame that everyone didn't still do that.

We'd wondered if the bus pick up point at ten pm at night would be a bit dodgy but it was like a busy city centre, so many buses, so many people moving about the country. There were lots of travel agents near our hotel and we passed many more on the way. In front of the buses before leaving men did a blessing, lighting a small fire on the road and saying prayers.

Sometimes I had the urge to check that the young women travelling alone were okay; us being together and older and sometimes I thought of their parents who I was probably the same age as. I also thought that if I were travelling on my own I might feel nervous. A Western woman was waiting outside the office at our stand, I walked up to say hello but she was engrossed in her laptop; I walked up the steps and back again feeling slightly foolish. Another woman also alone, and young was standing nearby us, I went up to say hi; we had a little chat, I asked if she was okay, she said she was fine. She was from Israel and going to Pushkar.

Our coach was green and luxurious, the cubicles had green curtains and shiny green cushions, very plush and there was no stuff in the aisle. The people around us were friendly and mainly young middle class Indians. It was a little cramped in our sleep area but very nice. A short time into the journey we realised why these had been the last two beds: they were over the back wheel arch and the road to Hampi is very bumpy!

***

We arrived in Hampi on Christmas Eve. In the early morning it was still dark. Three men were waiting for us offering autos and we got in one. The driver seemed to drive unnecessarily fast around the bends in the dark, one of only a few times that I felt slightly unsafe.

The auto driver dropped us at the market area, slightly outside the main village where the local buses stop. It was still dark and most things were closed except for a couple of chai stalls and the public bathrooms. We sat down at a chai stall. It had narrow wooden benches; we put our bags on the bench beside us. The woman at the chai stall asked us if we wanted big or small, we said big. She gave us glasses; I didn't see any paper cups and was too tired and too polite to ask. Around us the stalls, mostly closed and brown, the streets dusty and grey. The moon was almost full. I sat on the bench looking at the moon, and at Hampi coming to life.

I watched a group of stray dogs hanging around and following a man. He bought biscuits from the stall and fed the dogs, one packet of biscuits each. I saw him and another man get chai, they were given paper cups. I should have asked after all. Buses arrived and autos came to meet the new arrivals. People were wearing cardigans, woollen bonnets and padded anoraks. Anthony had gone to the loo. Coaches arrived, a group of school children wearing white uniforms, walking in pairs in a long crocodile. Another group walked past, the light hitting bits of colour in the dusty grey dawn, a pink skirt, a purple skirt. Sitting at the chai stall alone, thinking, realising: Every place is something new, a new start, a new state of mind.

Anaconda who had looked after us last time arrived! We had a big hug. He drank chai and chatted to us for a bit before he went off in his auto to 'Catch some tourists' arriving by bus like we did. He said if we waited he would come back and take us to our guesthouse. We were so tired just sitting was enough and we were very happy to wait, we drank one chai, and then had another.

Anaconda came back and took us to our guesthouse. The moon was almost over the temples. I felt so happy we were ending our India journey in Hampi, where I first fell in love with India back in April. We asked after the Chillout restaurant. Anaconda said, 'The banana palms are very big now.'

At our guesthouse the staff were asleep on the seat-mattresses in the restaurant. They got up and began straightening the cushions and mattresses and sweeping.

'Oh, we woke them up,' I said.

'It's waking up time,' Anaconda said, 'It's (the tourist season) only for a few months, they can sleep the rest of the time.'

Anthony went off to see our room.

'Manage your expectations,' he said when he came back. 'Don't worry I've checked everywhere,' (meaning spiders.) Wrought iron steps led from the upstairs restaurant to a ground floor courtyard with rooms off it.

Later we went out for a walk. At the main temple I saw a monkey eating scraps from a bin. I bought some bananas and dropped them into the bin which frightened the monkey and it came after me, teeth bared. A man shooed the monkey away and gave me back the bananas which I fed to some much less intimidating cows. Apparently the monkeys get fed up with bananas and prefer peanuts.

The scenery was almost too much to take in, so surreal looking but so peaceful at the same time. There were lots of people at the water; families were asleep outside, just lying on the big flat boulders beside the river. People wore coloured fleeces and cardigans on top of colourful sarees or long lace skirts. Tiny black birds with flashes of Kingfisher blue at the throat or head flew over the river. Dazed with travel weariness, we suddenly ran out of energy. On the way back Anthony said, as he had done once in Thailand, 'Don't look.' Afterwards he told me there was a monkey cradling a dead monkey in its arms.

In the evening we went back to the main temple; we had heard there was a big festival. Inside the temple whatever had happened was mainly over aside from a few musicians quietly playing but there were tens, hundreds of people asleep on the temple floor, lots of families including little babies. Some little oil lamps were still burning, some had gone out. Earlier outside the temple I'd seen people selling little shallow clay dishes and what I now realised were wicks and little bottles of oil to make lamps. The stone floor under our bare feet was slippery with oil and with occasional broken pieces of clay to avoid. The scene was breathtakingly, tender; holy, what a way to spend what was for us Christmas Eve.

On Christmas Day we went back to the main temple and hand fed the monkeys peanuts in shells. An Indian woman told me to hide the peanuts under my scarf or the monkeys will take them! Peanuts became the new cigarettes, sharing them with people, prompting interactions. People with no English would put out their hands for peanuts or we would offer. We bought coconuts to drink and sat in the shade and cooled down. We made Christmas phone calls, as much as we could as the reception was very poor. Anthony struggled with missing Maeve and Jude.

On Boxing Day on the way back from the temple we threw peanuts on the ground for some monkeys who were quietly sitting about. 'They look languid, should be okay,' I said. One of them quickly sprang up and jumped onto Anthony's bag where the nuts were. '*Never* describe a monkey as languid,' he said when he had recovered, 'they scared the life out of me!'

Our room was okay, it had a kind of rustic charm but it was a bit mouldy in places and smelled a bit from the sink. Plus the toilet seat was broken, or rather it wasn't broken it just wasn't attached to the toilet. Couples who argue about how the toilet seat should be left might have fallen out big time as it needed to be lifted on and off each time. Also the room was by the staff area and work started very early the first few mornings; running water into plastic buckets, beating laundry, chopping food and talking loudly. And at night through an open vent between ours and one of the staff rooms came some very loud snoring. Anthony said, 'That was my karma, they asked me if I'd wait longer for a room and let this one go to some other people and I said no.'

We saw an empty room on the other side of the courtyard and went to have a peek. It looked and smelled better, had a Western style toilet with a fixed on seat plus an Indian style toilet in the same room. I joked that we would both be able to go to the loo at the same time, although fortunately that wasn't necessary. It was on the other side of the courtyard to all the taps so it was quieter in the mornings and the snoring was a lot less intrusive from there. There was no sink, just a low-ish wall tap and a shower, and the fan was either full blast or off but as we said to ourselves you can't have it all.

The new room had lots of shelves, wide enough to put piles of clothes on as well as toiletries. I felt very at home with all my stuff unpacked. On the windowsill were our regular companions Odomos for mosquitoes and Oreos (accidentally vegan and available almost everywhere.)

One day Anthony went to go out of the courtyard but there was a very large cow with extremely big horns standing in the entrance between the wrought iron gates. 'Er, I think I'll go out the other way,' he said.

There was no Wi-Fi in our room or the restaurant, 'Monkey broke wires,' they said, but it was bad everywhere. I did internet stuff in the Chillout where the Wi-Fi was sometimes okay and we ate most of our meals there: eggplant curry and roti or finger chips and vegetable sandwich.

When we had been to the Chillout in April the password had been 'Are you single.' This time it was, 'I don't know.' Later it changed to 'New password' which was always amusing for guests and staff. The staff were fun, it was always, 'Pay later, no change,' (it can be really hard to get and keep change in India.)

There was a big brown dog in the Chillout restaurant. I thought I'd heard the dog growl at Anthony when he came in so I asked the staff, 'Is he a good dog?' 'No, sometimes dangerous,' the staff answered. I love India, so matter of fact. No apologies, no excuses and no concern re having a dangerous dog in a restaurant.

In Hampi food waste was put out for the animals- cows and dogs- in big plastic tubs and buckets, not in a pile on the ground and not in plastic bags, it was like the old days that our guesthouse manager in Varanasi had told me about.

I'd so wanted to stay at our old room with the green glass windows which looked out onto the banana palms, the scene of my tablet being stolen and then rescued by the boy from the house below, but it was too expensive now that it was season time. Every day when I went past one of them would ask me, would I come, the boy's father or mother or an old man presumably the grandfather would be sat outside, he had no English except to gesture to the room. All I could do was hold my heart and say, 'Next time.'

In Varkala we were ill, in Bangalore we wandered around the Botanical Gardens wondering about The Future and in Hampi we got happy again. So much to love: the temples, the people, the monkeys, the scenery, buying peanuts, bananas, coconuts and chai from little stalls.

Follow the rabbit hole, as long as you're alive. The blogger SMUT and Self-Esteem was important again here. In April she'd written about spirituality when I'd had my spiritual moment in the Chillout; this time she was struggling and we exchanged messages on Christmas Day and Boxing Day. It's okay that I feel in some ways closer and find it easier to help people from the internet or new friends than I do my family; it is normal for adults to live their own lives: me, my mum, my son. Keep moving forwards. I don't have to have everything fixed; I'm not setting myself up as a guru. And sometimes accepting things just as they are *is* fixing them.

I saw Indian squirrels again which made me happy. In my mind if I see an Indian squirrel it's a sign that everything is okay.

There were lots of school trips and families in Hampi for pilgrimage, sleeping outside in the temple area or at the roadside.

We met a family, mum and dad, brother and sister in the main temple. We spoke mostly to the girl, a teenager. The father spoke proudly of her, her and her mother sewed and the girl hoped to become a fashion designer. I gave her one of my bangles from Pushkar. The dad was about to take a photo with us but his battery died, he looked absolutely crestfallen.

So many kids saying hi to us. One day it started with one or two then more and more came until I was surrounded by children wanting their photograph taken, girls in beautiful colourful dresses, the crowd growing bigger and bigger with each picture.

It was lovely but tiring! It was good that we'd been to Lalbagh so that when we met parties of schoolchildren and their teachers and they said they were from Bangalore we could say, 'Ah, yes, Bangalore, we went to Lalbagh,' and they looked pleased.

We'd been for a walk, past a tree decorated with material and with piles of stones. The piles of stones were made by people wishing for houses or for extra storeys on houses. Big groups of kids came past; I put my hands in prayer position and said Namaste. They wanted to shake hands which I was happy to do but there were too many kids; the group was moving and there was not enough time to do each in turn, so as they passed by their hands piled on and on until both my hands were covered in their hands.

Whole families had set up camp and were sleeping at the side of the road, out in the open. One family were cooking dinner and invited us to join them, we declined, not wanting to take their food, but later we brought them some sweets for the children.

Last time we'd come in April when it was quiet. Now in December it was full season time and Hampi was busy with tourists. The demographic was different too, there were lots of Indian tourists come for the New Year and one day we were the only foreigners in three cafes on the other side- the hippy side- of the river. It looked as if Hampi was being developed for tourism, with roads and paths being improved.

The Western tourists were different this time, coming in from Goa like we had in April, but these looked like wealthy holiday makers, middle class families who mostly didn't respect the dress code. One day a younger group were lounging in the Chillout. 'That's my blanket,' one of the staff said. 'Oh,' they said. They didn't say anything else or put it back, the only bit of personal space he has when tourists sit on his bed all day and he's there all day and all evening every day.

Essentially there was no 'nightlife;' in the evening we would go out and get chai and feed bananas to the cows. Cows around the village became familiar to us; one had horns joining up above the head, one had horns curling down to the head. A caramel coloured beauty hung about near the Chillout. Two youngish cows slept cuddled up near the chai and street food stalls. Once we saw a tiny calf maybe newly born, spindly legged, being licked clean by its mother. One evening I saw a cute sleepy baby cow, other cows were asleep nearby. I was late and had missed my bananas woman so I bought a few tomatoes from a street food stall. I placed the tomatoes gently on the ground in front of the sleepy baby cow, but it couldn't pick them up and they rolled away, which disturbed it and then the sight of one being fed woke the other cows up.

Late at night there were people going to the toilet near the main temple but mostly people seemed to all be in bed. Once when we walked back at 12.30am we passed an old woman ironing outdoors. Nearby were people asleep outside under mosquito nets.

***

Twenty years ago Anthony had visited a chai stall near the Rama temple and met Hanuman and his wife and was very pleased to find that they were still there. We visited most days and had chai and coconuts and watched the monkeys in the tree nearby, sometimes feeding them peanuts we'd bought on the way. At Hanuman's and other stalls, chillies were dipped in batter and fried and served in paper. It was mesmerising to watch Hanuman cooking.

On the way to Hanuman's chai stall one afternoon we saw monkeys going from one side of the car park to the other to go into a tree, to go to bed? There was a banana stall right beside the tree but I said, 'I won't wake them again by feeding them,' 'Yes,' Anthony said, 'You upset the eco system, feeding cows when they are ready to sleep, don't go waking the monkeys up as well!' There were loads of monkeys including babies and some very small wet babies on their mothers, all crossing to the roosting tree but I resisted. But then some Indian people fed them biscuits, the monkeys came down so we bought bananas for them and then even more people bought bananas and started feeding them. The man at the banana stall told us all to move, to feed them away from his stall. He had a big stick;

we wondered if the monkeys ever ganged up and robbed his bananas. One grabbed Anthony's hand but they were the easier black face monkeys like in Pushkar.

Hanuman told us about an 'Italian Baba' who lived on the other side of the river. He had built an ashram there forty years ago. Hanuman explained how to get there and a couple of days later we set out to visit. We had to walk beyond Hanuman's chai stall to a place where there is a man who takes people across the river in a coracle.

I'm not at all good with directions let alone ones involving just pointing across the way, walk there, then come to water, coracle, go there and wait, man will come, offer you lift, it should cost this. We didn't really understand where to go; we came to a chai stall near the river, there were signs warning about alligators or crocodiles and a policeman who seemed to be guarding a ruined monument, we thought he probably had one of the easiest police jobs. We stopped for chai and bought three packets of crisps, one each for us and one which I put under a tree for the crows. We asked the chai people about the boat, 'No boat,' they said.

We went back to Hanuman and tried again. I was surprised we didn't give up, usually we might not have bothered but we did, and we got to the coracle place and explained we were going to see Italian Baba. The coracle man told us that he had died the day before, 'Heart problems;' he'd been taken to the Government hospital, 'The doctors tried their best.' He said it was still okay to go to the ashram and pay our respects. The coracle was beautifully made and being rowed across the still expanse of water, surrounded by the otherworldly scenery of Hampi was absolutely magical.

Before the ashram was a small temple, we hesitated unsure if we were allowed in. An Indian family beckoned us and showed us the way, we followed them down a low-ceilinged stone passageway. At the end was a shrine within an alcove in the rock with a very old Baba sitting there. Copying the family, we gave some money to the Baba and received a blessing. The coracle man was still outside and pointed the way through scrub and old garden to the ashram. I had imagined lots of mourning devotees and been unsure if it was even appropriate to visit, but there was no one about. The ashram looked as though it hadn't been active for a few years. A caretaker lived there but no other residents.

An Indian man who spoke good English showed us around. He had grown up knowing the Baba, who had come to India when he was seventeen or eighteen in the 1960s; at first he had lived in nearby caves then built the Ashram. For the past four years the Baba had been living between Italy and Goa as he was very old, and hadn't been to the ashram. The man told us that the Baba had planned to return to see the ashram and do little bit of cleaning in the garden. The Baba travelled from Italy to Goa with his family, then travelled from Goa to Hampi, which is quite a journey along a bumpy road. He had stayed at a guesthouse in Hampi rather than the ashram as he needed somewhere more comfortable with a fan. When the Baba arrived in Hampi he began to feel unwell. He died on 28/12/18 aged eighty-five. He didn't get to the ashram but he did get back to Hampi.

The man explained that the body may not come back today, 'Lots of work if foreigner dies in India,' he said. He showed us the Baba's bed and a picture of him on the wall and invited us to take photographs. We met an Italian woman who had come especially to see him, she was very moved to have arrived the day after he died, and we all had a hug. The man took a photograph of all of us together in front of the Baba's picture, 'To remember this day.' I asked the Italian woman if the Baba was famous in Italy. She said not exactly famous but known because of a book that had been written about him by a fellow Italian. She said the title translates as 'Barefoot on the Earth.'

The story of a Westerner making an ashram in India, living in caves was inspirational to us. Was there was a way for us to play the universe, to say, l live between India, Southeast Asia and the UK?

Later in bed I asked Anthony, 'Is there anything you want to do, be a pirate, climb Everest- substitute alternatives- be like Matt in Nepal and be a nomad?' Anthony said nothing like that but that he would like to do some travelling alone and to go away for the odd weekend and be out of contact, that freedom of feeling 'off grid.' I understand that, I enjoy time alone too. We even spoke about the unthinkable, would we stay together, would we get divorced. We both said that we didn't think our relationship will break down; it would just be if we decided that we wanted to live on our own, to play the game of life by ourselves. Or to have more space; we spoke about Helena Bonham Carter and Tim Burton who are married but live next door to each other, and Bill from next door who lives on his boat and speaks to wife every day but she lives somewhere else.

***

The Wi-Fi worked properly on the other side of the river and we went there a few times so I could do my blog. Like the difference between how Renate and Michelle perceived Varkala, I noticed my perceptions had changed from when we were in Hampi in April. Then, going over on the ferry for the first time, the ferry man had seemed like Siddhartha. This time, waiting for twenty people to come so he would go, it seemed like a slightly annoying business.

Yogesh told us that he'd been in situations there of offering them ridiculous amounts of money to take him across to catch a train, and the ferryman saying, 'No, the police,' and Yogesh saying, 'What police, where?!' exasperated, and the ferry man saying, 'No, not until twenty people.'

While waiting one day for the queue to fill up we spoke to two women, they said they had arrived at five am and had to wait three hours for the ferry to start running to get to their guesthouse on the other side. They were from Bangalore and explained about the salt, 'It's a superstition, not allowed to lend neighbours salt;' they sounded almost apologetic or even slightly embarrassed. We told them that's one of the reasons why we love it here, things like that make it interesting.

On the other side of the river were the steps where the motorbikes went up the hill, the concrete made into ramps to the side of the steps which had so scared and impressed last time. This time I watched a kid not make it and have to get off; it was nothing dramatic.

We visited the guesthouse we'd stayed in on the other side. The loo was upstairs at the back of an unused room off the peach coloured balcony where we stayed before with the cat and kittens, the swing seats and the courtyard where Jude and I saw a monkey close up for the first time. I walked to the end of the balcony and stood there looking down onto the dusty road, the rice fields beyond, the people below, a solitary auto. My heart swelled, to have this second chance.

***

Just before we left Anthony met a couple in the Chillout and arranged to meet them the next day with me. They were a similar age and like us had sold up and gone travelling. We were excited that we had met 'people like us,' but when we met the next day it transpired they were a lot wealthier than us. They had sold up but had an extensive property to go to. Realising the wealth disparity caused me a minor wobble.

'You have options,' they said, after recommending places and properties which were out of our price range. No we don't, okay we do, but fewer. Doubts, why did we spend so much on a boat? Compared to many people we have so much and plenty of security. Compared to what we had, compared to what others have and us being older, not so much. Fear! What if Anthony dies first and I'm left alone on the boat, versus we had a house... Even though no one has any real security.

What next? Life on the boat, work... Mind whirring, so get it out, write it down and then get back to living in the moment. The only thing off that list I need to do now is write the book and maintain the blog. As I was typing the 'What next' piece, writing about managing fear, a smiley face emoji appeared in the text by accident. I deleted it and kept typing. Immediately another smiley face, this time made of a comma and dots appeared, another magical typo!

A faint nip appeared on the air. We saw a group of women in shawls and cardigans. Near the Chillout we stopped to say hello to some super cute babies in woolly multi-coloured crocheted hats and cardigans and cuddly fleeces. The second to last evening I had a cold shower and used my lungi as a towel. The cotton lungi stuck to me and my feet were cold. I didn't notice until almost the end that the door of our bathroom in our last proper room in India was made of the tiniest mosaic...

Even the monkeys at Hanuman's chai stall had been the most entertaining ever on our last visit there, flying from the temple across branches, up the tree and back again, causing a commotion, crashing into the chai stall's empty metal oil drum bin and knocking it over, apparently just for fun.

On our last visit to the main temple we watched people who had been staying in temple loading a truck with gas bottles and cooking equipment. There were lots of people selling ornaments and tourist souvenirs and we managed this with good humour on both sides, 'Good luck,' 'Try someone else,' 'We're no good.' We didn't want anything and couldn't buy extra stuff to carry anyway. There was a man staring at me, perhaps unfamiliar with Western women, it felt creepy and Anthony told him to go away. Inside the temple grounds we sat and watched the many monkeys, adults and babies but people hassling us for selfies got too much; we couldn't sit quietly even for a minute and our usual friendly patience started to wear thin.

We saw a man feeding fish at the temple lake, a monkey wanted some of the food and put its hand into the water to get it. The man gave the monkey some food. He saw us watching and invited us down to join him, we climbed down a steep flight of steps to the edge of the lake.

'You do this every day?'

'Not every day.' He and another man had big sacks of puffed rice. Just like in Pushkar, where we regularly saw a man feeding bread to the fish, these were just ordinary local people feeding the animals. The fish feeding man said the same thing, 'All animals are free here.'

Last time we'd left Hampi it was early in the morning, as night was turning into day. This time we left in the evening and day turned into night during the auto ride. There were palm trees against the orange sky and smoke from the evening rubbish fires. Tiny humble houses beautifully painted in pink, pink and jade and multi-coloured squares. India sadness. Sadness at leaving India. At the same time it was also good to leave India sadness behind; India can be very intense and sad sometimes. We planned to party and have fun in Cambodia; I was looking forward to being able to wear anything and relax.

At Hosapete train station a few people stared at us. There were a few people begging. There were some stray dogs around, one came around the back of bench near our backpacks, I clapped it away, thinking it might pee on the bags. Then I saw it had teats and was obviously a nursing mother. I had biscuits for the journey in my bag but thought I won't feed it; there were a few dogs around and I didn't want to attract a lot of attention or for them to fight.

Later on the platform far away from the bench, too late, I regretted it. I saw a man in a lungi who did not look well off, feed another dog a bread roll. 'My' dog had teats, a nursing mother! How could I? I am not usually mean but nor am I always nice. It's about acting nice not just having nice thoughts. Shame, I even had biscuits!

Being in India can mean hardening your heart against things you see simply in order to cope. Hard heart versus heart open depends on choices being made all the time. Sometimes, like Greg from Poland and the woman with the chocolate you can get it wrong and I realised I'd got it wrong with that nursing dog.

The announcer was announcing our train over and over, using the new name for Bangalore, which she pronounced in a delightfully sing song way as Beng-ga-loo-roo. My thinking brain said, 'Well you can't help all the animals, you only occasionally help them anyway. You can just feed a dog in Bangalore to make up for it.' But my heart said, *Please give me another chance.* We were way down the platform from the bench where we'd been. The train was overdue and the announcer was still announcing our train.

From the distance a dog appeared coming towards us. As it got closer I knew: brown and white, slightly skinny with teats. I waited until she was a little bit past us and emptied out two packets of biscuits on the floor for her.

'That was nothing short of a miracle,' I said, breathless.

'Well, miracle might be stretching it,' Anthony said.

The train was an old fashioned model with burgundy seats. We were sharing with a family and once everyone had got settled we all started to talk. They asked us what we liked best about India and as usual we raved about the colourful houses of Kanyakumari. They said it's a new thing, colourful houses, and that people in Delhi had started painting their houses pink recently. They were a nice family, a middle aged woman and her husband who had lived in New York for twenty-seven years. Every six months they come back to India, 'I miss my mum,' the woman said, looking at her mother who was with them.

Everyone got ready for bed; we turned the lights out for the mother in the lower bunk. Her daughter was above her, reading a Kindle. Anthony and I were on the two bunks opposite. The son-in-law was across the aisle against the window. I was in the top bunk and lay there teeming with everything as usual and trying to write things down in my notebook in the dark. Our last night in India was on a train, which felt like a good way to end it.

***

Arriving in Bangalore at five am, people were wrapped in fine woven fawn coloured blankets, others wore cuddly bonnets. Our flight to Cambodia wasn't until eleven pm so we had booked a hotel room for the day. We had just run out of data and hadn't bothered to top up, thinking we could manage for just one day. As we got closer to the hotel, the taxi driver asked us to phone the hotel for directions. The hotel wouldn't give directions without our confirmation number which we couldn't get without internet. We asked them just to tell us the directions and we'd sort it out when we got there but the man on the phone refused to give us directions.

In hindsight, we should have tried harder to find it; I mean what did people do before smart phones? We could have got the driver to stop and ask an auto driver. But at the side of a main road in Bangalore in the semi darkness not knowing where we were, feeling tired and vulnerable, we gave up and asked the taxi driver to take us to a hotel.

'Oh you need a hotel? That's easy, no problem.' He took us to somewhere far too grand, then another, then to another before finding one that had a room. Suspiciously, he rushed ahead in front of us ostensibly to translate, 'Your language' or in case they were asleep. We didn't realise the first time, the second time we did. We've never need a translator or intermediary at hotels. Finally he took us to a hotel in a run down area. It was shockingly expensive, almost three times the price of the room we had booked and was clearly overpriced. We tipped the taxi driver well for running us around and said goodbye. After we had checked in and taken our bags upstairs I went downstairs to ask for the Wi-Fi password. At the desk I saw our taxi driver, who had said goodbye and left, talking to the man at the desk. We suspected that he and whoever was at the hotel had made some kind of a deal to overcharge us and split the money. It was the only time anything like that happened to us.

The plan had been to try and sleep in the day, I did a little but across the hall was a child with a very loud squeaky toy and then some building work started in another room.

We looked on Google maps, found somewhere to eat and booked an Uber auto. The place we went was very friendly and had loads of staff, we often thought that in India. The staff served our food onto our plates for us, veg biryani and cold juice. It was hot and dirty outside, inside the restaurant was cool and clean. We felt better. After all, we hadn't planned that it would be any different than this, rest in the room, go out and eat; it's just that it had seemed to be difficult.

The online booking people gave us some money back to say sorry which covered about half of the extra expenses and the day woman at the hotel gave us some money back too, 'Taxes' she said, we didn't understand why but were pleased we'd got some money back. Maybe she realised we'd been overcharged by the night man. She also booked us a cheaper taxi than the night staff had.

At the airport things went well until passport control where we were told off for not having registered; we hadn't realised that we should have done that, although we had been in three times and out twice before anyone mentioned it. Later I had a calm look at our visa in good light with my glasses on and saw that as well as in the centre where it says you have go out and in after six months which we aware of and had done, at the bottom it also says in even smaller writing if you are staying over a certain number of days you need to register. Oops!

We had our most expensive meal ever at Bangalore airport. Then our flight was delayed. At the gate we met a British couple, it turned out that one of them built narrowboats which surprised us all since we live on one. They looked like regular tourists, they'd been to India to go to Goa for a beach and sun holiday rather than for enlightenment. We spoke about the pressure on tourists to buy.

'He can't say no,' the woman said.

'I bought so many shorts and t-shirts and I didn't want any of them!' the man said.

On the plane to Cambodia a young Indian man sat down next to us as if taking his seat then just took selfies and left and then laughed with his friends. It was in sharp contrast to our first flight out of India where we met a young Indian man on his first flight who took selfies with us which we were happy to do.

But maybe it was good that our leaving day wasn't so smooth. It stopped us being too sad. Compared to our last ten days in Hampi, if all had been beauty and sweetness how would we ever have borne to leave? So perhaps it was a gift after all.

I just got lost for a while: Cambodia

Phnom Penh

On the inside of the door was a sign with the rules and information for the guesthouse. Top of the list was *No Drugs, No Prostitutes, No weapons.* 'Well that's our holiday ruined,' we said, laughing.

Suddenly it felt like we were on the tourist trail. It seemed expensive. 'Everything's going to seem expensive compared to India,' Anthony said.

Our taxi driver had a big, lived in face, open and strong at the same time. I noticed a lot of the men looked like this. Near our guesthouse men sat in social groups chatting at tables outside workshops and garages with cans of Red Bull or beer. One of the first things I noticed was that the Cambodian men don't look. In fact I looked more! I couldn't help noticing men working on engines, not wearing tops, their bodies fleshy, soft, just natural.

An old Lonely Planet I read in a cafe in India advised Western women travellers to wear dark glasses and avoid making eye contact with Indian men; of course this is a huge generalisation. But in Cambodia it wasn't just that men didn't look at me, no one looked at us at all. Not one person hassled us except one person offering us a bright pink tuk-tuk. Not one selfie request. 'Don't you know who I am?!' we said laughing.

Our first meal, at a Western owned restaurant mirrored the sexy-in-the-mouth-noodles of our first meal in Bangkok; even the lettuce was tasty. Sometimes in India we missed fresh crunchy vegetables, and right then we were happy to be away, from the bad tummies and just relax.

From our table we watched a little street food van with lights and music blaring like a disco, a scooter with two adults and a child holding a toddler, women on scooters holding giant teddies; big shiny new cars, tuk-tuks with silky shiny curtains, another decorated with Astroturf, one white with neon lights, another full of monks in orange robes. Cycle tuk-tuks with the passenger seat at the front like a Victorian bath chair; one was carrying a woman with an orange cat on her lap.

After dinner we went for a walk, a woman walked past carrying a big circular tray of bottles of nail polish and hair scrunchies on her head. We walked down a road full of bars with young women dressed in mini skirts and mainly older men drinking. There were lots of women walking little fluffy dogs on leads. In the streets and alleys were lots of cats, most of them had short tails. There were buildings with spiral staircases visible from the outside like I'd seen in Tokyo.

In the 7/11 type shop was a woman wearing a very short peach-pink lacy dress; she had long shiny hair, shimmery legs and high heels; she looked as if she had just stepped out of the pages of a magazine, a vision of loveliness. She was with a much older Western man. The '7/11' sold soya milk, face cream, body moisturiser, brands including Vaseline and Nivea, luxury four blade razors and all kinds of biscuits. Almost all the face creams was whitening and sunblock went up to factor 100. I bought a big tube of thick sunscreen; I had slacked in India and let my skin go chicken skin-ish, never mind, the tiger stripes or stretch marks of the experience.

Near the river there were groups of people doing outdoor exercise classes to music, outdoor gym equipment and a running track with distances marked out. A tuk-tuk driver standing beside his parked tuk-tuk was cheerfully doing exercises, hands on thighs, swirling his knees. Beside the river were little food stalls with tables and chairs and mini charcoal burners, scales and dumplings in a big pot. People with little hand carts filled with ice and cans sold drinks including alcohol. Even though alcohol was the same price as Coca Cola, the night life didn't seem to be all about drinking; people were just out, playing cards, sitting at the little tables. Further along the prom were big neon screens with ever changing and moving images; tulips, rain water falling.

We found a cheaper place to eat in the market with plastic tables and chairs which spilled onto the pavement; inside the restaurant was a glass fronted wooden cabinet full of nail polishes, as if someone had a sideline doing nails. They gave us free iced Jasmine tea; we risked it the first time, later we looked up about ice. If it is big chunks with a hole in, which this was- chunky cylinders with a hole through the middle like very large beads- that's good, that's for drinks. Otherwise it could be from ice used for packing; we saw great slabs of ice on trolleys, beautiful like glaciers, with air bubbles and fractures and the light shining through it.

Cambodian women wore wraps of printed cotton like lungis as skirts with shirts or short skirts with t-shirts, covering up their tops from the sun like in Japan and Thailand. There were lots of bright colour design printed t-shirts and shirts; I saw a woman's shirt, so bright and with two large faces on the front, one on each side. In the evenings women often wore silky button-through shirt and three quarter length trousers pyjamas in the street; one evening a woman walked towards us wearing pink shiny pyjamas, luminous in the dark. We went to the night market and saw Marilyn Monroe style silver lurex and red velvet plunging neckline dresses, alongside cheap jeans and t-shirts.

But... it soon didn't seem enough, after India it seemed too touristy. After all our complaining towards the end of India about selfie takers, I missed the attention. Not because I liked feeling like a celebrity (okay maybe a little…) but because it was positive interaction with the people of the country. We missed India. All the things we had been annoyed about, we missed.

At the guesthouse I drank good strong French press coffee and wrote downstairs in the restaurant. The coffee was great for writing, not so good for sleep; I caught myself out a couple of times having coffee too late in the afternoon and then wondering why I couldn't sleep at night.

I finished the 'What's next' piece I had started in Hampi, and then the word document disappeared. As always I had emailed it to myself as back up so I could have found it in my emails but would that really be best? Is it beneficial to live in the future? No. Was losing my 'what's next' ideas a coincidence? There's no such thing as coincidences. Rather than trying to plan for or worrying about The Future, it came to me that a useful self support system could be to make spiritual enlightenment or awareness the guiding aim or principle of one's life rather than anything else. That way you'll always be okay because you can do that whatever, wherever and anything can help.

***

Koh Rong

The wooden boat painted red, the island, the sea so blue, it was all so totally Instagrammable that I didn't want to. Again I felt as if I was supposed to feel something that I didn't. Sometimes too much beauty doesn't resonate; it's impossible for me to feel. Give me an orange cat on a dusty wall or raindrops glittering on shutters in the dark; those things are more likely to get me there than the big stuff.

The man dropped the anchor a little way from the shore, hooked a ladder over the side and we stepped down from the boat with our bags into the water above the knee, past the bow which was beautifully decorated with flowers and onto a paradise beach with well off looking tourists on sunbeds and little beach front restaurants. 'Are we in the wrong place?' we asked ourselves.

We were in a tent, nearby were huts and glass -fronted tree houses. It was luxurious camping though, the tent set up on a wooden platform, a tarpaulin above for shade and a deep thick mattress, electricity and a fan.

An English woman helped out with online bookings and English speaking queries at our place, we asked how she'd ended up here, she said she'd come on holiday and fallen in love with the place and come back to live. She had been on the island seven years and had a Cambodian partner and a little boy.

'He understands everything, but he's a little late in talking, which is normal as he's learning two languages at once,' she said.

In a way it was a bit boring, being stuck on a small beach with nothing to do, 'I feel like Robinson Crusoe,' Anthony said. It was good for me and writing though.

I got up early and drank black coffee at the restaurant attached to our place, poor food, poor service and sometimes the staff would play really loud music even if I was the only the customer 'and obviously writing' as I egotistically thought to myself. Still, sitting at a wooden table looking out of the open front to a great view of the sea, when it was quiet it was a great place to write. One of the nicest things was that even in a sloppy type up of old notes I saw patterns that matched other sections or the present.

We walked to the village in search of culture and authenticity, up a hill, watching motorbikes going up the steep paths. In the village decrepit buildings, small rubbish piles, the children very poor and dirty looking. The harbour area was beautiful with wooden piers and buildings. We stopped at the first little shop which had cans in coolers and a few plastic chairs.

When I went to the village alone that was all I did, walked to the shop, sat and had a drink; Sprite, Red Bull or a soya drink in a can and watched the chickens and chicks on the other side of the path by a small rubbish pile. The chickens ate a big sheet of polystyrene; it got smaller each time I went, shedding little fragments like rough beads.

On my walk to and from the village I paid a lot of attention, making a mental note of all the markers: a building with a blue roof, a cafe which was never open, sacks of building materials, a truck that was almost always there. Scrubby plants which led to a sandy path. Broken planters. Tiny shells, periwinkle blue, violet and indigo scattered in a messy semi circle. When I went with Anthony we walked another way. I was momentarily confused, looking for the shells.

'All roads lead there,' Anthony said.

On the beach were tiny shells in beautiful arrangements like art, and lots of tiny holes and tiny piles of sand made by crabs, each one different, some like comets, some like asymmetric snowflakes, all so delicate and pretty.

***

Evening swims, the other people in the water couples happy on holiday, the water warm, the sea green and glossy, the sunset reflected in it. We used to float in the sea and talk about enlightenment: Is this all there is? If you gave up the search, put all the focus on this life- like being in the moment, or even richer.

Think of it like a game, if that helps you to take the gas bill less seriously. But don't have half your mind on the otherness- the brain in the tank, the Green Mist theory, the after, the what's next. Just like the what's next in life it stops you being in the present. If there's nothing else and nothing after then you've wasted that time.

People realised they were in a mortal life, found that scary and so invented the possibility of otherness as a comfort.

Just live, enjoy, make up and imbue meaning- or not.

Robert from Switzerland said that belief comes first, then knowing. Experiment with the hypothesis, practice believing it and seeing how that is. Forget about spirituality, it's a cul-de-sac. I'm interested in it; it appeals to my imagination. Waking up= enjoying life. Sadness prevents us seeing beauty. People say the 'first step' is seeing beauty. What if the first step is the only step? Simple life, slow, no smart phone, minimalism, enables you to notice the beauty and really engage with your own experience physically via the senses and emotions. No demanding job that caused me to adopt an inauthentic persona. Waking up and leaving work and travelling was waking up and enjoying my life.

Like Robert from Switzerland, if you want to reinvent yourself maybe it is much easier to do with no contact with your family. Your family might just think you're a bum with no job. But if you think, This is what I'm meant to be doing, this is what I always intended to do, therefore you are successful. Like me, this is what I always intended, to live on a boat, and WRITE as I did as a child, as I've always done. I just got lost for a while, that's all, for twenty years.

In the sea the day after the enlightenment conversation I felt pinpricks as if something had stung me on the outside of my thigh, then at my wrist it was as if a tiny spiky thing like a prickle was caught in my bracelet. Then I felt it again, stronger, stinging, on my right breast. Anthony said, 'Are you getting stung?' We couldn't see anything. We got out after a little while; whatever it was had caused tiny bumps like little TB markers which disappeared quickly. That evening we saw a shooting star, orange like a firework with a tail like a comet; I had never seen one like that.

We had dinner with a woman Anthony had met earlier and her companion, both from Italy. The woman, Vanessa, had left her job and been travelling for two months. She planned to go home and work then go out again. Not all her friends understand; 'Everyone just wants *things*,' she said. Before they left she gave me a four leaf clover.

Digging a hole on the beach and then leaving it is anti social, I realised. I had fallen in several holes on the beach especially at night in Thailand. As a child I fell headfirst into a muddy water filled hole straight after my mum's boyfriend had said, 'Don't you ever stop talking Rachel?' On the beach in Koh Rong, also holes.

'Even my chair fell into a hole,' I complained one day.

'Perhaps it's a metaphor.' Anthony said. (I'm always say that things are metaphors.)

'What, I'm in a hole?!'

'No, you're going down the rabbit hole.' Oh yes, I like that, a reminder every now and again, my own personal mindfulness bell: *Remember to remember. You followed the White Rabbit down the rabbit hole. You took the RED pill.*

***

I'm not friends with my son on social media; it is Anthony who monitors things. Sometimes things seem terrible on social media but then when we call things are fine. Or they've been fine on the phone and then they seem awful on social media. Or on social media some kind of terrible disaster is reported and then when we call or even if we don't, within a day or two it's actually resolved. Adie (millennial WordPress blogger) said millennials use a lot of hyperbole, maybe that's part of it?

So it was Anthony who saw a news interview he had done, and who gently, piece by piece, told me what it contained. My son is an upcoming artist, being interviewed about his backstory and one of the things he said was that he was kicked out of home as a teenager. It's true, I kicked him out as a teenager.

When he was a child, I would never have thought that would have happened. For years I had saved a leaflet I had picked up when I was on a work placement at a child and family place when my son was eleven. Me still so smug, a confident and loving parent. My friend a social worker in child protection saying she'd driven past us on her way home from a horror-filled day at work and seen us playing with the dog on the grassy walkway and said that we'd made her feel that there was good in the world.

The leaflet said, 'Parents of teenagers often feel that they have failed.' Much later, when things had gone wrong, I over related to two mothers from an autism organisation who said, 'As a mother you feel like you've got 'Guilty' stamped on one side of you and 'Failure' on the other.'

Those words weren't meant for me, I just borrowed them. Like I'd do a depression questionnaire on myself at work, I never hit the criteria; I ate, I got up for work, I liked to have sex, but did I feel like a failure, did I feel hopeless, did I feel like I wanted to die, yes, yes and yes again.

When my son was sixteen I phoned up the housing department of the council. A woman answered, 'You would have to ask him to leave; he would come here with his bag and we go from there.' 'I can't do that,' I said. 'Well, then you haven't reached the end of your tether yet.' She added, 'I did it to mine, and it was the best thing that ever happened to us.'

It took another two years until I reached the end of my tether, sitting at the top of the stairs, screaming, wanting to hurt myself, my boyfriend at the time locking away paracetamol and knives in a suitcase.

In the long years prior, truanting, refusing to go to school, a social worker threatening me, school saying I needed to take more responsibility, my son trashing the house, getting in trouble with the police.

Of course, when I look back maybe there were loads of other things I could have done, if I had been a different person. I took his things to my mum's, he stayed round a girlfriend's, sofa surfed, and several years later we are all still alive, I am available to help and we get on fine.

It's not like I've ever forgotten any of that, but to be dragged back there so completely and publicly more than a decade later was almost more than I could bear. It was a hilarious contrast that we were on a paradise beach in Cambodia at the time. Oh, the shame, I could barely move, and yet of course I did.

In the water, in the heat, over dinner, terrible shame that I couldn't get away from and the guilt, the guilt. Imagine the worst thing you've ever done, something you did years ago when you couldn't do any better, not only brought right back, but now it's public.

'People do things to survive, and then after they survive, they can't live with what they've done.' Adam Johnson, *The Orphan Master's Son*

I didn't hear anything from anyone. Anthony reminded me that those who knew me would know that there was more to it than that.

Having a famous person in the family could be like a time bomb, what if he tells people I had loads of different boyfriends? I wondered what it was like for Damien Hirst's mum. Anthony said, 'No one gives a fuck about Damien Hirst's mum, no one knows anything about Damien Hirst's mum or even cares; even if he had said anything about her, no one would remember it now.'

Anthony said it's hard to think of your child as an adult or a complete adult with totally their own identity, that's why famous people like to go home, to keep their feet on the ground. And it's hard if you don't always get the art- or want to get the art in my case as it's all about my son's mental distress which I find distressing. Again I wondered about what it was like for Damien Hirst's mum, her little boy slicing open a cow and putting it in a glass case and that being his most famous work. *(No offence is meant to DH or his mum, this is the actual conversation we had at the time and he is the person who popped into my mind as we were talking; I guess he's the most famous male artist I know, which hopefully is a compliment.)*

A string of epiphanies: Cambodia

Otres Village

I had read about the development in Sihanoukville, Khmer owned
small shops and restaurants were being sold to Chinese developers
and the land redeveloped for hotels and casinos. Westerners were
selling up and moving out, fed up with living beside constant
building work, and bemoaning the loss of familiar restaurants, bars
and shops. Sihanoukville was as 'bad' as we had feared; one large
building site, but fascinating, huge hotels half built, and so many.
Some covered in green netting, others almost done, we could see
through the windows to big dormitories of beds, and developments
of small huts with little space in between; a different standard of
personal space to that of Westerners.

From the tuk tuk, the occasional pretty sight: a navy umbrella
with silver edges, a burgundy shirt with sequins, the sun catching
them and making them sparkle. In the tuk-tuk, the road long and
dusty with building work all around my main concern was dust after
so much pollution on the trip. Luckily where we were staying was
something of an oasis, away from the main road.

On a beam above the door of our wooden hut was a bag of weed,
some papers and a lighter, left by the previous occupants, probably
because they were taking a flight. The paths from the huts to the
showers were paved with tile mosaics. Past a now-closed
'Alternative Pharmacy' there was a biggish room with 'Good vibes
only' written in chalk on a blackboard. I brushed down the top and
underneath of a small table and chairs and set up a place to work.

Outside the onsite restaurant were some umbrellas hanging upside
down. The umbrellas were faded maroon, pink and brown, with
delicate and flower patterns. We drank Sprite with ice; the ice would
melt almost straightway and I'd get extra glasses of ice and keep on
topping it up. There were three kittens around the restaurant who
would play, sit on laps, eat noodles and curl up to sleep beside
us. One day when I was watching and playing with the kittens
outside, a young couple stopped to admire their cuteness. They said

that in The Netherlands where they were from there was a reality tv show of kittens living in a kind of giant dolls' house with a voice over narration. The show was especially made for adults at home suffering from burn out, what a wonderful, wonderful country.

Nearby was a lake. A person tipped big plastic food buckets into the lake and the water became alive with fish in a feeding frenzy. I saw husky type dogs with pale blue unreal marble eyes. I wondered why there were huskies in Cambodia when it was so hot. On the main road were wooden buildings, bars and restaurants, many owned by Westerners and almost all with 'For Sale' or to 'To Let' signs up. We saw a woman, blonde and skinny with dreadlocks, be dropped off by a man on a motorbike. She had a bloodied face and her expression and walk made her look like a zombie. We watched her for a while and saw that she went into a pharmacy, hopefully for some first aid. We saw a vegan street stall selling, unbelievably, homemade Vegan Snickers. He was a young Westerner. We asked him what he was going to do. He said he was thinking about going to the Andaman Islands. In the dust I saw a glass ball, clear white, faintly blue. For a moment I'd considered picking it up before I realised it was a marble, later I saw boys playing with them at the side of the road.

Sitting outside on our balcony I saw a woman walk past our hut a couple of times. 'Friend' I said to myself, and resolved to speak to her next time she passed. It was the same for her; she'd said she wanted to speak to us too. Of course at first it's the outside things: our kind of age, kind of hippy-ish in a natural way, no makeup, loose natural hair, a printed cotton smock. Rupa was Spanish, as a young woman she had left home and gone off to Osho's ashram in Pune, India, which explained why my husband 'recognised' her, he has known several sannyasins.

Rupa runs workshops in Italy and Spain on family relationships and consciousness raising. She created a life totally her own that was nothing like her parents' lives or their expectations for her. When her mother became ill she returned home to care for her. She decided to just be herself, 'Here I am, I run these workshops, I am a teacher,' rather than try to 'fit in' by being inauthentic. She said it was very hard, going back. Back, 'in the collective,' as she called it, the fear comes: security, pensions, savings, all those things she had happily not worried about for years. We all spoke about our times in more touristy, holiday maker areas. 'You can have your own experience even in a party place,' Rupa said.

We often had dinner or lunch together, 'You are an angel,' Rupa said to our regular waiter on the last day. 'You have come down from heaven, an angel.' She expressed herself so easily, like Renate, who when we said goodbye had said to me, 'If I'd had a daughter like you, we'd have had such fun,' whereas I sometimes find my English reserve gets the better of me.

We told Rupa about Baba Cesare, the Italian Baba whose ashram we had visited in Hampi. Rupa spoke and read Italian, she had a book she had borrowed off another guest. It was 'Barefoot on the Earth,' the book that the Italian woman at the ashram had told us about!

I knew I was working too hard, trying to tackle and complete a big section that I had long been intimidated by, along the way finding more to do and then doing that as well. My hand and arm needed a rest but at the same time I was feeling a burst of inspiration and energy. This temporary feeling helped me to access good work, to see patterns everywhere, and to dream of it being completed.

I went for a walk to the beach, on the road nearby was a mini funfair with small rides, stalls of garish plastic toys and brightly coloured balloons. At a canned drink stall a woman in a pretty dress was semi asleep, she woke and we caught eyes and smiled. It was unusual for me to go out alone and even more unusual for me to go off and not say anything; the appeal of a bit of interstitial time, unknown, unexplained. I stood on the beach facing the sea. The beach was busy with people. There was a big hotel block almost like a skyscraper, lit up. It was the end of the day; all the lights were coming on. I was in the moment then.

We got an overnight sleeper coach to Siem Reap. We arranged our bags in the cramped compartment and sat top to tail. Just sitting and feeling okay was such a nice feeling. I had been feeling anxious-checking my bag, bank cards. So just sitting happy on the bus, thinking, or just letting the thoughts think themselves, about the next section of writing, the overall plan, as if it's just going almost by itself, me just recharging myself so that I can write it. The light on my water bottle in the window made it beautiful; a pale blue light like the marble in the dust, like the dog's eyes, even.

***

Siem Reap

To our eyes the hotel was like a pop star's luxury residence, with a cream facade and a blue swimming pool. The outside was neatly paved with pots of bright pink and orange flowers and lots of pretty summer shoes on the paving outside the entrance.

The headboard was solid wood, shiny and carved. At the other end of the room was a wardrobe with double sliding mirror doors; it was like having my own private yoga studio. The room, although no more expensive than our average, felt luxurious.

I had read about travel fatigue in someone's Instagram post. As well as the normal missing friends and family and dealing with the stresses and strains, unfamiliar foods, new places and the travel, some people also over schedule, moving from place to place too fast, packing the days with long tours and over photographing everything. There was no danger of us doing that but we still got tired sometimes, especially when we were ill.

I laid on the bed looking at the aura around the just-turned-off fan, thinking of a screen free day. Surely it's okay to have a day off after a night journey? Also I am giving space for discussion and inspiration, and I'm sharpening my axe!

We had a look around an indoor market. I became temporarily enamoured with glazed and decorated bowls made from coconuts, elephant purses and checked scarves, the prices going down as I looked without me doing or saying anything. Other than a pair of sunglasses to replace mine which had broken, I didn't buy anything and the feeling of wanting things soon wore off.

There were lots of big Westernised bars and restaurants, one had a sign: 'Order beer with your breakfast we won't judge you,' and street stalls with small plastic tables and chairs on the pavement, set up from the back of motorbikes and plugged into power supplies installed on trees.

The room in Siem Reap represented real comfort and luxury; especially after a week in a tent, with everything sandy. On the polished wood bedside table I set my lip balm, my kohl eyeliner, my earrings, a charcoal face pack I was excited to buy from the 7/11 nearby and my new glamorous but cheap black mirror sunglasses which I always kept there, the ceiling fan reflected in them.

It was the first day that I felt the fistula healing sufficiently to feel okay to do a forward bend: Bliss. Then back to earth with a bump: period, blood on the white sheets, Aghh! Mess! But no shame or stress through; I cleaned the sheet as best I could and told staff the sheet needed changing, knowing it would be better to wash out blood straightaway.

Suddenly, in Cambodia, at Koh Rong, there had been women in bikinis, men in shorts, flesh everywhere, it seemed so strange. A beautiful dark haired woman had walked past me; she had a lovely curvaceous figure and was wearing a white vintage style balcony bikini. In terms of impact it was like Ursula Andress emerging from the sea in the James Bond film. I had got used to being modestly dressed and my sexuality being completely switched off in public which probably also had an impact in private too, if only because I didn't always feel attractive in my clothes. And then all that flesh which isn't necessarily sexuality it's just people dressing for the beach in what is a totally normal way for Westerners. Anyway it gave me a self esteem wobble in Koh Rong and Anthony had to spend a bit of time reassuring me. We also talked about how maybe we hadn't always felt like sex as much as usual, due to the heat, and maybe due to our 24/7 proximity to each other.

In Siem Reap one morning Anthony watched me doing yoga and then I came back to bed. After sex, the sheet, the duvet, white, soft, perfectly comfortable. The light on the turned wooden legs of the table, I counted the four turns. The smell of my husband. No smell really but perfect anyway and everything feeling so good. Wondering, will I remember this? Anthony often says, if you look back on your twenties, how many actual days do you remember? Actually waking up, being somewhere in a room? Maybe one or two at most.

Shrines in the hotel foyer and restaurants had cans of coke, tea in a glass cup, a bunch of bananas, stacks of money, something new every day. It was like the morning rituals we watched in Pushkar, shop keepers sprinkling water and lighting incense before the working day began. I wondered if we should do it at home, make a shrine, have a morning ritual, make a tea for the shrine, light incense, set an intention; not directly from or connected to a recognised religion. Anthony said religious practices look like a kind of OCD sometimes; he once had a friend who used to walk around the room fifteen times before he went out, everyone thought it was a big problem but Anthony always wondered why was it a problem, why not just accept that it was something that he did, like a kind of ritual. Like I could change my OCD checking of the taps before I go out into a mini ritual, to say thank you for having water?

We talked a lot over meals at the restaurant. I noticed that we were able to discuss things like politics better without annoying each other or getting annoyed. It's not so much that we disagree on big picture stuff, more that the way we approach things is different and that used to cause conflict during discussions. Each difficulty this year has moved us forward in terms of how we handle discussions, personal issues and the way we are together.

Anthony watched road rage videos and laughed; people in the UK going crazy over what would be nothing in India. I watched a couple of YouTube videos with Anthony about 'the matrix' and felt trippy and inspired. I scribbled down quotes and ideas: words are spells that programme you, make friends with your body, subconscious, conscious, make all one. People inside same age- body irrelevant look past this. Don't live in the past, don't live in the future, stay in the NOW. Don't live in fear, raise your frequency. Dream where you are now.

One of the comments mentioned language and conditioning; would we be freer without language? I'd talked about this before when thinking about Raul at Osho's guesthouse in Kerala who couldn't read. If you didn't see any ads, if you weren't exposed to all those ideas and conditioning... But it is double edged: the good books get you there, wake you up, the bad ones keep you sleepy and distracted. Who defines good and bad though? I've had an inspiration moment through a car ad.

Anthony had seen *The Thirteenth Floor* and told me about it but I hadn't seen it. In Koh Rong I had a conversation with a fellow blogger who had written a blog post about *Westworld* and its effects regarding thinking about consciousness. I mentioned *Battlestar Gallactica* which we had recently finished and which had similar themes. Anthony said, 'Tell him about *The Thirteenth Floor*.' It turned out that *The Thirteenth Floor* was kind of like his (the blogger's) *The Matrix;* he had gone to see it with his cousin, hadn't known what he was going to see and unexpectedly had his mind blown. The internet wasn't strong enough at Koh Rong to download it. We tried again in Siem Reap: success.

We switched off *The Thirteenth Floor*. I went into the bathroom and looked in the mirror, still kind of in the film, feeling or imagining that I had just 'arrived.' I noticed two new moles on my body. I came back in, still feeling floaty as if I was a film character. I looked out of the window. There was an unrecognisable animal sitting on top of a car. I couldn't process what it was and I couldn't find the words to name it. It was black and about the size of a monkey. But at the same time it looked like a cartoon; with big orange triangles inside its ears and an orange 'O' shape for a mouth. It was as if my brain didn't recognise it at first. A monkey? A cat? A completely unrecognisable animal; before coalescing into a recognisable creature, a black cat. Or possibly a small monkey. I remember returning home at seventeen and thinking the cats were enormous, having not seen them for a while. Anthony didn't look until it was almost too late; he thought it was a cat, although he admitted it did look weird.

We went outside, me tripped out on a drug free high, everything colourful and sparkly. I pointed to a building, struggling to speak: 'Look- orange- no- purple-.' I couldn't find the words, couldn't say the colours. I was looking at a small purple house set back from the road. Next door to it was a bigger building, a guesthouse peachy orange with shiny chrome balcony rails. Draped in front were sparkly tubular lights, plastic tubing, it was still daylight, sunny, and the lights in the tubes were subtle like a prism or glitter.

I wanted to talk about the cat. I kept telling Anthony off for not staying with me; I used to say this a lot when I was trying to explain something strange and he was either trying to ground me or finding it hard to follow me. Plus he was hungry. We went into the 7/11 nearby. I told myself: 'Don't think about coffee or deodorant or mascara (things I wanted.) Don't speak. Wait for him to eat and go back.' (To the cat, the insights)

We sat outside the 7/11 on a bench. *Don't let me get put off. Don't look at anything. Pick the most boring thing to look at.* But even just sitting on the bench, it was hard to keep my focus on my ideas; a man walked by, some interesting dogs, always distractions, distractions...

To wake up is to realise. To unplug is to disconnect- no distractions, no phone, no unconscious actions and interactions; no actions or interactions that aren't conscious. *Act in awareness. Wake up.*

We walked down to the river. I had to sit down again. Even under normal circumstances I can get overstimulated walking and talking. It's easier for me to be still when talking about something serious, and if the visuals around are interesting I can't take both in and process everything. So we sat down on a bench. I looked down- it was made of shells, like a mosaic. Like the paving in Otres Village, like the path to the village in Koh Rong. Even the bench was overstimulating. Shells and mosaics seem to be kind of a thing for me, maybe they signify arrival?

So are there blank lives we go into, available slots that we light up on the circuit board? I have visualised this like a ball of stiff string, with many intersections, our lights/us moving around it and lighting up different places. Like a circuit board crossed with a ball of wool which has been attacked by a kitten. Like *The Thirteenth Floor?* Or is it remembrance of other lives?

It was hard to focus on thought. So many distractions; a man acting weird, on drugs, two weird dogs. Keep focussed, wits about. It felt like it was a matrix. Experiment with thinking it's a matrix. Stop saying hi to everyone- waste of energy. Don't worry about what others think; people near/walking past. Parents, possibilities; if it's not real then it's not scary. Personal power.

We kept looking for a quiet road but it just got busier and then the neon lights of Pub Street with the multicoloured tumble-blocks of lights. Eventually we came to a dusty road, three stools were set out at a mini table, I felt like I could sit there.

'I think that's just where the staff go for their breaks,' Anthony said; it was the back of a hotel.

Even underfoot, so many distractions, so much to focus on, sand, uneven paving of all kinds, constantly watching and feeling footing, small chairs in the path to go around, being aware of obstacles, constantly aware and/or distracted, how much variety and stimulation can there be?

Home.... The plastic cable lights of the orange-pink and chrome guesthouse were brighter now that it was dark; I could see all the different colours, blobs on a loop.

For most of the time we were in Cambodia one of us was ill, finally in the second half of our time in Siem Reap, our last week in Cambodia, we were both well at the same time. As we were going on a plane to Vietnam next it was now or never for taking the ketamine that Anthony had managed to buy in Phnom Penh. It is sold in liquid form and needs turning into crystals. We weren't sure what to do so Anthony messaged Harrison, the young Australian we'd met in Nepal and asked how to prepare it. Harrison sent us back a comprehensive reply complete with pictures of his set up. We made a contraption out of metal containers and tea lights and pierced the rubber seal with one of my earrings that I had serendipitously just found. Anthony prepared it in the bathroom, lighting incense to mask the smell, which fortunately wasn't too strong.

My legs felt a little spongy but otherwise I felt okay to go out. Walking outdoors felt a little hard; when we had looked up risks one of them was crossing roads as perceptions of speed and distance can alter, and falling over as one of its uses is as an anaesthetic. I was hungry too. Rather than going out of the world, it was like going into the matrix; enjoying food: deep fried mushrooms with sweet and sour dipping sauce, drinking mojitos. It wasn't difficult to interact normally at the restaurant. Seeing the matrix for what it is, appreciating it, versus the rest of time, being outside of it or at least trying to be. Yet at the same time I could really see it as and believe it to be an illusion.

We went to Pub Street and sat on red velvet chairs. Anthony took more ketamine in the toilets. We started talking to a man, a Westerner; big, loud, opinionated, interrupting- Anthony was up for a fight though and held his own.

'I've written fifty books,' the man said.

'I've read fifty books,' Anthony said, refusing to be put down. The man's previous companion took the opportunity to flee. I had taken an instant dislike to the man but I tried to practice being open and relaxed.

Anthony had read up about ketamine; its use in therapy but mainly about it as a psychedelic with many people reporting similar esoteric experiences. Getting the dosage right was the thing, more than the small amounts (bumps) that kids take on a night out, less than the amount that sends you into the K hole. Anthony spent a few hours one afternoon watching a serendipitous episode of Star Trek that fitted perfectly with his 'experiments,' taking more and more to get to the place he wanted. Because it wears off quickly it's possible to adjust the dose and effect as you go, if you are careful and pay attention. We'd tried it before and ended up in the K hole, but we hadn't really known what we were doing and certainly hadn't known what to expect; later a young person told us you can control it and avoid the K hole experience. I sat writing at the desk, my back to him, checking occasionally. 'You don't need to do anything, I'll tell you if I need anything,' Anthony had said beforehand. 'I'll just look around now and again,' I said.

I had picked an area I thought would be good to visit on ketamine, a quieter looking road with a few bars, slightly alternative looking with quotes on walls. Normal- Boring, was written beside the open door of a lit up bathroom which was painted cerise pink and glowing out of the dusty black surround. But when it came to the night the bars all seemed too noisy and not worth it just for the cerise toilet.

On a new drug it's hard to know what you need. We wandered around for a bit then came to a bar that seemed perfectly created for my needs at that moment. It was kind of neutral, not minimalist, not cool, not noisy, not intimidating. On the walls were old style plaques and signs, framed photographs of a random selection of singers and a handful of recognisable sports people. There was even a cheery regular at the bar who said a random comment as we came in. He had left his phone charging on our table, like an excuse to chat just to put me at ease. It was okay service, no hassle. We had a beer. It was perfect, but I didn't feel the need to stay.

We walked past furniture shops selling heavy ornately carved mirrors like our headboard, like junk shops full of piles of antique looking furniture. We saw a bar with a cabaret. Would that have been more exciting? Am I just not adventurous enough? Or am I not interested?

We got nearly home and went into the 7/11. A Western man was wearing a bag, on the bag it said, *'Do something important.'* I looked and read, showed Anthony, the man saw, I complimented him, but he looked like, 'Whatever,' like we were a bit crazy. I said to Anthony afterwards, 'It's like you don't even know what you're saying to the world. You have that written out loud to all but it's meaningless.' Let alone when people do it more subtly via dress and that's meaningless too. Like when I think people who look like hippies are vegetarian and they aren't necessarily. They would have been when I was younger but now that I'm older it's harder to read tribes and subcultures and some are just fashion with no corresponding beliefs.

But of course I'm being too harsh; you can't seriously expect a slogan on a bag to be serious or to actually mean anything. Like when I was on the Tokyo subway and saw a young man wearing a t-shirt with *The Matrix* film red pill blue pill speech on it; I was so tempted to say hi, luckily I didn't. Or it may mean something but just privately to me and whoever I share it with, not the actual person. Like seeing a shop called White Rabbit; I wouldn't expect to go into the shop and make a connection, that's too weird. So I'm the weird one really. And also, I don't make it easy for people to read me. Sometimes (okay, occasionally...) I dress smart and all in black. More usually 'country-ish,' scruffy and uninviting. Once described as looking 'Happy, friendly and approachable' on wearing bright colours by my son, 'More like how you are.' But I don't generally gravitate to bright colours on me although I love to see them like on the women in India.

A friend of ours, a musician had said, 'The problem with ketamine is, I don't know what music to listen to on it.' We looked up, ketamine music, what came up was YouTube nature mixes which didn't do it for us AT ALL. And then we watched Netflix, Sex Education. It wasn't to watch something intentionally sad but that episode blindsided me, it was so quietly and realistically and so well done.

A girl has an abortion. That's what it would be like. No dramatics, no counselling. Someone else gets assaulted, he doesn't even tell his parents let alone the police or get any counselling or support. The pro lifers shouting at her. Her alone back to a trailer park where she lives alone (her mum is an addict) to do her homework (she is super smart). Her friend who goes with her doesn't take her back to his home to be scooped up by his mum. Children; not the same as adults or not the same as us watching would want but real life isn't like that and would adults have been much better anyway? Kids dealing with adult stuff, supporting each other as best as they can with their limited experience and resources; a sandwich, a text.

Oh the sadness! I shut myself in the bathroom. Tears rolled down my face. It was like I was opened up to all the sadness of the world. I was still very much aware, having not having taken loads. After wondering 'what do I do on it,' 'what's the point of ketamine?' Watch something sad; I hadn't even known or thought about that but that was the perfect thing.

Later in the white bed with the white duvet and pillows, watching the fan and two tiny lizards on the white ceiling. Hadn't I always wished for a white room, silence and simplicity? Realising what we've had, the experience. Changing perspective and looking down. Thinking, reviewing our trip and how well we've done together. I can remember that.

As if *The Thirteenth Floor* wasn't enough, we also watched *Vanilla Sky*. The film explored decisions and consequences; most importantly how the little things, the small decisions people make change everything. 'There are no bigger things,' was a line from the film.

The day after the ketamine, egg off the menu, had I changed reality? I used to order an avocado egg sandwich without the egg almost every day, a wet, full sandwich chock full with avocado and salad, absolutely delicious. Now it had a blank sticker over where it had said egg! I was excited, Anthony not so much, he said he tends to just notice and accept things like this and move on rather than focus so much on them as I do. Aside from whether it was exciting or not, we agreed it was a sign of being in flow, like Instagram synchronicities, like all synchronicities. Like 'conjuring' sheets, towels, beans on toast at the 'wrong time,' in Kerala. Why so hard to believe, when people have vision boards of Porsches and trips to Australia? Because people think the little things are just coincidences.

Opposite the clouds: Vietnam

Hanoi

Narrow houses got narrower from bottom to top, some had nail bars in the front rooms, some had the Vietnamese flag outside, red with yellow stars. Everyone was preparing for Tet, the Lunar New Year. Mopeds drove past laden with big bunches of flowers, branches and even trees in pots. A woman on the back of a bike was wearing a primrose coat embroidered with flowers. Another woman walked past us wearing a beautiful long red velvet dress. The market was full of balloons, branches of yellow flowers, orange trees in pots, red lanterns and pink plastic pigs. At the front of a rack of clothes on a stall was an orangey-pink jumper embroidered with the words, *'Venture out of your comfort zone, the rewards are worth it.'* People let off big party poppers, pieces of gold sparkly paper landed on the ground. It was the 'Biggest assault on the senses since India,' as Anthony said.

Hitting Lunar New Year, when everything closed down for several days except for the odd convenience store, was a challenge. In the ground floor of the building next door was a supermarket, it was like Christmas, with boxes of biscuits, a shopping rush and things running out, no lemons, no bananas. I stocked up as best I could before everything closed. In the morning the pollution hung over everything like mist.

The past like a grenade. First me, then Anthony. News from home. A foolish conversation, a careless discussion we had at the height of our existential crisis just-into-India shell-shock, came back to hit us- or rather Anthony- like a truck. Anthony had his own experiences of grief. To bond and have and love children and be hands on and then to have to move out, to not see them every day, to miss their faces so excited when you get home from work. The fear of not being allowed to see them. The pain when you say something wrong and they won't speak to you so you can't fix it for days or weeks. And even I as only a very part time step parent felt the sadness when Anthony's children grew up and stopped coming up every couple of weekends.

Having children can be a world of pain, the guilt, the anxiety. Not just birth, not just when they are little. *Because you love them.* Having children has given us the experience of love and responsibility like nothing else. The pain and guilt, that's incomparable, and that's what's made up our lives. But life is both, as Pema Chodron says, be open to it all, the beauty and the pain.

The experience of raising children, the fun and creativity of that, when my son was little, a child-centred world of mad pets, crazy kids' parties, riding bikes indoors, an easel and washing line of paintings in the kitchen. The mural I painted on his wall with the boat from *Where The Wild Things Are.* The sparkly fish I stencilled on his wall while he was asleep. Later with Anthony's children, the fun fun fun, the house so full of laughter. Having had them, had the experience, we can't imagine what not having had children would feel like.

Anthony got ill, we thought due to getting too much pollution. It started as fatigue and a tight chest and then got more like flu, with him sweating and shaking uncontrollably. We had to leave the place where we were staying the next day. I had relied on Anthony to do all the booking and suddenly faced with it I felt overwhelmed and anxious. In the end Anthony found somewhere else online and we managed to get a taxi. The woman owner came straight away and greeted us. She was wearing a red velvet dress for Tet. She said she opened the guesthouse ten years ago so that her son and daughter could learn English. She told us all the restaurants were closed but that they would cook for us. The family brought us huge bowls of steamed rice and lots of fresh chunky vegetables, and tea in pretty china cups.

Beside the bed was a big stained glass window with lots of fish. During the day natural light came through it and at night the lights on the landing lit it up. It had curtains but I left them open and lay in bed looking at the fish wall glowing in the dark. The bathroom window at night was a cracked mosaic of blues and purples; the light through the coloured glass was broken up by the leaves of a tree pressed against the window.

The guesthouse woman kindly walked me to an open supermarket, waited for me while I shopped and then walked me to an open pharmacy where she translated so that I could get some medicine for Anthony. On the ground were shiny pieces of paper from TET, multicoloured cut up squares like rough confetti.

Even though it was unlikely, we got scared that Anthony might have malaria. We were more scared about health now that we were not in India. After seven months there altogether, India was more familiar and many more people spoke English. But I just thought, there's loads of ex pats and foreigners in Hanoi, what do they do, and looked up online, found a hospital popular with Westerners and saved the details. They were open twenty four hours and even had an ambulance service. Then I felt better, which is probably why people say to research and note down the details of local hospitals and doctors when travelling.

When I went out alone, I orientated myself by the big tall new buildings beyond the main road, many with neon names, some flashy and done, some just a metal-framed shell but still kind of beautiful, and beyond them, the sky, pink in the evenings. Nearby was a smart looking college with inspirational quotes outside; 'Be someone you'd look up to,' 'Go wherever you want,' 'Question the answer,' 'Why ask why.' I found an open coffee place. They brought me a dear little brown earthenware cup and saucer with a tiny metal percolator on top, the coffee dripped out one drop at a time, an exercise in patience.

Anthony and I went looking to see if any food places were open. A Vietnamese family walked past; using sign language we said there was nowhere open. They beckoned to us. We followed them all the way around the block, past bushes and plants in wide shallow stone pots on the pavement, past a woman's garden with bonsai and lily pads and coriander, the smell delicious, to an open restaurant. A woman greeted us warmly and said she could make us noodles. They were served in a white bowl on a white plate, beauty in simplicity, the instant noodles made beautiful with coriander; on the side a leaf-green oval dish with two pieces of lime.

***

SaPa

As we grew near to SaPa the road became winding with steep drops. I thought about us putting notes on our bodies, in our pockets just in case. *We were very happy, we had a great year, a great life.*

The town of SaPa was pretty; the buildings were painted faded blue with giant pots of big plants with huge red flowers outside. The people were dressed for the cold. I was delighted by the clothes; a little girl in a swingy A-line skirt with pockets, the skirt made from thick beige fleece. Hill tribe women wore bands of material like cummerbunds around their waists over the top of their coats. On top they wore shiny navy blue padded overcoats and tasselled beaded leg warmers. The women carried baskets on their back and wore big silver chain necklaces like giant chain mail. Men wore black jackets with colourful embroidery and waistcoats with jewelled tassels.

TaVan, our village was a half hour journey by taxi. Along the little roads were strings of village houses and home stays, the buildings wooden or stone. Out the back of our place was a terrace area with chunky wooden sun loungers and little square stools made from pallets. I moved a stool into a sun spot and looked at the view: rice terraces, hills, the hairpin road bends and a big wooden abandoned looking hotel we had passed on the way. The mist hung low in the hills which made it seem as if I were sitting opposite the clouds. On the opposite side of the road a man on the balcony sat blowing huge perfect smoke rings. It was the first time I'd been so close to rice terraces. I watched a group of ducks in a feeding frenzy in the rice terraces; they were shooed off the top layers by a man, but remained on the bottom layers feeding at a hundred miles an hour. I watched strange animals be herded, three at a time towards the road. I don't know what they were, big grey animals, unfamiliar, almost prehistoric looking.

The outside wall of our room was brick with a big window and a view out onto the fields and the strange animals; they were herded right past our bedroom window and along the road. We had a sumptuous mattress, a foot thick, a mosquito net and an electric blanket. I sat in bed in my Nepal burnt orange roll neck jumper, my thick sweat pants from Tokyo and my two India lungis over me, writing and blogging. The plywood walls between the rooms had slight gaps, you could hear everything and even see through to the next room if you looked. Next door there were new people in, speaking a different language, playing music- Amy Winehouse, the man singing along, not well but it was sweet, and the proximity of us all felt kind of nice.

The place was like a hostel with lots of young people in Lycra and walking gear. Hill tribe women hung around either waiting to guide people on treks or trying to sell handicrafts. I liked their clothes, one woman wore green beaded leg warmers, a pink waistcoat, a purple t-shirt and a green classic style hat like the Queen would wear. We ate big chunks of bread and jam for breakfast, and for dinner big homemade vegetable spring rolls and plates of cabbage sautéed with garlic and ginger, a traditional SaPa dish. In the restaurant inexplicably they played children's nursery rhymes, Twinkle Twinkle Little Star, Old Macdonald had a Farm, Pat-a-cake Pat-a-cake Baker's man.

One day on my own in the restaurant, I looked out onto the other side of the road where there was a small house with a stony garden. An older woman holding a baby, presumably her grandchild, was hanging out washing. I watched the woman pegging out little baby waistcoats: So tiny, so cute, I thought. I wondered if she was thinking the same as me. When she had finished there was a row of tiny baby clothes on hangers on the front fence near the road. As the sun moved, the woman still holding the baby, moved the hangers around. Everyone had gone and the restaurant was unusually peaceful. For once they were not playing nursery rhymes but the most beautiful music. I asked the woman in the restaurant what it was and she wrote it out carefully for me into my notebook.

From the restaurant I watched someone kill a fish at the side of the road. I wasn't sure what I was seeing at first- was he just chopping it up, or did it move? I watched the next one fully: he lifted a fish out of a covered container attached to the side of his moped- ingenious, a fish tank attached to his moped- and hit it over the head. People stopped, he reached under the cover, got out a fish, killed it, weighed it, cut it up, put the pieces in the ubiquitous blue bags made of thin flimsy plastic. The fish I watched struggled, tried to escape, he pulled it back and hit it again, its gills still moving on the weighing scale, then he cut it up and put it in a bag. When all the customers had stopped, or he'd run out of fish, he packed away his things and rode off, just the blood left on the ground.

A short while later a woman walked past where he'd been standing, a plastic bag of groceries in one hand and a live duck in a carrier bag in the other. One of the duck's feet had pushed through a hole in the thin blue plastic and was paddling frantically, its head and beak sticking out the top of the bag as the woman walked on down the road.

The mainly young people went off for treks, either guided by small hill tribe women whom the tourists towered over, or in some cases on their own. But for me just a walk along the road was enough. One road was busy with stalls and people selling handicrafts in the street, hill tribe people chatting or asking me to buy. Women in knee length wide, soft, thin black velvet trousers, a baby in a purple velvet suit with a hood. In a quiet area I went past a cafe. I thought I saw a television screen of a mountain. I looked again and saw it as a lit up picture. Or was it a mirror reflecting a picture of mountains? No, it was actually a hole in the wall. Out beyond the hole was a blue crumpled tarp with a covering of grey dust, blue-grey in the light. The light must have caught it just right for me to see it.

I stopped for coffee and to write everything down. Again it was like those overwhelming insights or too much beauty; things kept slipping away even as I was writing them. 'Grey houses made colourful with washing.' I was thinking of my favourite Kolkata line and at same time I saw grey dwellings or outbuildings with washing hung out opposite where I was having coffee and writing. Or did I see them first and that sparked the line, without me noticing consciously? The coffee place was wooden with a low wall beyond which was a river. Outside there was a small waterfall where the river went over some rocks. There were swallows outside and inside; I could see a nest. My coffee came in a glass with a metal percolator and saucer forming a lid on top. Why do I so often deny myself, when to stop somewhere and write with coffee is so nice? The activity and the coffee the same, but the view, the table and chairs, the percolator and cup arrangement a little different each time. Was it shyness, social anxiety, money? But maybe I stop at the right places and appreciate it so much because I don't do it as often?

On the way back I paused to look at the view: little wooden shacks, rice terraces, hills. I saw one of the strange grey animals, like a very big pig or a yak, with their baby snuggled beside them. If you pause, even for a moment with intention, you see. Sitting at the cafe with coffee, writing, looking at the waterfall, this feeling, not high happiness per se, perhaps it is better than that. Maybe the aim is to feel in power again, like the best most powerful version of me. Recharging self. Simple. Don't forget to do.

***

Dong Hoi

At Dong Hoi station small shops with plastic chairs outside sold oranges, bananas, baguettes, boiled eggs, sticky rice, noodle soup and coffee. The shops were packed like the little shops in India but with huge stacks of instant noodles and crisps. A man at a table nearby was eating a big bowl of noodle soup. Dong Hoi seemed strangely quiet; the side streets were quiet and even the main street which our hostel was on was wide and empty.

Our room was at one end of a long marble corridor. The curtain pole in our room looked as though it were made of silver hologram wrapping paper. The white pole had a serrated curved and curled finish, as if twisted, and with the light shining on it the surface sparkled like glitter. At the other end of the corridor was a small balcony with a view out onto the street below. In the middle divider of the wide empty street were bright pink flower signs, like metal sweets, precise symmetrical cut out shapes. Within the row of pink flower signs was a small cube on a pole with screens showing orange and red flowers, like a much smaller version of the big screen wall of waterfalls and advertisements by the river in Phnom Penh. At night the pink flowers became just lights and looked completely different.

We found a noodle place and used a translation app to write our order in Vietnamese. Two beautiful dishes of food arrived, tasty fried tofu with spring onions and mushrooms. By pointing to the menu we also ordered peach iced tea. It came in tall glasses with long spoons, a deliciously sweet cold drink with lots of ice and big slices of slippery tinned peaches, probably the most delicious thing we had tasted all year.

We walked to the market. On the way there were big flowers fallen on the pavement, with thick lush pinky-red petals. The market was full of flowers and fruit. We saw live frogs tied up. On the way back we stopped under a tree and ate lychees and oranges.

Little huts stood on stilts in the river behind raised nets like the Chinese fishing nets of Kochi. We watched a person in a coracle go from the hut to under the centre of the net, check the middle of the net which hung down like a nipple above the water. Then he went back to the hut and lowered the net into the water via ropes. In the river there were blue plates, square or rectangular, a gold lamp, with broken flower glass or shell bits. Were they put into the river as a prayer? Were they simply discarded or broken? The things shining, beautiful and strange looking in the murky water, amongst thin plastic bags floating upside down like jelly fish.

It was an ideal place in a way, but we probably got a bit bored. We had lots of time to think about The Future and that can bring us both down individually. Anthony said, 'When we get to the next place, I think we should start meditating every day again.'

After writing I stood on the balcony to wind down. I had had a period on and off for two weeks, it wasn't too bad but I felt a bit ropey. In the street below was a woman on a bicycle, she was wearing bright pink trousers and had full black bin bags loaded onto the bicycle. Another woman in a thin purple velvet top and matching loose trousers with a traditional conical hat was carrying a thin plastic carrier bag in each hand.

One evening there was a big storm with lots of rain, thunder and lightning. After it finished we stepped out, from our room through the noisy hostel bar and out into the street and yellow flowers with a nice, strong smell permeating the air.

We watched the film The Lady in the Van which was very timely given how much time and energy we spent worrying about The Future. Anthony said, 'But she was okay, she lived in a van, in the end, rich or poor, everyone dies.' The point being that lack of security didn't really matter, she lived anyway, and no amount of security can stop you from getting ill and dying.

***

Hue

There were shrines in the trunks of trees, one had concrete dragons built into the tree, another had once-lit cigarettes, now pillars of ash standing upright alongside the incense. Near our guesthouse was a nail place, the decor all bright shocking pink with Astroturf on the walls, bright pink beds close together and giant teddies. A child and two fluffy dogs, one white, one brown were running around the room and bouncing about on the beds. It looked like the set of a wacky children's television programme. Women's clothes shops displayed black knee length office skirts, short skirts in black and neutral with women's fitted shirts, little denim shorts and t-shirts, pinafore dresses with white blouses, amazing sparkly princess dresses; one shop just sold pyjamas. In the street women wore traditional style long dresses and trousers, lacy dresses, jeans or sweatpants and t-shirts, and pyjamas.

There was an chay (vegetarian) restaurant opposite our hotel. The woman wore a cotton dress printed with cherries and had immaculate waved hair. We ordered hot pot, we'd been scared to order it at other places in case it had meat or meat stock in it. A metal hot pot- a saucepan with a lid- was brought to the table on a gas burner very hot and bubbling away, with a separate big white plate with uncooked mushrooms, the long thin white ones with long white stems, on top of a bed of greens, plus a plate of cold rice noodles and small white bowls. You add the mushrooms and the greens into the hotpot, which has already has tofu, some vegetables and herbs including big sticks of lemongrass, turn it down, wait for a few minutes, and serve yourself. You put some of the cold rice noodles in a small bowl and add some of the hot pot on top, this heats the noodles and also the noodles help cool it as it is so hot, and Voila! It's a work of art, an activity and a nourishing meal, simple and complex at the same time.

Vietnam had the best fruits of any country we'd been and Hue had the best fruits of Vietnam. Anthony bought a bag of fruit from one of the women selling fruit on the pavement in the market area. 'I don't know what I got,' he said, 'She just took control and gave me stuff.' One looked a bit like a passion fruit or a pomegranate from the outside, inside it was pale pink and fleshy with a white centre and a stone, and the fruit dripped milk. Another kind of fruit was dark purple on the outside, inside there was a pink firm and spongy layer which seemed not to be for eating, inside that were white segments a bit like lychees but arranged in the round in segments like a satsuma.

At a cafe I got coffee and Anthony ordered ginger tea. We both got the standard free iced tea, it had a hint of caramel. The ginger tea was a work of art, various saucers with a ginger tea bag, a slice of lime, an orange slice, fresh ginger and balls like hard dried truffles- maybe a herb bundle or root of some kind, and salt and sugar.

***

Indoors we watched Netflix's The Umbrella Academy, and meditated. The first day we woke up in Hue Anthony said,

'Meditation, we said we would.' We meditated every day, some guided meditation and lots of our own just sitting, watching the thoughts, free meditation or follow the thought (Krishnamurthy). See the patterns. I thought, that girl in the shoes (one of my most horrible childhood memories, being teased over some 'horrific' shoes). All that I am now, the life that I am making, that I am choosing to live, is not to 'show' the bullies,' it's to show HER, that girl in the shoes. It's to make all that worth it. And of course without that exact childhood I wouldn't be the person I am now, so of course it was worth it and I am grateful for it all.

In Umbrella Academy: she had stronger powers than everyone but as a child she was tricked and medicated to think she hadn't any power at all. All that childhood stuff I went through wasn't so that twenty years later I could squeeze myself into their world, going against my values, acting, dressing, feeling unreal and being inauthentic. But I did all that. I stayed late at work, I tried extra hard to be perfect. As Elizabeth Gilbert said in *Eat Pray Love* of her old life which she realised she didn't want anymore, 'I was a willing participant in all of it.' I can't blame my mum, or on being a mum. I did it all. As Anthony says, 'You have to do stuff to find out what you don't want.'

Umbrella Academy was about children being prepped for something. In Battlestar Gallactica Starbuck was being prepped for something as a child. What was my childhood prepping me for? Not to just stay in career and house. Not to be so happy just to have 'made it,' to have done all that despite anxiety. That's not the goal. That's a waste- and hence I woke up. Or, I woke up, and realised it was a waste. I woke up and I realised all this.

***

Hue to Nha Trang by train was a fourteen and a half hour journey. Anthony was reading *Sapiens* and he read some bits aloud during the journey and we had a few discussions about the topics: capitalism-people who fear money hide it under the bed versus people who aren't afraid use what they have to make some more; history and religion. Sapiens is fascinating because it takes a long view of everything. And apparently the author went vegan after researching what humans do to animals.

Anthony also read me some of The Power of Now- the insane person muttering to themselves is the same as all of us but they do it aloud. We identify with the mind and it's like we're possessed. Go behind the chatter and you find You. What do you do without the chatter? Rest in the present moment. That's enlightenment. It linked interestingly to the Krishnamurthy style of meditation we had been doing i.e. no real method, just watching your thoughts, going within and knowing yourself.

Arriving around ten pm it was dark outside. Near to our destination only a few things were lit up. A grand looking white-cream building with yellow-white lights. A pink house with the ubiquitous red plastic chairs, lit up amongst nothingness, surreal.

We spoke only at the end to our train companions, they were French, she was quite chatty, him less so, 'We're just staying one night,' she said, 'Then we go to Da Lat.' 'We're here for a week,' I said. I saw his face react but to his credit, he didn't say a word.

Lord give me a song that I can sing: Vietnam

Nha Trang

As soon as we arrived we knew it wasn't us at all, a glitzy shiny lit up holiday resort with late night shops and restaurants, full of tourists. We watched dazed from the taxi and then our driver dropped us off in amongst it all. Although as it was so near the end of the trip it was even easier to just go with it, to say it doesn't matter, it's all experience.

Nha Trang was the site of a Russian naval base; used for R&R by the Russian navy it had become a tourist destination popular with Russian families. Russians had opened businesses such as travel agents, jewellers and shops with everything written in Russian. The menus were in Russian first and sometimes not in English at all. Like in Sihanoukville in Cambodia it was a useful reminder that we aren't the centre of the world. We'd travelled around India and been spoilt with so many people speaking English. In Sihanoukville we had realised how many Chinese tourists there are now and how important they are. And that we as Brits are insignificant, numbers wise anyway. We met no other Brits in Nha Trang; we heard only one group of Americans. The other tourists were Russian or Chinese. Although the US is a big, wealthy country, we met very few people from the US on our travels. A US Instagrammer/traveller showed a photograph of herself on a boat full of people, in the caption listing all the different nationalities and saying, 'Yet again, I'm the only American in a sea of Europeans.' We didn't meet many British people either, especially not in India outside of the main tourist areas of Goa and Kerala.

All around were hotels, lit up after dark, their names in lights, one was called 'Happy Light Hotel.' The hotels were huge with only small gaps between them. One hotel looked like honeycomb; so many hotel rooms. It was hard to take it in, the numbers, the facilities. 'Things to do in Nha Trang,' still came up on Anthony's phone several months after our return to the UK, which always made me smile as we found very little to do there. But the fact that the outside had little appeal gave us space to go inwards.

The first night we ate at a restaurant on our street, we ordered vegetarian food but I found tiny flakes of meat in it, either cross contamination, stock, or not understanding us. It kind of set the tone for Nha Trang food wise and knocked my confidence eating in restaurants that sold meat,- and everywhere was meaty. The next day we ate at another place on our street, a fairly simple looking place, the woman had a tiny baby, her granddaughter. On the walls were photographs of all the animals they served, before and after, a photograph of the animal alive next to a photograph of it prepared to eat or in a meal. A live chicken and then a whole chicken raw and plucked, a frog, an alligator, an ostrich, a snake, next to a photograph of the animal cut into chunks in a meal. This became known as 'the place with all the animals.' But nowhere else was any better, everywhere was the same.

All the restaurants had tanks, aquariums, at first glance they looked like fish tanks for decoration, then we realised no, it was to eat. Outside almost every place, all along from the corner of our road and all down the main road were bowls, like large plastic washing up bowls, some stacked overlapping on top of each other. In the bowls were what looked like every kind of sea creature, as if every sea creature you could imagine had been captured. Crabs with their claws bound with a rubber band, I couldn't tell if they were alive or dead. Two big fish in a plastic bowl the same size as them who looked almost dead; there was obviously a limit to what they can endure. Lobsters that were clearly alive, all sorts of small creatures, strange kinds of squid. They changed the water and it spilled out onto the pavement; every day we walked past and through the poor creatures' water, the floor slippery underfoot. As well as all the sea creatures, shops sold dead baby alligators with pearls in their mouths as ornaments. Heated barbecues on the street cooked lobsters and other creatures.

Shops and street vendors sold ready cut up slices of fresh fruit on polystyrene trays wrapped with cling film. The street food was all meat but just outside our hotel was a coconut stall run by a woman, with a couple of red plastic chairs and a child's table. If I squinted my eyes and blocked out all the shiny tourism around, I could imagine I was somewhere kind of homely, a quiet street stall somewhere, a chai cafe in India. It was a tiny island of sanity, not even that really but I tried to pretend that it was. Through Happy Cow we found a tiny food stall, a little cart, run by the same woman for twelve years serving Banh Mi (filled baguettes) with all vegan ingredients; different kinds of seitan meats, sauces and salad. We started off just getting two, then another two wrapped to take home, sometimes even more! This stall was our saviour in Nha Trang. There were loads of shops selling pillows, shaped memory neck pillows and mattresses. Small tourist shops sold water, toiletries, bikinis and sun clothes. The Vietnamese shop assistants spoke Russian, a few times they spoke to us and we didn't understand and then they realised we weren't Russian, 'Oh you are not Russian!' A Russian man outside a bar gave us a flier, 'I thought you were Russian,' he said. We went out for a meal at an Indian restaurant, the Indian head waiter spoke Russian to the other diners. I was so impressed; maybe he already knew English, maybe not, but certainly he had had to learn Vietnamese and then learn Russian as well.

It was interesting to observe a different group of tourists. Many of the Russian tourists wore white cover-up shirts in the street- loose casual almost Indian style which were for sale in the little tourist shops. In the evening their skin was often bright red against the white. Walking alongside the beach we saw the Russian style of sunbathing: standing, arms outstretched, baking in bikinis or brief trunks. Although when I reported all this to my cousin back home in the UK she said that she sometimes sunbathes like this too to make sure she gets an all over tan. We kept off the beach during the day; it was very crowded and in any case far too hot for us. The Russian style of sunbathing was in sharp contrast to the Chinese tourists who covered up from the sun with hats and tops and who also wore pollution masks. Many of the Chinese women wore pretty flower print dresses with shoulders and sleeves, and we saw a cute young couple wearing matching comic strip pop art t-shirts.

I went out alone a few times; for breakfast one day I bought fruit from a shop on our road and sat in the shade on a low wall near the beach to eat it, delicious slices of fresh mango, a little moment of peace in my quiet corner. I went out alone for coffee and writing a couple of times, the coffee was good and strong. In Siem Reap in Cambodia we had booked our flights home and in SaPa we had booked a Travelodge in London for the first night as well as our train back to Northampton. From the room in Dong Hoi we had paid the boat insurance. In Nha Trang we paid the boat licence and arranged the car MOT. Picking up even the slightest of our old responsibilities felt weird and tiring.

One day on a beach walk, I wanted to stand and look. Anthony walked off, thinking I wanted to be alone. Being left behind is a trigger for me. A misunderstanding; over sensitivity, a bad atmosphere. The atmosphere between us deteriorated. My mood plummeted. Thinking, 'It would have been better if I hadn't woken up.' Thinking about the past, imagining going back and preventing things with my son turning out as they did. Better to be an asleep person, who could take pride in having had a successful family. Decisions, my responsibility. But what did I actually do that was so bad? And it wasn't Anthony's fault, I'd already fucked everything up by then. And on and on, thoughts spiralling down and down. 'I left my children for you.' Anthony said to me once. Oh God, and I'd painted myself as so good, getting their room ready, buying things, cooking. It wasn't only my kid I messed up. Lots do it- women break up families. But they'd already been separated for years. But he did move to me not vice versa.

The ultimate destination of these thoughts of course is suicide. So many reasons to die: As a punishment. As a 'I don't know how to live with myself.' As a solution to every other worry or concern. In order to take responsibility. All I do is harm. I do no good. My son's doing well without me. Wow, The Matrix really did a number on me. Such dangerous thoughts: If he's done this well when I stepped back, and done even better when I went away for a year, then how much better would he do if I wasn't here at all?

I remembered in Thailand lying on the floor. Me: 'Why do I feel so bad?' The answer seemed to come from the light above me: 'It's your programming.' It's the mother of all battles undoing this. Do I want to? Or do I want to die? The argument, depression, so much talk of suicide as a future option. All this talk between us re The Future and getting older; who am I kidding? One day I'm going to kill myself and this is why. I've not yet got the method planned. Maybe I haven't reached the end of my tether yet. Maybe I don't want to enough. Maybe when I do, I will.

Walking along the beach, going into late afternoon, grey light, me thinking of methods of committing suicide, thinking about drowning myself, getting up early or coming back late. On the sand there were big chunks of mosaic. I remembered there was mosaic on the stairs at the hotel too. Mosaic is special to me. A grey bicycle was chained up on a ridge of sand so that it was set against the grey and cloudy sunset sky. A shiny apple lying on the sand with only a few bites out. Some beautiful driftwood. A sparrow pecking at a discarded corn on the cob on the sand. Another sparrow, another corn on the cob. A light koru, the symbol of new life. 'It's no good showing me all that,' good stuff I'd usually like, things of beauty I'd normally connect with, I said grimly, in my head. Then I realised: *All that stuff is always there.*

An old Vietnamese lady walked past selling buns, bags of tiny sponge cakes. She smiled and was friendly. I smiled at her, was friendly, and bought some. I felt bad about being so sad, as if she could catch it. On the beach on one side on a spit were mountains, partly concealed by high rise blocks of hotels ranged in front of the mountains, the juxtaposition was shocking.

In a cafe in Kerala I'd read an old newspaper magazine pull out. In it there'd been an article by a food and travel writer. In the wake of two recent celebrity suicides he'd written about how he'd travelled to all these amazing countries, stayed in great hotels and eaten all this wonderful food, that was his job but at the same time he said, 'For two years I wanted to die.' I thought it would have been better if he'd written about that too. Like the social media thing of people tending to only put up the good stuff. 'No one posts photos on Facebook of themselves sobbing.' I often say. I know there are sites of self harm, but are they another extreme, all bad; would it be healthier if we all put everything or at least a balance out there?

The trigger to all this was another news interview raking over the past of twelve years ago when my son was a teenager and out of control, and a few cross words between me and Anthony, both of us probably too cooped up and bored on top of anxiety around the end of the trip and going home. Even he as my best friend can't really help. Whatever he says will just sound like platitudes or niceties, him trying anything, searching for the right words, because how I'm feeling scares him. Obviously Anthony had his own stuff going on as well, and this was exacerbated by my silence. This has to be alone. Once awake, awake. 'Enlightenment' is accepting all of it, somehow, and somehow making peace with it.

Back in the room, thinking about how just a short time of silence and awkward atmosphere will plummet my mood. One to two hours of it and I'm at suicide methods and my mind is dangerously 'out of control.' No, I said to myself, I may not be in control of my thoughts but I can control my actions. I hugged myself and thought of the suicide prevention workbook (that I wrote!) 'Curl up into a ball, you can't hurt yourself then.'

In bed something in the room screamed method: the curtain pole. Compared to Dong Hoi, where I had admired the curtain pole's glittery beauty, here the pole was a suicide option. I was scared of it. Would I just do it, like I slapped myself the other day, involuntarily? That night so depressed. 'Just get through the night,' I said to myself.

Later, talking myself out of it: You think committing suicide will wipe out (or atone for) all the bad you did; but of course it doesn't, and actually makes it worse. It's another bad thing. A really terrible thing. It *adds* to the sum of the harm you've done. If you were to ask them if that's what they wanted, of course they wouldn't say they wanted that. But of course even to ask would be an awful thing to do.

The 'logic' of a suicidal mood state can be terrifyingly dangerous. In the past I've even thought people would *want* me to do it and would agree with me that it made sense and was a good idea were I to ask them. One particular time, after an awful Mother's Day of petty crime, a one hundred pound phone bill, I decided to go to bed, sleep on it, and if I still felt definitely that it was, I'd run it by my friend M, ask her if she thought it made sense and if she did, I'd do it. Of course I woke up and thought there's no way she would, and crisis averted.

I woke later, realised it was no threat- the method I'd been scared of, the curtain pole. Is what I did worse than people who have affairs and break up families? Even murderers can get born again. Umbrella Academy: 'We're not kids anymore, there's no such thing as good people and bad people, there's just people, living out their lives.'

When I woke up the next morning, I saw that the curtain pole had a screw loose, it wouldn't have held, it was not dangerous, and me, feeling better, noticed glitter on my leg which reminded me to include the nice Dong Hoi curtain pole in the story.

Anthony apologised, he said it was him, his mind. He showered me with specific compliments which I acknowledged but was too depressed to feel. He read aloud from Eckhart Tolle *The Power of Now.* I listened and then we meditated; I could feel a peace, the place where healing comes from, the method of healing I used to do. Later as I wrote, I wondered if maybe it's where actual healing comes from?

We had a long talk over breakfast about suicidal guilt. I felt like we were at a fork in the road. But it's not a mind decision, it's not one thing, it's each day just carrying on. Anthony talked about the moment his relationship with his children's mother ended, about being curled up in the foetal position in the bathroom. About all the thoughts of killing himself; ways to make it look like an accident. Suicide as a punishment, and because he couldn't live with himself.

I brought up religious forgiveness, about born again murderers in prison. Anthony doesn't believe someone else can forgive your sins for you. Can we do it ourselves? He thinks that is the only way.

As Anthony and I have discussed previously, just because you're conscious doesn't mean you're happy. This 'last' bit is a lot of pain.

Being conscious doesn't mean you're nice. Some heads of big businesses that destroy the environment and people's health for money to fuel their pleasure lifestyle may well be conscious. They may have decided it's all an illusion so just do what you want it doesn't matter. But even if it is only a game, I will still recycle, I still won't hurt animals. And being conscious definitely doesn't mean it's fun. Sometimes you'll wish you were still asleep.

But I made all the mistakes before. Before I woke up, while I was still asleep. So was that all my script? My back story like in *Blade Runner,* to make me guilty, miserable, sad, easier to control, less likely to wake up? In Blade Runner they gave the robots memories, a family, 'To make them easier to control.' Or if we don't believe in some malignant power, that it just made it more of a challenge for me to wake up. Like the George Harrison song *Isn't it a pity.* And some people say that the sadness triggers you waking up; the cracks let the light in. And Now provides the chance to go off script and to deprogram myself, should I choose.

I went for a walk by myself. It was the middle of the day and very hot. I wanted to go down the new road; we had passed it on the way to the Banh Mi stall but not been down there. Like in Cambodia, there was lots of building going on, unlike in Cambodia, here they seemed to build the infrastructure before the hotels, so that there was a big wide new road leading nowhere, still, I wanted to see it. The road led to hotels and hoarding beyond which there was more building and beyond that the mountains. I could see part of the mountains above the hoarding but they were half concealed. Once the hotels were all built you would only be able to see the mountains from up high inside the hotels.

The wall outside a new hotel had bricks sticking out at angles; at first I thought it was a creative design then I realised it was unfinished with wires going in and out. Inside looked done, the foyer wall was decorated with a painting of a flock of birds, from the ceiling hung two huge candelabras designed to look like giant birds' nests. Just around the corner was another new hotel, the staircase visible from the outside, a zig zag in a glass box. I watched people going up, it looked like an art installation. I stopped and leant against a wall and made notes and drank water. On the walk home I took deep breaths, pausing to look, and in spite of everything I could feel a sense of peace. Outside the entrance to the hotel I noticed a white pottery tea pot with flowers on it sitting on a red plastic chair. However bad the night had been, I could feel myself recovering.

Halfway down our street, opposite our hotel, a young Vietnamese woman and I walked past each other. She was wearing a bright red t-shirt. Printed on the t-shirt, over her heart area, were the words *'It's broken here.'*

Nha Trang abounded with patterns and metaphors, the trapped huge variety of beautiful/fascinating animals dead/alive, the non-communication; outside of staff we spoke to other people only twice. The man giving out fliers outside a club who thought we were Russian. I had an urge to stop and chat to him but he probably just wanted to get people into the club and anyway we can't speak Russian and he may well not have had much English even if he had wanted to talk. In a restaurant a Russian tourist had come over and asked me something about my beer, assuming I was Russian. Again, I felt a longing to connect; I like to help people but if you can't understand or speak anything in Russian and they're asking you a specific question in Russian... I wished we could all speak the same language or that I knew another language but to really connect you'd need to be absolutely fluent and how long would that take and which language to choose and how few people I can absolutely connect with even in our first language... Even Anthony and I lost each other for a while...

***

DaLat

I arrived feeling rebellious, wanting a cigarette and a beer. There's always a push, I want to go somewhere, sit and have a drink, Anthony wants to just get to where we are staying, I won that time. We sat outside on a small terrace area. DaLat is in the hills and it was just beginning to get cold as we arrived.

Straightaway we loved DaLat. All of a sudden there were old buildings, full of character, old shops and old flats above shops. Apparently there was a tacit agreement from both sides not to bomb Da Lat during the American/Vietnam War hence all the old buildings. It made us realise the contrast with where we'd been before, that all the boxy, functional buildings were new buildings built after the war. There were street food stalls with great big pans of eggs, some like chicken eggs, some small like quail eggs and big pans of stew or noodle soup. There were grills with tortillas on; beaten egg was poured on to cook omelettes on top of the tortillas. In the street were stalls with piles of scarves and furry hats with ears and long furry scarves attached. From the window of the taxi we saw lots of hair dressers and shops selling cool looking vintage clothes.

We went to the wrong hotel at first, it looked too expensive for us but both had similar names, something like My Dream and Dream Hotel, both with dream in the name anyway. The guesthouse was run by a woman; her son was there sometimes and there was a young man there all the time who was unable to speak. In the reception were two little dogs. In the room we were aware of the change in climate; the room smelled very slightly damp and it smelled a bit of mildew when we opened the wardrobe. In the wardrobe and in a neat folded pile at the bottom of the stairs were the thick synthetic blankets that were so popular in Nepal. I always like to know there's another blanket, just in case. Across the road from our guesthouse was a van parked outside which beeped all day; apparently no one complained.

I continued watching *Atypical* on Netflix which I'd started on the train to Nha Trang. The show is about a teen with autism; in one of the episodes I saw in DaLat he goes to stay at a friend's house for the first time. His friend has done his best but we see the unfamiliar environment through the main character's eyes; there's a waving cat, (the gold cats with beckoning paws), an aromatherapy diffuser glowing a colour and puffing out visible scent and a gold and noisy halogen heater. All these things loom large and become too much for him to cope with. The next day I saw a waving cat just like the one in *Atypical*. And on the stairs of our guesthouse was the very same aromatherapy diffuser, the same style but in a different colour. Mind you, as it turned out there were waving cats everywhere. One day we sat at a cafe eating vegan cookies and drinking tea. On the sofa next to me sat a small orange cat who let me stroke it and purred. In the window of a shop across the road was a waving cat positioned at such an angle that we were facing each other, both at matching angles, me turned slightly towards the real cat, the waving cat turned slightly towards me, so that it seemed to be waving directly at me.

We meditated in Hue, Nha Trang and DaLat. In DaLat I found that it was helpful for my anxiety. In meditation I felt my anxiety change to excitement or maybe I was able to reinterpret the anxiety as excitement and to change fear into possibility or excitement; rather than fear of the future, excitement about life's unknown possibilities. In meditation I was distracted by wanting to think about to my do list. With great effort I dragged myself away from that and asked myself, why do I want to do this? The answer: because I'm anxious. Beyond anxiety, there was calm and in meditation I was able to access that; the calm that is always with us. For every meditation in DaLat I sat on the end of the bed facing the window with my eyes open. There was a pair of silvery white curtains, a net curtain and a slight gap where I could see out unhindered. Outside the window there wasn't much of a view. I could see two electricity wires. In meditation these represented free will and fate or free will and possibilities or 'you' and 'environment.' I thought about how molecules bond. About how if you raise your frequency you attract 'better' things or at least you attract a match.

The mind tries everything: the past, the future, guilt, 'shoulds' and to do lists but if you step back from that and let it go you realise that in order to have peace that's all you have to do. Not do anything the mind is telling you to, or not then anyway; most of it is not practical or possible, you can't go into past for example; so just experience peace, without thoughts. Choose not to think about it. Even if it is practical or possible you can't do when sitting. Deal with stuff in its present moment when the time arises. Or not... I thought of what Peter Klopp a blogger on WordPress had said, about light and shadow. 'The brighter the light the darker the shadow.' This was different. People say the darkness lets the light in, know suffering to know happiness. But this seemed to be saying that if you have a bright light you have a dark shadow as well, as a kind of balance or side effect, something that has to be managed, or accepted maybe.

In meditation I often thought about *Atypical;* that's okay I thought, at least I'm not thinking about stuff I'm anxious about. I felt a pain in my right arm and the centre of my chest. I thought about heart attacks and the tarot man in Thailand telling me I needed to look after my heart. Both my granddads died of heart attacks; I hoped that'd be how I went, easy, one in his arm chair, one at the side of the swimming pool. We are animals that have become conscious. We know we're alive and that we're going to die. It's not 'spiritual' or new age or complicated. It's just if you realise, really realise, I'm a being, I've got a life, I'm here, wow, it's going to end, I don't know when; then that's so exciting! Is that waking up/enlightenment? And maybe that's why people in the East seem to enjoy themselves more, because they are okay with death, whereas we in the West tend to push it away. Oasis in Nepal saying matter of factly, 'So I die, I die, they be sad for a couple of weeks.' People of all ages in Vietnam and Cambodia dancing and exercising and socialising simply and cheaply, our Thai friend in London always laughing and joking.

I began to see the benefits of yoga and meditation after the low period in Nha Trang. Even my arms felt a little different. I used to do loads of yoga and arm exercises at Sea Win in Kerala although at the time I didn't think it was that much or very good. Just like hitting x number of followers; I look forward to it but when it comes it doesn't actually do anything. Or when I was one stone lighter, yes I was pleased but I don't think I ever felt I was 'there,' I always wanted to be thinner, I never felt my body was perfect. Although I didn't have a sense of it being wrong, even before that, just kind of neutral. I could wear all these clothes, buy stuff on eBay, anything fitted and felt good but it didn't really *do* anything, I knew it was just a surface thing.

In a reverse to the waving cats aromatherapy thing which I'd seen first on *Atypical* on Netflix and then seen in real life we saw a cockroach in the room and then cockroaches were mentioned on

Atypical. We couldn't catch it and so ended up living with it in the room which I was very proud of myself about. We never saw it again; they stay on the floor, they like the dark, they avoid humans. That's what I said to myself anyway.

We found our way back to the area we'd seen from the taxi, a street full of vintage and original fashion shops. Nearby was a yellow wall where we watched countless tourists take photographs of themselves against it. At a juice bar we talked about keeping it all going. We almost booked flights back to India for September but chickened out/thought we should let our future selves decide/be responsible. A man at the next table was wearing a t-shirt, *'Do what you want go wherever you want,'* it said.

In the market women sold strawberries, displayed in baskets in tall perfect piles which they built one by one, layer by layer in an expanding wall, fascinating to watch. We sat on some the steps with a thin blue carrier bag of grapes and satsumas with their leaves on like we'd have at Christmas and relaxed. It was good to just look. Behind us was yet another hotel called Dream something. *Nice Dream,* maybe. 'It's like we're being told, 'It's a dream!'' I said, and just like that, everything felt trippy and shiny again, the two of us feeling high, feeling like it's a matrix or an illusion. Before we left we thought, 'Why not?' and took photographs of ourselves against The Yellow Wall of DaLat; Anthony put them on Facebook and Heather from Pushkar said we looked like rock stars!

***

Ho Chi Minh City

The man at the bus stop in DaLat asked us if we lived in Ho Chi Minh City. We marvelled at the possibility. There are ex pats. There are digital nomads. There are retirees. There are people with all sorts of businesses. It's not strange but at the same time, the thought that it could be us seemed somehow hard to believe. And yet, of course, it's possible.

The place we'd booked was a hostel, our room was one of two small private rooms off the main dorm. The room seemed unfinished with bare concrete floors, albeit with a nice rug, a comfy futon bed, a clothes rail and a desk. The key to our room didn't work so we had to go in and out via the balcony doors. We thought about moving, especially as the first night it was very loud outside.

But it turned out okay, as always. There's a sense of having to bed in to a new place. We got settled into the room and the hostel staff were really friendly and one had a cute little dog that she brought to work. Later we even enjoyed the noise outside or at least appreciated it.

I had been anxious about the shared loos; only three toilets for all those people but there was hardly ever anyone else in there. Sometimes there were young women in the bathroom area playing music, I wondered if it was a privacy thing, like in Japan?

The dorm room had eighteen beds in it; you could even stay as a couple sharing one. Occasionally walking through I caught glimpses through slightly open curtains, people had their tablets propped up like televisions and small bags of possessions and food. Their big bags and suitcases were on top of a bank of lockers along the wall of the dorm. Could one live like that all the time, I wondered?

Inside we had AC as powerful as we wanted. Outside on the balcony it was hot, I needed sunglasses and I couldn't stay out there for long. There were some untended window boxes and plant pots with overflowing ashtrays and the floor was dusty with old leaves and soil. There was a wooden stool and a small chair. Sitting out on the balcony was a way of feeling a part of it from a distance, being able to watch the people and the business of the street below, without having to go down and be out there in the heat. The alternative was to be in the sealed AC room, totally cut off. A room with a balcony felt like a real luxury.

Our road was busy with traffic and people day and night. Below the hostel was a cafe bar with tables outside which was busy late into the night. Like in Japan, Thailand and Cambodia, the women covered up during the day to protect their skin from the sun. They wore sundresses at night, white cotton strappy dresses and pretty print dresses; it was still so warm in the evening.

We watched a man with a kind of bicycle, at the front it had two wheels with a burner and on top a big basket of sweet potato and corn on the cob, it was ingenious. The man walked the bicycle-stall down our road and paused for people to buy. In Cambodia there'd been noisy coconut stalls, this one was the same, the sound on a loop coming through a speaker. It sounded like 'Up down huh, Up down huh,' repeated over and over.

Opposite our balcony on the other side of the road we saw a man set up a restaurant on the pavement. He had a small area with plastic buckets for washing up and a neon sign on a tree- like in Cambodia there was a power point on the tree. He put out lots of children's plastic tables and chairs on the pavement, pushing them together to make one long table. Earlier he had jet washed the pavement in preparation. What looked like a big family party came and sat and ate dinner, everyone looked well dressed. A woman on a bike stopped, she had a Karaoke machine, a big box on the back of the bike and a microphone. She sang right next to one of the men, it was very loud even from our balcony but he just carried on eating, looking totally relaxed. It looked just like a big easy dinner party but all on plastic tables and chairs on the pavement, the seating just functional, no environment, no 'restaurant' as such and all done by this one man.

Steep stairs led down from the hostel to the street. Across the road was a pharmacy where we both got medication for going home as getting to a doctor's while living on the boat wouldn't be so easy. Just along the street on the corner was a coffee place. They served strong coffee in small cups and tall glasses of peach iced tea; there were rows of tinned peaches on shelves behind the counter. Once a big cockroach came out and went across the floor right in front of me. I startled and one of the waiters looked at me. I pointed to the cockroach by way of explanation. He squashed it under his shoe. I hadn't wanted him to do that, I just didn't think.

There was a feeling of things to do, a kind of anxiety. In Nha Trang we'd been low, in DaLat we'd been high. Here, it felt like a balance between the two, a focus on the practical, shopping for warm clothes and presents. 'Just do what's in front of you'- method of dealing with anxiety. It felt still, in the eye of the storm, 'It' (home) upon us, surreal.

We looked for presents, searching for waving cats and bargaining, out of the habit of buying and shopping. We bought trays of prepared fruit and went and sat out of the way for a breather at a woman's little stall where we bought coke and beer and ate the fruit. People came past trying to sell us things but we were totally done with shopping.

The walk to the night market took us past very expensive looking creatively decorated hotels with glitzy receptions and gold walls. Everywhere felt lively, busy and vibrant. 'We could live here for two weeks a year,' we said, 'Phnom Penh for a month, India for seven months, the UK for three or four months.'

On the way back we walked through a public park. There were huge fallen leaves on the ground. A man sat on a bench smoking what looked like a crystal meth pipe, another man stumbling around nearby. There was music in a pavilion with formal dancing lessons going on, first young people then in the next pavilion, older people also doing dancing lessons. In the streets there were people of all ages out late, eating cheap food, drinking cheap beer. It seemed easy for people to be out having fun, socialising and enjoying themselves in the evening. Being somewhere where it is dry and warm late into the night helps to make this possible. HCMC had a nice vibe, people seemed happy.

We went to the area popular with tourists, where there were narrow alleyways, lots of massage places, street food stalls, packed little shops selling everything and nice little bars and restaurants. We stopped at one and I ordered a mojito.

Two punky, cool looking people came in, a man and a woman, and sat at the next table across. They looked kind of preoccupied as they sat down and didn't make eye contact straight away. When they had settled down they looked across and we all started talking to each other. They had lived on a narrowboat in London, we lived on a narrowboat; they even knew Anthony's friend who lives on a boat in London. It was a demonstration of soul connection, cosmic recognition, and timing. We'd been in a temporary slump, experiencing a lack of confidence, and then we meet these two. Their boat in London had needed too much work doing so they sold it and were now on the road touring Vietnam, Cambodia, Laos, just the two of them. They had been in a band but the other band members had full time jobs which they didn't want to leave. 'So we said, enjoy your life, we're off,' said Virginia. Their equipment fitted in the back of a taxi. We talked about music, what we liked; we shared many of the same music tastes.

The next night we went to see them play. It was a half hour taxi ride to an arts bar in a different area. The skyline looked as if it had been designed by David Lynch. Tall skinny blocks of matching buildings; square blocks of flats with outlines almost drawn around them in white light; a collection of buildings in various neon lights and best of all Building 81, the second tallest in Southeast Asia. We had seen it coming in from the coach, like a children's building stack getting smaller and smaller until a thin point; interesting in the day, spectacular at night, lit up like a computer motherboard. In front of it chunky blocks of flats looming black out of the darkness and lit in patches, looking like something out of *The Matrix* or *Blade Runner*.

I thought about the man at the bus stop in DaLat asking us if we lived in Ho Chi Minh City. I allowed myself not to think but just to feel the glittering possibility of the idea... So we were already halfway there before we even arrived...

In *Billions*, which I had been watching on Netflix, Taylor and Oscar go back to Oscar's after their first proper date. He has a very classy apartment and a great sound system. He presses a button or waves or whatever, something magical and hi tech, and on comes *The Killing Moon,* by Echo and the Bunnymen. 'Is this okay?' *Oscar asks.* 'It's what I would have hoped for, had I thought about it.' Taylor answers.

The bar tender moved a big wooden bench and tables for us so that we could sit with a good view of the stage. The room was lit with huge white chandeliers and the band's pink and purple lights. What would we have wanted, had we thought of it? Turns out it was Geography Of The Moon.

Much is written about how people as they get older stop listening to new music. It's hard for anything new to compete with things that are so loved. Or for things not to remind you of something you already know, and prefer. And sometimes it's about wanting to lean on someone older, even though they were young when they made it. And having seen so much music, been to so many gigs, its easy to get picky and hard to impress.

From the first song: *Play for me my Lord a song that I can sing,* we liked their music, psychedelic enough for Anthony, mournful enough for me and a song that could have been written just for us at that time: *I want to travel, I don't want to work/The future is unknown/Enjoy the present, the little things/The universe will provide/Remember you will die make this an interesting ride.*

We talked at the bar then got a taxi back together. A lot of the lights of the big buildings had been turned off, leaving an echoey shadow. The four of us talked about *Blade Runner, The Matrix* and *Black Mirror.* I admired and appreciated Andrea's easy vulnerability and openness, 'I find it (*Black Mirror*) too freaky to watch,' he said. I feel the same; the blogger who wrote about *The Thirteenth Floor,* he too said he found it hard to watch, and advised me to 'Take it slowly.'

Swapping seamlessly into everyday physicality, talking about missing European food, 'I could set out fifteen different types of cheese and eat them all, right now,' Andrea said. I smiled, knowing what was coming next. 'I hate cheese,' Anthony said, 'It's almost like a religious fervour,' This has nothing to do with veganism, it's always been this way, and has long been a point of amusement amongst friends; when people first find out they reel off every kind of cheese and ask, 'But what about Philadelphia, what about halloumi,' and on and on, even texting him afterwards, 'What about Wotsits?'

We sat outside at the bar below our hostel and drank coke. A little boy, one of the bar staff's children came to see us, asking me what all the colours were on a Lego/Playmobil catalogue, practicing his colours, except it was me having to say them to him while he chose smaller and smaller corners and edges of colours until I could hardly see. We broke off, me and Virginia, Andrea and Anthony, talking about more personal stuff; kids, guilt, energy, mystical, spiritual, PMS, creativity, emotions, mental health, tattoos, drugs. 'I knew you took heroin,' Andrea said to Anthony, 'I could see it in your eyes.' 'Yes, a long time ago,' Anthony said.

It was good for Anthony and I to have a night out, us dressing up (as much as we could.) We were out until 2am and up much later, the noisiest ones in the hostel yet again, except for the staff downstairs who were smoking marijuana, listening to loud music and hugging inflatable balls. I had only had one beer and two cocktails; one mojito and one cinnamon one called 'The Struggle,' invented by a previous bar tender, 'She was going through something,' the bar tender said, with lots of space in between. But I got a contact high from Anthony smoking. Such a high of happiness. Loved up sex, up almost all night.

Later I lay there loved up, him asleep or resting, me thinking, appreciating him, thinking he may die, what would I be like. The next day I said, 'I thought, Oh my God what if you die, I'll scream and I won't be able to stop.' I'd had a dream like that, like being out of body, trying to get a hold of myself and stop screaming. Anthony's face was a mixture of sad and horrified.

'No you won't,' he said firmly, 'You'll say to yourself, 'We had a great time together, and now it's time to get on with the next phase of your life.''

With two days left, I wrote a 'Words are spells' action plan/wish list. It's interesting that post success life looks the same as what we are/have been doing... I imagined what I'd want, how it could start, someone could approach me about the blog... And they did. What next? Jim Carey, 'You can fail at what you don't want, so you might as well take a chance on doing what you love.' The alternative is what we'd do anyway, get ordinary jobs, not suicide. And what is being a failure anyway? Leaving with nothing? You can't take anything with you anyway.

Just before we left we went back to the mojito place where we'd met Geography of the Moon. We had one last thing to buy, incense, we thought we'd have to go to Chinatown but we were fed up with shopping. Like everywhere the restaurant-bar had a shrine with incense burning. We asked the woman where we could buy some. 'Are you Buddhist?' she asked. 'Well we meditate, we use incense.' 'Easy,' she said, and told us to just go down the alleyway and ask at any shop, and wrote us down the Vietnamese word for incense on a piece of paper. Sure enough, at the first shop we came to we were shown a box full of big tubes of incense, perfect for presents and for us to take back for the boat.

In the coffee shop we had a conversation about The Future, Anthony saying I must finish the book and that he would support me, over coffee and iced peach tea and more free iced tea; so much liquid. Anthony said, 'It's funny how you get a free drink when you order a drink.' And that at least in the case of coffee the free drink is often much bigger than the ordered and paid for one (a last metaphor!)

'Lord give me a song that I can sing. Sing for me my lord, a song that I can sing.' Geography of the Moon.

Much as the mournful request is hardwired into me to love, I know really that you can sing the song yourself. You can write the song yourself. You can write yourself the song you want to sing.

For photographs of the trip see Instagram @travelswithanthony

For blogs and info about the trip as well as my personal blog see http://thisisrachelann.wordpress.com

Front cover photograph: Rachel in Hampi, India, Christmas Eve 2018

Author photograph: Pushkar, India, February 2020

Printed in Great Britain
by Amazon